IMAGES
of America

AROUND CAROLINE

ON THE COVER: Mailmen line up in front of the store in Brooktondale on the first day of Rural Free Delivery, some on horseback and some with carriages. (Courtesy of the Caroline History Room, Caroline, New York.)

IMAGES
of America

AROUND CAROLINE

Patricia A. Brhel

ARCADIA
PUBLISHING

ISBN 978-1-4671-1579-7

Published by Arcadia Publishing
Charleston, South Carolina

Printed in the United States of America

Library of Congress Control Number: 2015954413

For all general information, please contact Arcadia Publishing:
Telephone 843-853-2070
Fax 843-853-0044
E-mail sales@arcadiapublishing.com
For customer service and orders:
Toll-Free 1-888-313-2665

Visit us on the Internet at www.arcadiapublishing.com

To my husband, children, and other family members and to the many kind and generous people of Caroline who have become family in my heart.

Contents

Acknowledgments		6
Introduction		7
1.	People Make the Town	9
2.	Churches and Schools	43
3.	Farming Feeds All	57
4.	Businesses Thrive	71
5.	Transportation	93
6.	Celebrations	107
Bibliography		127

Acknowledgments

This book could not have been written without the assistance of Caroline town historian Barbara Mix Kone, who has been a tireless collector of local history, a task made easier by her father, William Mix, and his remarkable memory. Taking over the job of town historian from her mother Prudence Shaw Mix, Barbara has worked for many years to promote Caroline history by creating exhibits and research space in a dedicated space in the town hall, writing a monthly column for the Brooktondale Community Center newsletter, *The Old Mill*, and by community outreach. She has organized reunions for the one- and two-room schools in Caroline, except the Brooktondale school, and served on the bicentennial committee. In 1994, with other committee members, she published a history of the town and organized numerous events to celebrate that occasion. She has also been a mentor to me and many others.

Ted Sobel has given a great deal of his time to help find pictures and information specifically for this book and has helped with many other history-related activities, including reprinting the *Caroline History* (originally published in 1994), creating a pictorial history of the Brooktondale Apple Fest, and republishing in booklet form a series of postcards originally donated to the Brooktondale Community Center by Gertrude Conant.

Other local historians who have provided information and inspired me include the late Molly Adams, the late Art Volbrech, and the late Leona Lasky-Tharp-Eastman. I would also like to thank the many citizens and former citizens who donated photographs and information, recently or decades ago, to the Caroline History Room. Without them, this book would be very very small. Obviously, any mistakes in the content of this book can be attributed to me, as fallible as any other human being.

Finally, I really appreciate the support and patience of my family: husband Robert Rehbock, children Michael Dube and Paul Rehbock, Paul's wife Jannah Matzen, my daughter Kathryn Rehbock and my grandchildren Joshua Brhel and Adrienne Cameron.

Unless otherwise noted, all pictures in this book are courtesy of the Caroline History Room in Slaterville Springs.

INTRODUCTION

Caroline, tucked into the rolling hills of upstate New York, is a thriving and progressive community that also appreciates its heritage. Caroline celebrated its bicentennial in 1994, but unlike many towns, it also celebrates a founding mother. The widow Maria Earsley, a mother of 10, purchased 100 acres in the Caroline Valley from a land agent in Owego. She and her oldest son arrived in the fall of 1774 to build a cabin for their family. They then returned to Owego to spend the winter and gather the supplies they would need to create a successful homestead. The following spring, Earsely brought nine of her children (one daughter married and remained in Owego) to settle permanently on the land. She was greeted by "Captain" David Rich from Vermont, who was camped nearby, beginning his own homestead.

I'm sure that these first settlers appreciated having neighbors close by in the great wooded Caroline Valley for companionship, as well as assistance and security, just as later citizens have. Wild animals, including predators, abounded, and Native Americans of uncertain friendliness lived, grew crops, hunted, and fished in this area. Still, there were many advantages to the new land. Water was in abundance, as were trees, providing lumber for houses and barns, as well as fuel to heat their homes and to cook their meals. Wild game, along with berries and herbs, were plentiful and supplemented what settlers could grow on their rough parcels of land.

Soon, other settlers came and several hamlets were formed: Caroline, Speedsville, Slaterville Springs, West Slaterville, Brooktondale (which was originally Motts Corners, Cantineville, and Brookton, before the "dale" was added), Caroline Center, Caroline Depot, Boiceville, and Besemer. Men and women with useful skills—such as blacksmiths and doctors—came, and the area grew rapidly when the Catskill Turnpike opened. The turnpike, authorized by Gov. DeWitt Clinton in 1804, passed by the home of Clinton's cousin Nancy Deniston-Mulks and her husband, Benoini Mulks, in West Slaterville Springs. Several inns and stables, including a stable owned by the Mulks and a tavern and inn owned by Captain Rich, sprang up along the turnpike. Just east of Slaterville Springs is a marker where one of the early gates was located. In 1875, the railroad came, increasing the demand for innkeepers, livery stables, and restaurants. From this humble beginning grew a town.

Nowadays, the local monthly newsletter, found online at brooktondalecc.org, features a history column. One-room schoolhouse reunions are a regular summer treat, and the shining white two-story town courthouse and meeting hall, which was promoted as a modern school when it was erected in the 1800s, stands next to a new geothermal heated and cooled, solar-powered office building.

This town of about 3,000 citizens has a library, a history room, a community center, three volunteer fire departments, several churches, stores, and small businesses, with people engaged in work ranging from traditional agriculture to computer commuters.

A trip to Caroline, whether through the pages of this book or in person, is a treat to be remembered for all time.

One

People Make the Town

Caroline town historian Barbara Mix Kone likes to remind residents that the history of a town is really a history of its people. From the first few settlers to the 3,000-plus people who reside here today, Caroline's residents have depended on each other for friendship and entertainment, as well as more practical considerations. Roads were initially maintained by neighbors who paid their taxes by the labor of themselves and their horses. The Grange and the Dairy League helped farmers and their wives learn new techniques while providing a way to socialize. Organizations such as Boy and Girl Scouts and 4-H kept—and still keep—area youngsters happy while teaching them valuable skills. Men and women joined lodges, and sewing circles were formed. During World War II, women got together and wrote the *Bugle*, a newsletter that went out to area men and women serving in the armed forces. That newsletter continues today as the Brooktondale Community Center's monthly *The Old Mill* and is now an important source of local news for the entire community. Three volunteer fire companies and a volunteer ambulance corps rose after World War II. When the local one-room schools were consolidated in 1959, the two-room school in Brooktondale became a teen center. Its successor is the Brooktondale Community Center, with the neighboring Old Fire Hall added to create a two-building complex, along with the concrete structure erected in 1964 to replace the school, which succumbed to an electrical fire.

Since the very beginning, over 200 years ago, Caroline residents have banded together to create a town that is welcoming to all. More recently, a new energy-efficient building with solar panels and geothermal heating housing a library and town offices was built beside the two-story school structure, which was revamped in 1976 and again more recently to create a courthouse and meeting room downstairs and a place to store and celebrate town history upstairs.

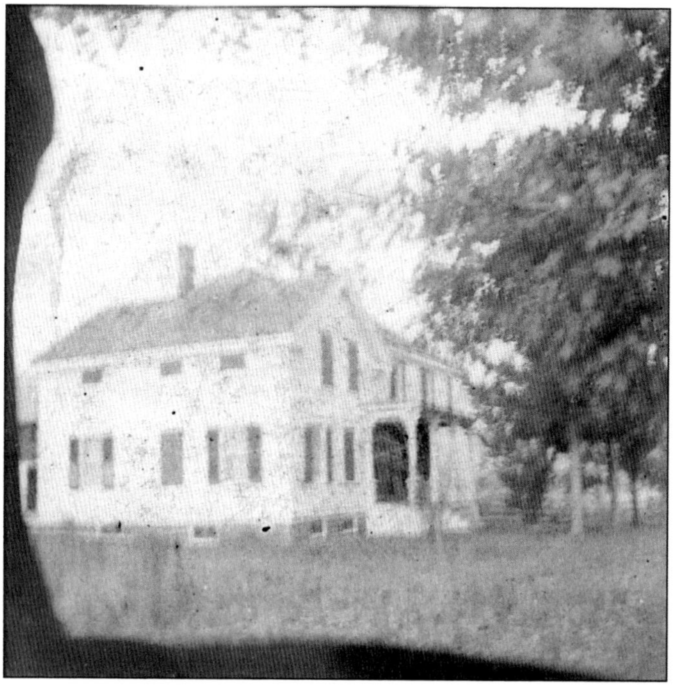

While the widow Maria Earsely and her family may have started life in Caroline crowded into a small cabin, they did not stay there. This photograph, labeled "Grandma Earsely's house," was found in the history room. Like most homes in the 18th and 19th centuries, the house was expanded to shelter a growing number of children and more than one generation. Many in Caroline are related to this early settler.

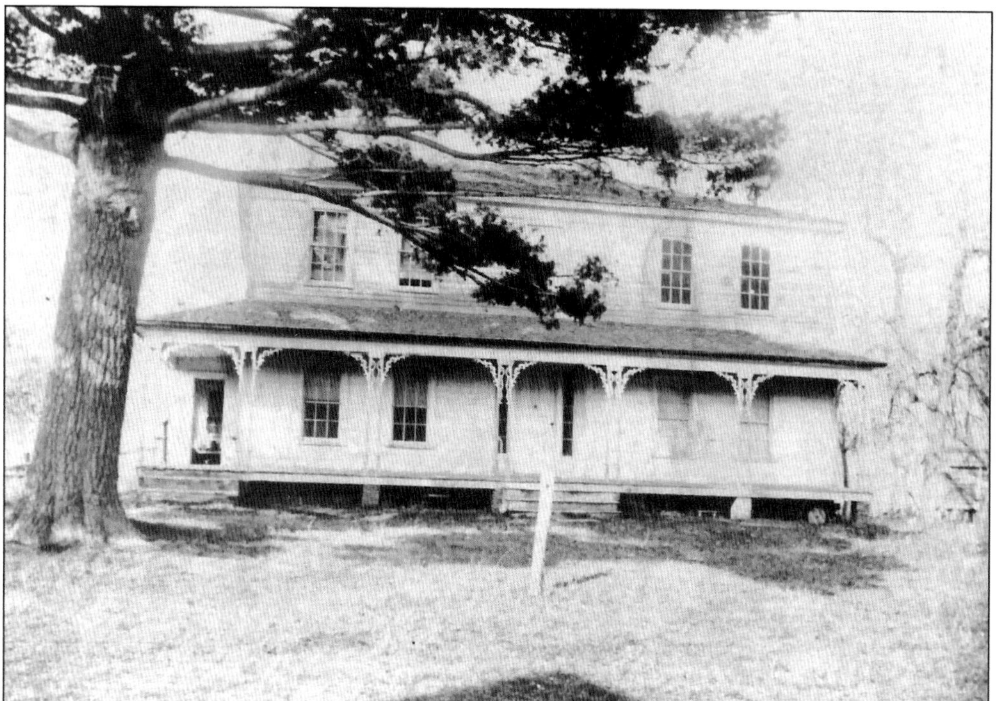

Captain David Rich, who arrived in 1795, one week before the Earsleys moved into their already built cabin, was an ambitious man and soon developed his property, which sat conveniently on the Catskill Turnpike, into a busy tavern. The house is now a private home. While the porch has been removed, it is still recognizable. A historical marker near the road lets travelers know the significance of this location.

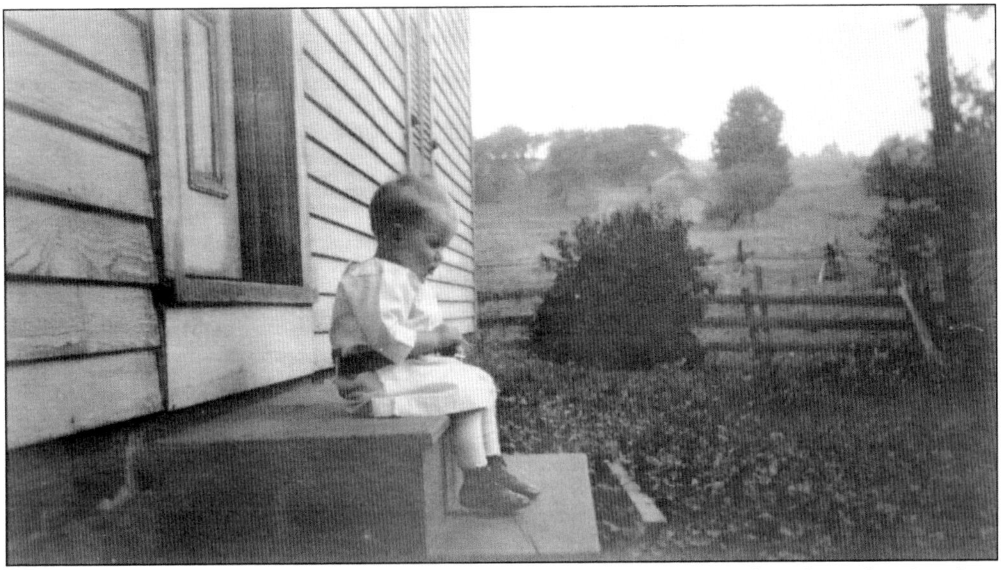

Richard L. Snow sits on the back stoop of the family home. The family has thrived in Caroline for nearly 200 years. Two of the three young men of the current generation are still involved in the dairy industry. John, with his father, Cal, takes care of the bulk milk production, while Cal and another son, Aaron, use some of the milk to make and sell cheese, like a previous family member.

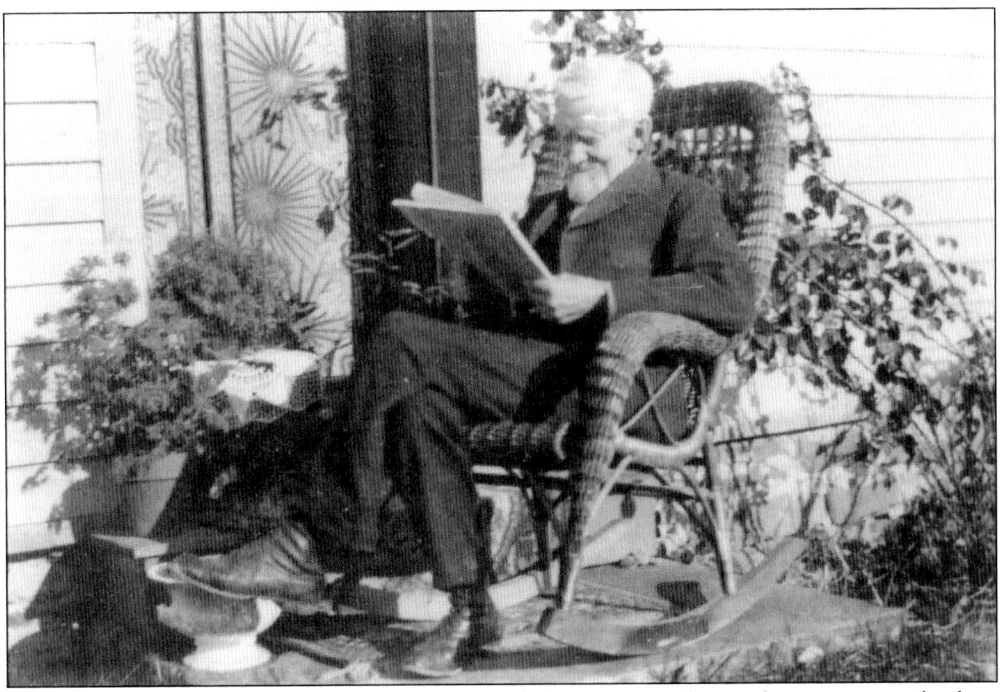

While little boys may be sent to sit outside the back door, contemplating their recent misdeeds or planning the next, the older generation might enjoy spending time on the back stoop. J.J. Peters relaxes in a wicker rocking chair, no doubt enjoying a snack, the latest farm magazine, and a little peace and quiet.

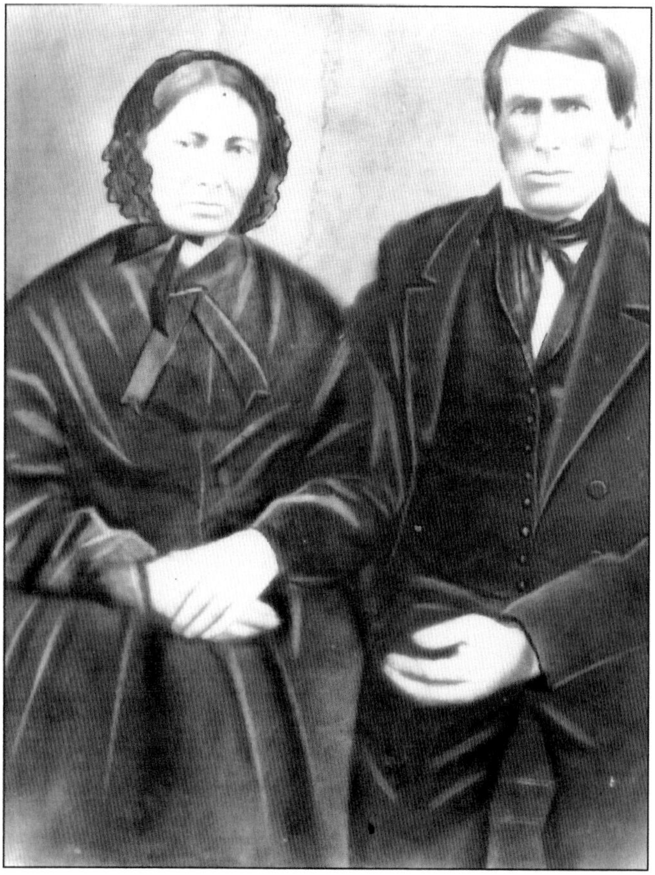

Rachel and James Van De Mark pose for a formal portrait. The Van De Marks, under different spellings, are one of the older Caroline families.

James and Rachel Van De Mark began housekeeping in this relatively spacious cabin. Early settlers did not begin life in the more elaborate homes seen today. Families may have started out in one- or two-room cabins, some without even floorboards for comfort and protection from the dirt and critters they had to contend with.

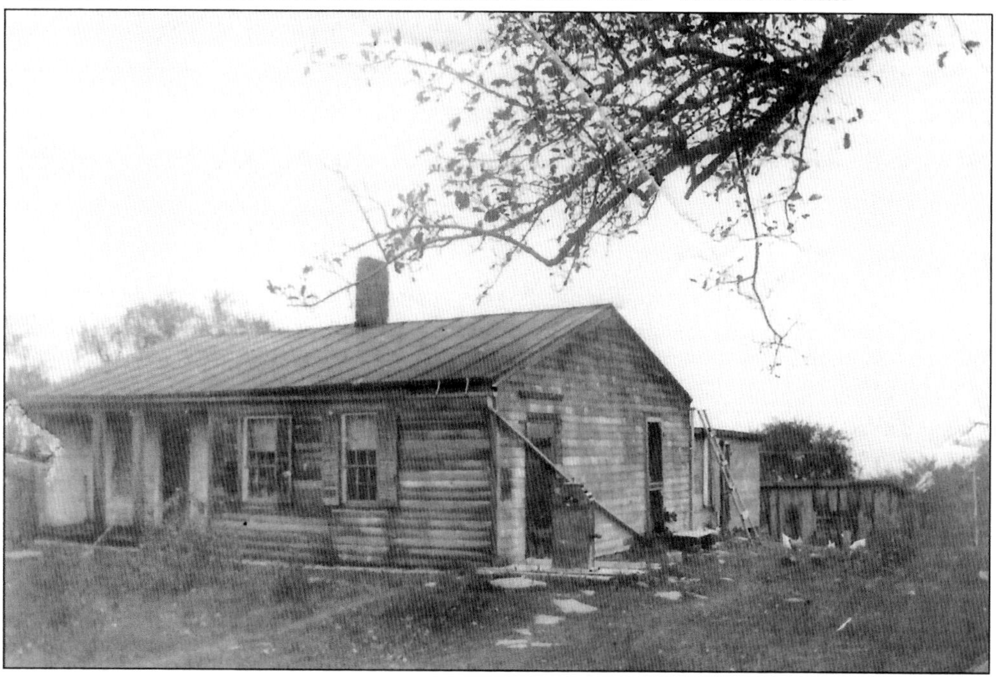

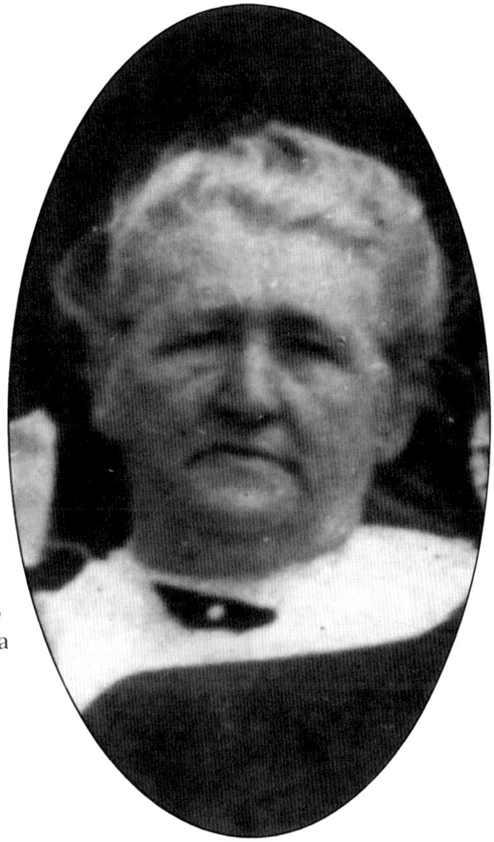

These pictures of James and Mary Van De Mark were cut out of bigger photographs and put into these oval frames. The pictures were passed through the family, and copies were donated to the Caroline History Room. (Courtesy of Teena [Decker] Abel and LeRoy Decker.)

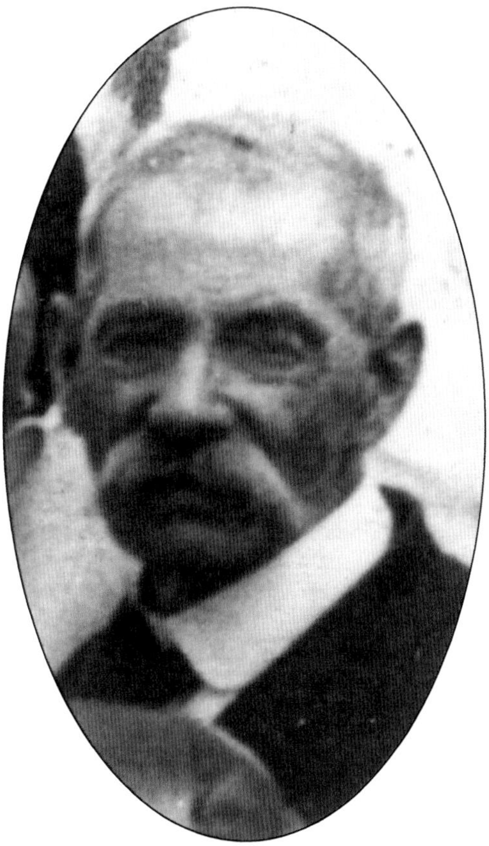

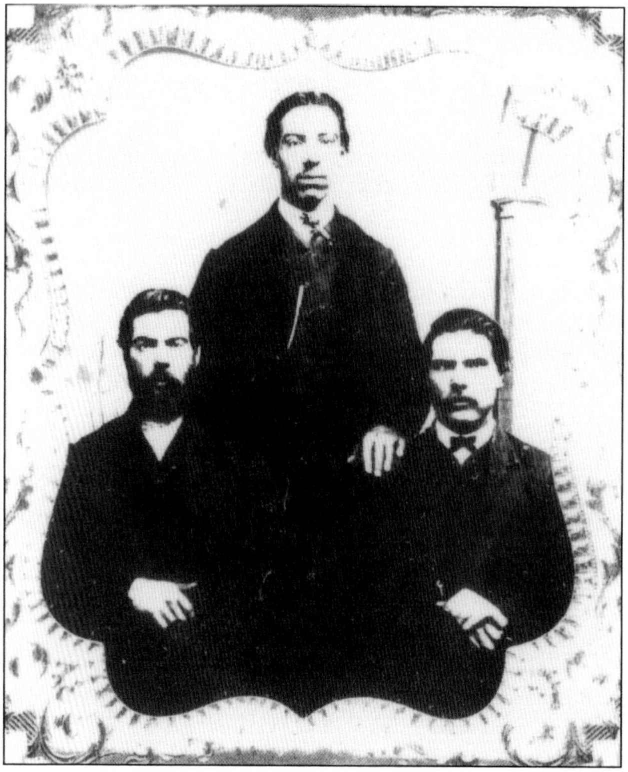

James, Valentine, and Hiram Van De Mark pose for a photograph, no doubt at their mother's request, as pictures of them and their three brothers were found in their mother's possessions by the Deckers in recent years. Teena (Decker) Abel has worked hard to create a family tree and an album.

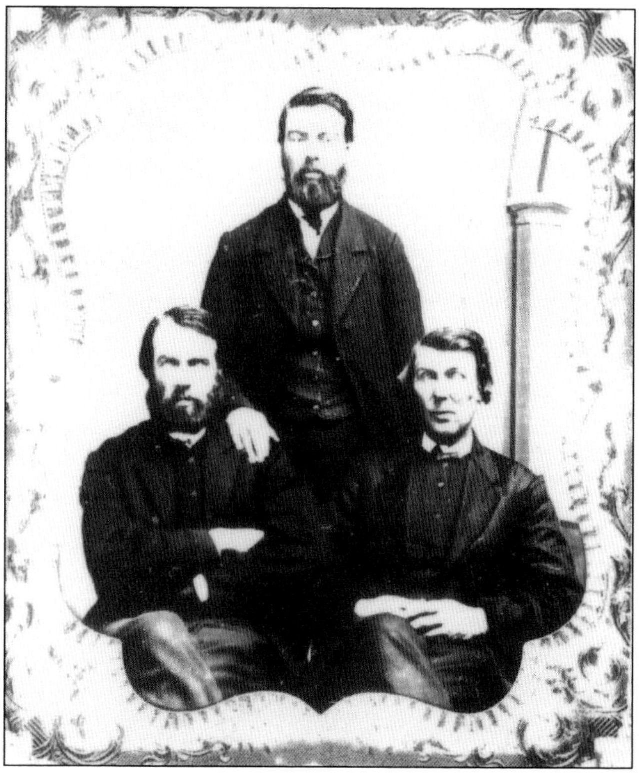

Isaiah, Justice, and Benjamin Van De Mark, like most young men of their generation, considered a photograph a formal occasion and something that could be a gift to their mother.

Grandma Van De Mark and her grandson Lawrence enjoy the afternoon sun at their farm. Milk cans and crates for fruits and vegetables are stored on the back porch.

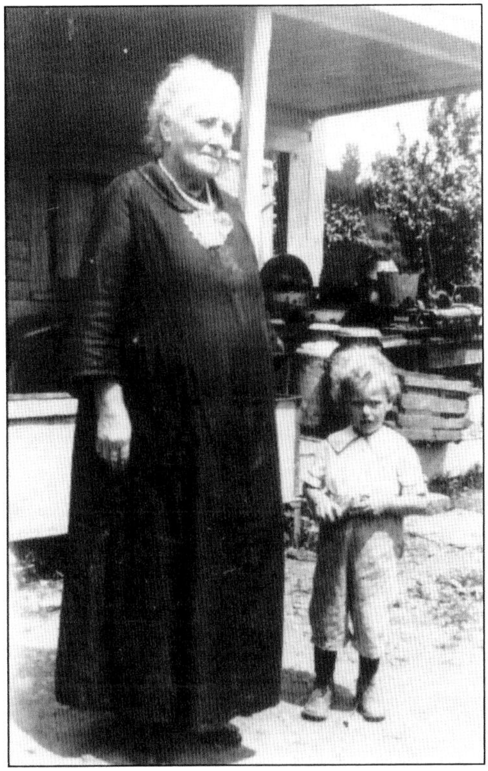

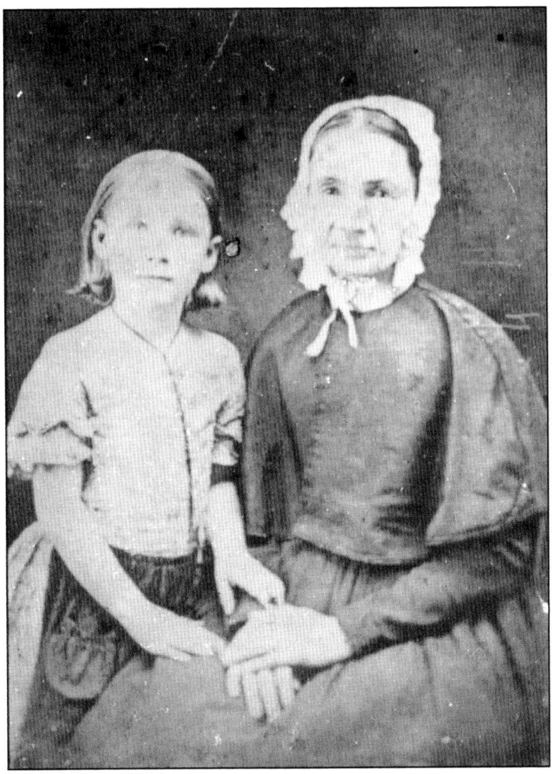

Mary Elizabeth Crane, later a Van De Mark bride, sits on her grandmother Mary Brown's lap. Older families married into each other, as well as newcomers, and many first names were reused to honor current relatives or ancestors, so the same names occur over several generations, making genealogy an interesting puzzle.

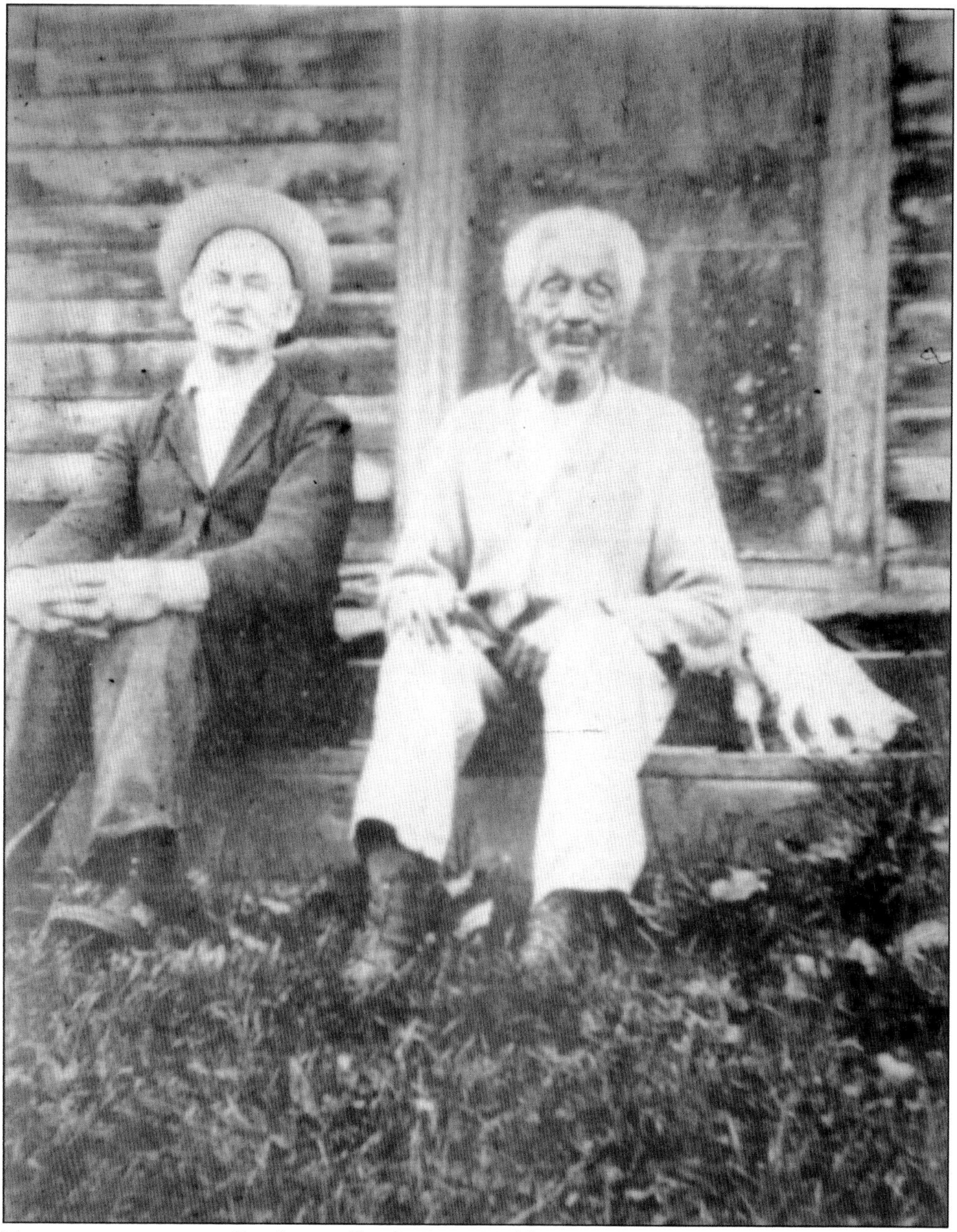

Not everyone came to Caroline willingly. Peter Webb was a slave brought up from Virginia by his master, John James Speed. Speed allowed Peter to work for others in the neighborhood after his farm chores were done and allowed him to keep part of any wages earned. By hard work and thrift, Webb bought his freedom in 1818 for $384 and later married Phyllis, who until her marriage never had a last name. They raised their 11 children in a log cabin near the farm that he had once labored on as a slave. This picture shows master and slave on the porch of Spring Farm on Level Green Road in Caroline. The farmhouse still stands and is in the hands of his descendants, the Bailors. Peter worked hard for his freedom and appreciated it. In addition to farming, he was active in the abolitionist movement, both in Caroline and in Ithaca.

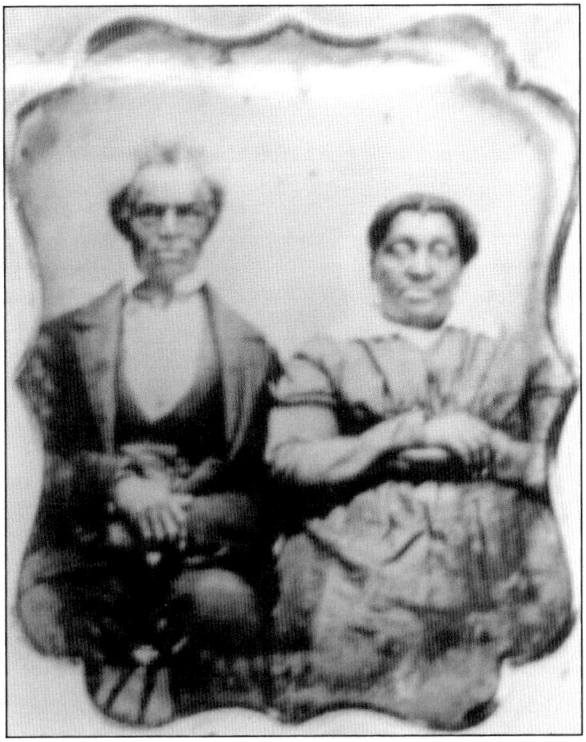

Peter Webb and his wife, Phyllis, seem to stare into the future, dressed in their best clothing and ready to be immortalized with a photograph, back when the process was still new. They are most likely thinking about their children and grandchildren and perhaps about how far they have come in life.

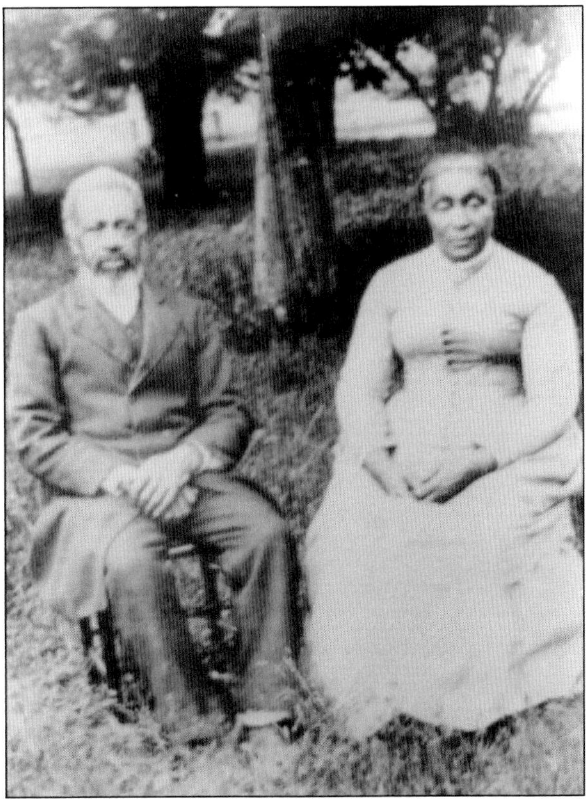

Peter and Phyllis's son Fredrick Webb and his wife, Lucina Barton, chose a less formal setting for their photograph. Here, they enjoy the shade in the front yard of the family home on Level Green Road in Caroline. Fredrick bought the farm his father had worked on as a slave, and it remains in the family today.

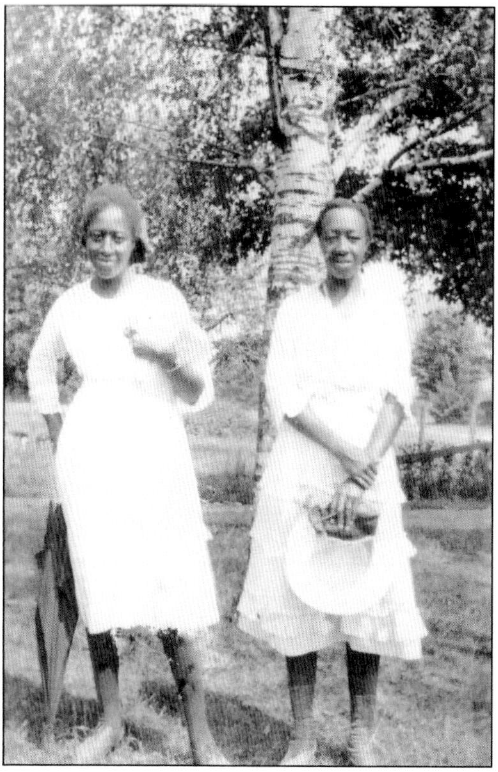

Sisters Lucina and Fredricka Webb enjoy a sunny day and one another's company outdoors at the family home. They are fashionably but modestly dressed, and both display beautiful smiles. (Courtesy of the Oscar Beam collection.)

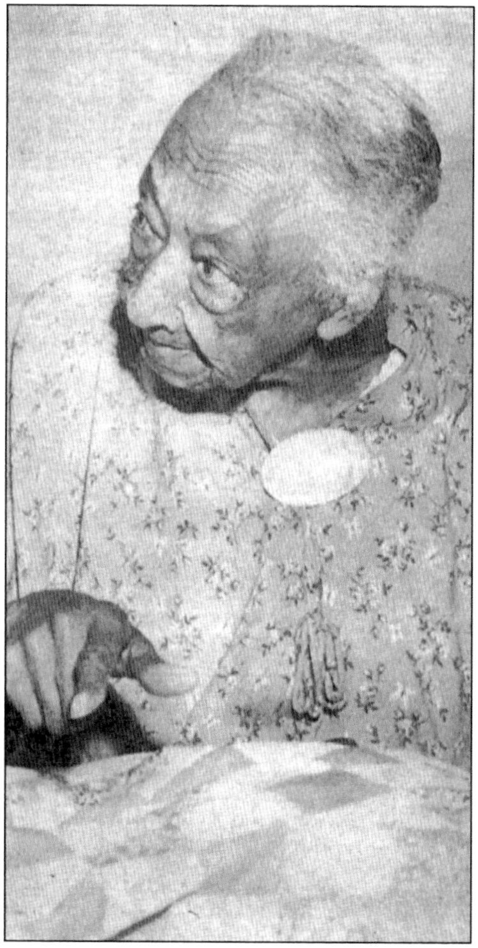

Mable (Webb) Van Dyke was first educated in Caroline schools and then continued her education by studying voice at the Ithaca Conservatory of Music, now Ithaca College. She was said to have played the piano beautifully, was an expert quilter and weaver, and was good at many other creative crafts. She was also a wife, mother of two children, foster mother of 21 additional children, and a much loved and respected practical nurse. She served as a Sunday school superintendent and ran the kitchen at the Nazarene Camp in Brooktondale.

This woman was able to afford glasses. She may have been too vain to wear them, though perhaps it was just that the photographer wanted to avoid glare. She is nicely dressed, but her widow's garb is relieved only by her broche and white lace cap. Like many photographs in the Caroline collection, it is unlabeled, a situation that frustrates many historians, who lament the inability to tell the rest of this story.

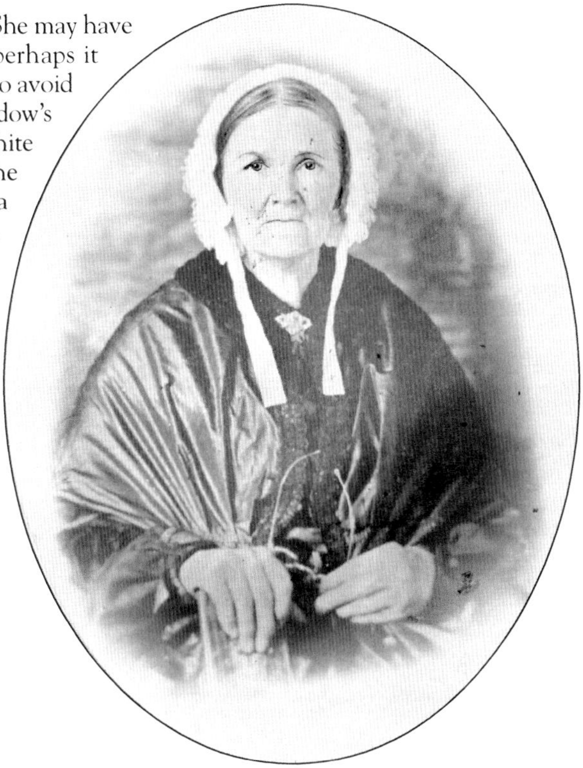

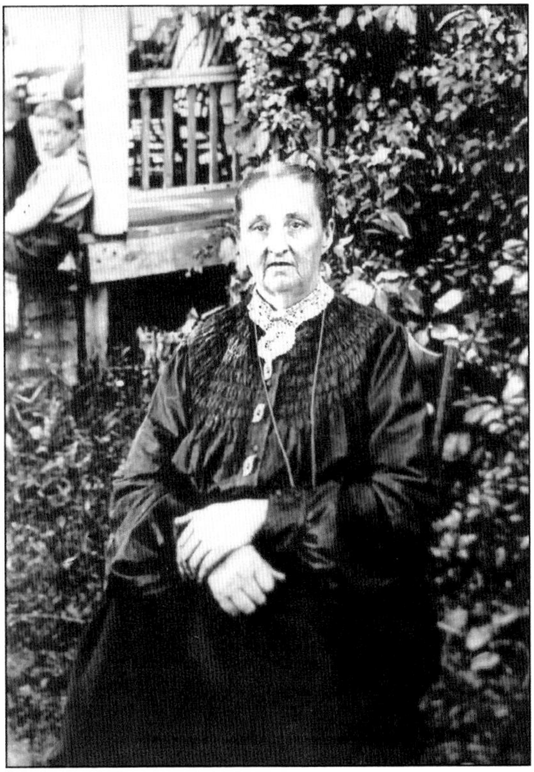

Hally Liddington, member of another longtime Caroline family, also wears a dark dress, relieved by a lace collar. She enjoys time in the garden while a small boy, perhaps a grandson, looks on.

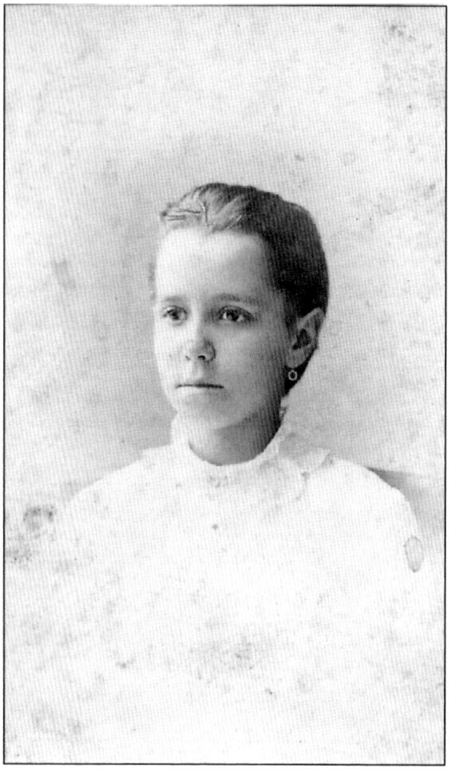

Young Fanny was the daughter of the prominent Dr. William Gallagher of Slaterville Springs and, like many a doctor's child, lived with a certain lack of privacy and frequently interrupted meals. This happened more so than usual, as the good doctor invited patients from Ithaca into his home to soak in tubs filled with the famous Slaterville Springs Magnetic Mineral Water, a purported cure for all sorts of ills.

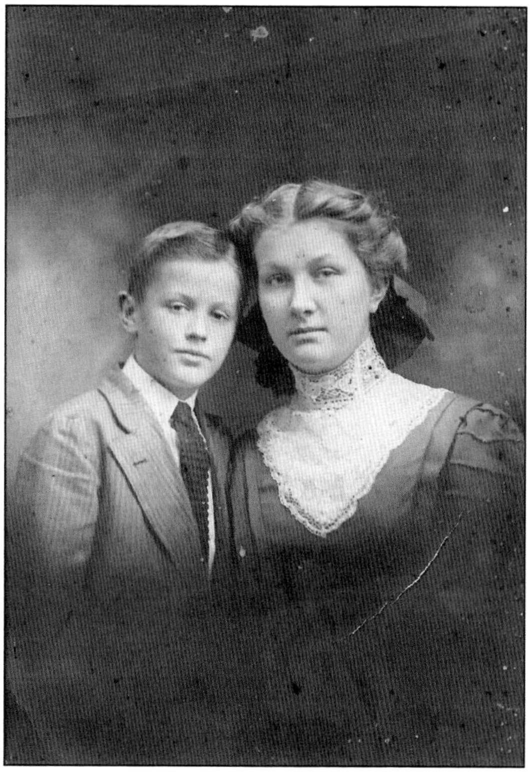

The Winchell mother and son pose for an intimate studio portrait.

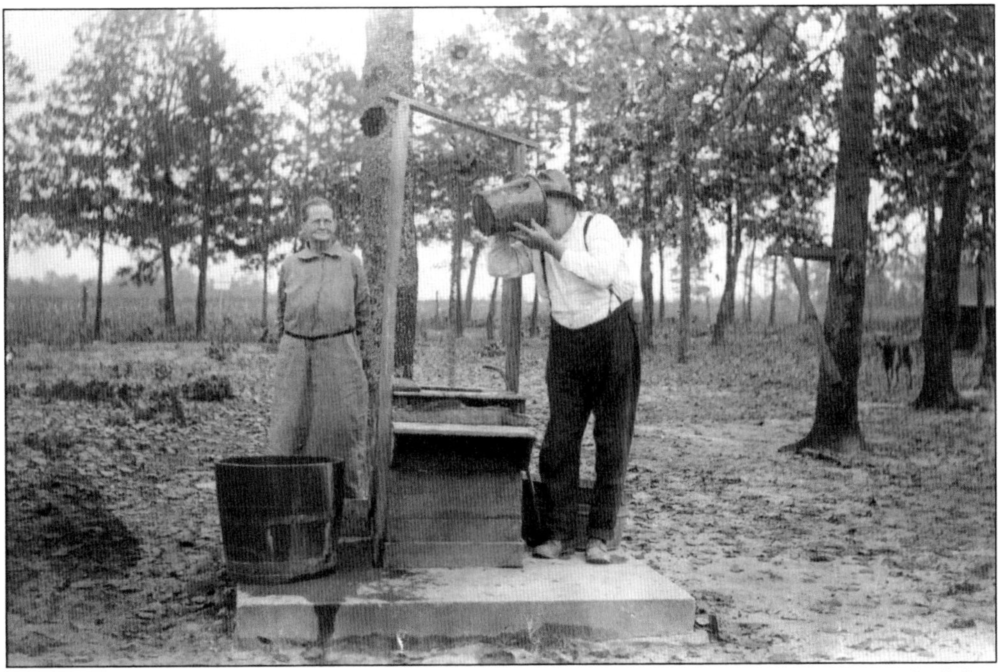

There is still no public water source in Caroline, other than the artesian well at the town hall, but fortunately, wells are now covered, and an electric pump provides water to modern households. This man seems to thoroughly enjoy his refreshment, while his wife gives him the same look that women today give someone drinking directly out of the juice or milk carton.

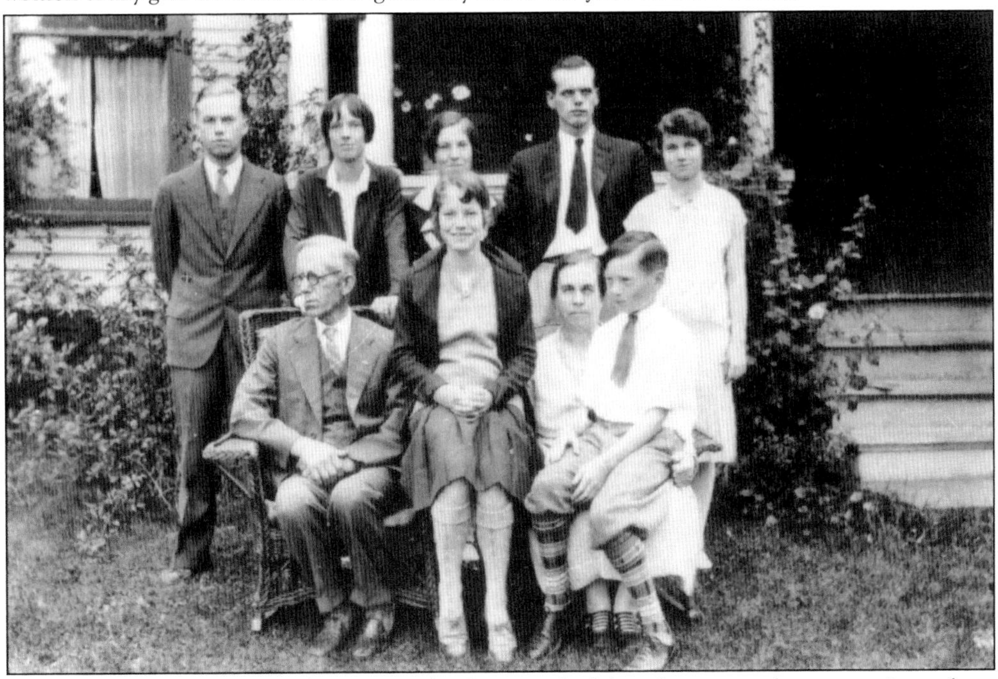

The Charles Lounsbery family poses in the front yard of their home on what is now Lounsbery Road. The boy on the right, perched on his mother's knee, is Charles Lounsbery. The family home is now occupied by his niece Lois and serves for family visits in the summer.

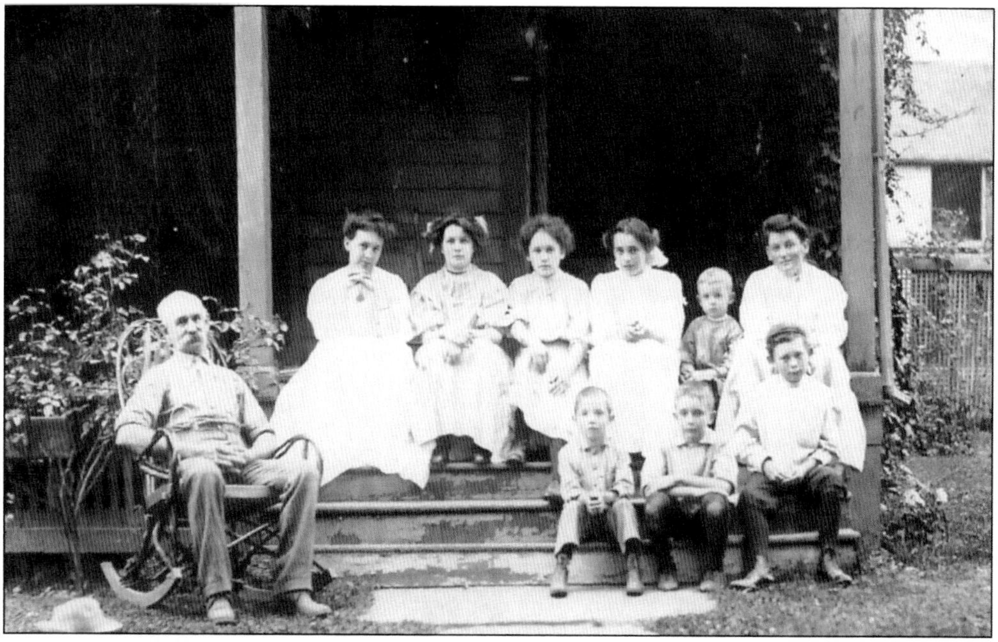

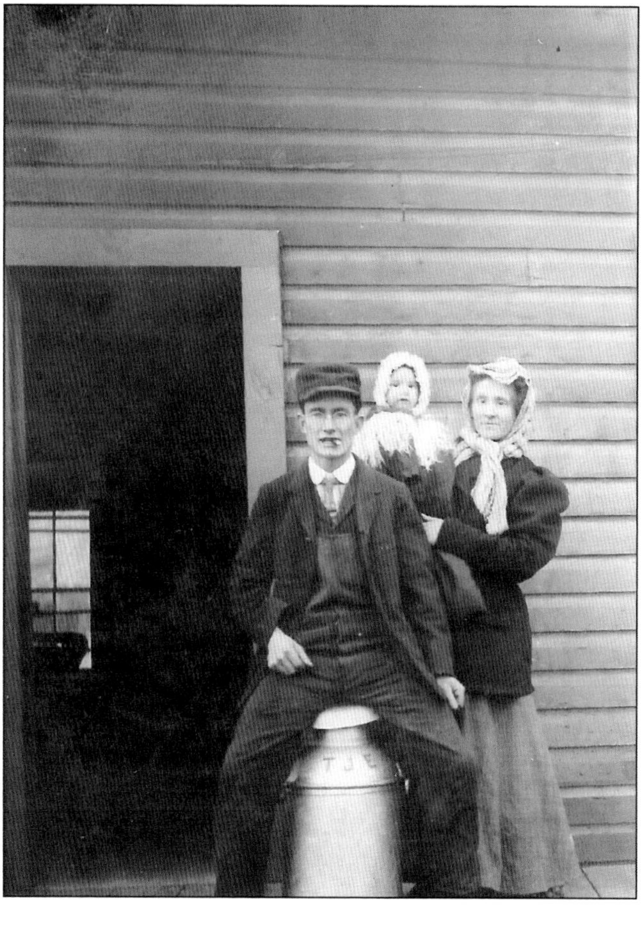

Henry Speed enjoys the comfort of his willow rocker while his family and some friends perch on the porch steps, enjoying time in the fresh air. From left to right are Henry Speed, Winnie Speed, Ruth (Speed) Davis, Elizabeth (Speed) Phillips, Marie (Speed) Davis, and five unidentified boys from Slaterville Springs.

In the hamlet of Speedsville, William Cornell perches on a milk can while his wife and child stand behind him, sporting bright smiles. Small dairy farms were common in Caroline's early years, and until industrialization and the fall of milk prices, it was a good way to make a living and raise a family.

Jesse Brewer ran a dry goods store in Brooktondale, selling fabric, ribbon, greeting cards, and other items. She took it over from a woman who had managed a grocery store in the same building and used the proceeds from the store to increase the family income and help support her widowed mother. She was also active in the Caroline Valley Federated (now Community) Church.

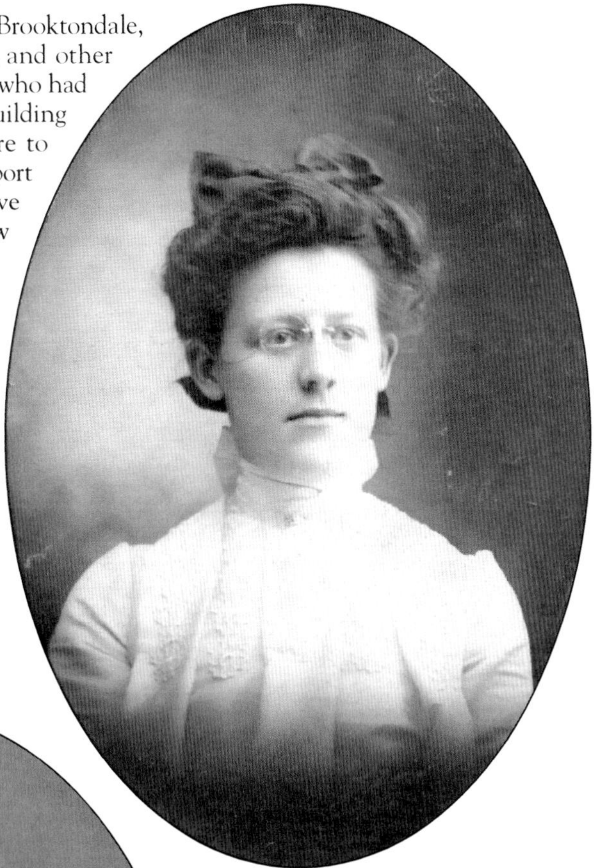

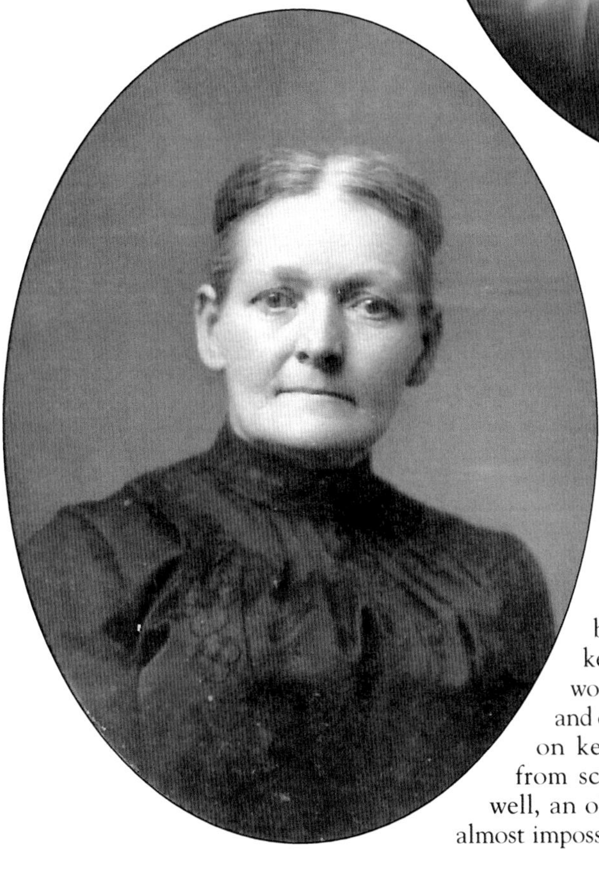

Jesse Brewer's mother lived with her daughter and son-in-law after her husband died. Nowadays, women can be far more independent, but when keeping a household meant chopping wood and stoking wood stoves for heating and cooking, filling and trimming the wicks on kerosene lamps, cooking everything from scratch, and hauling water from the well, an older woman would find living alone almost impossible.

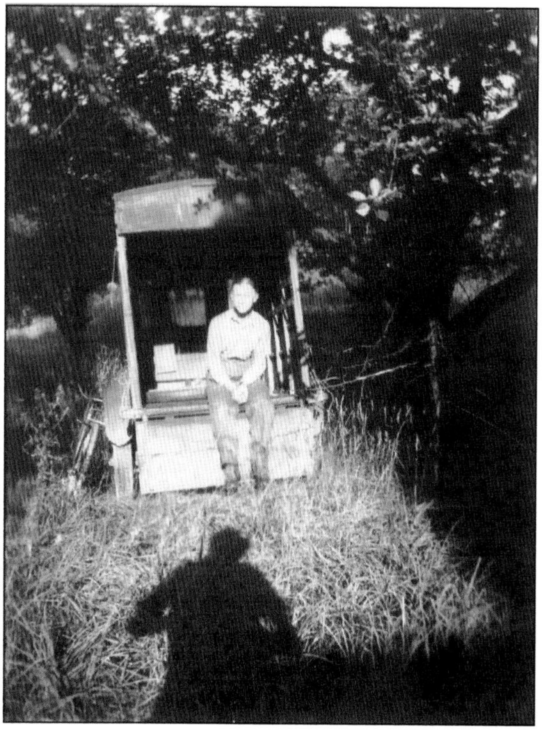

George Ward made several trips in this truck to move his family to Caroline. He and the truck both look tired, and even the bicycle is leaning against the truck frame, but Ward must take pride in a job accomplished and a future of independent living in the country.

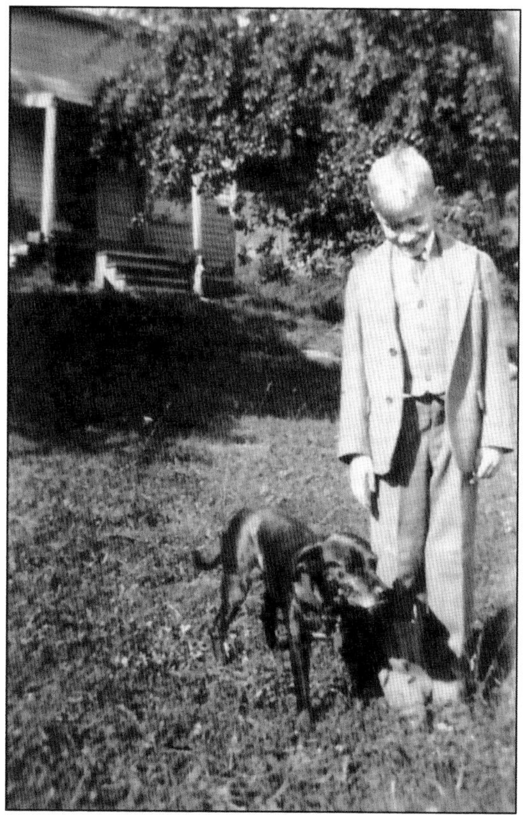

Young George Ward poses in his school or Sunday clothes with his young dog Major. Ward and Major can look forward to exploring the woods and fields and many exciting days on their new farm.

George was not the only person in Caroline with a best friend. This young lady is happy to sit with her attentive pooch. She wears a pretty white outfit and has her hair piled high on her head; the perfect image of a well-behaved young lady and her well-trained pet.

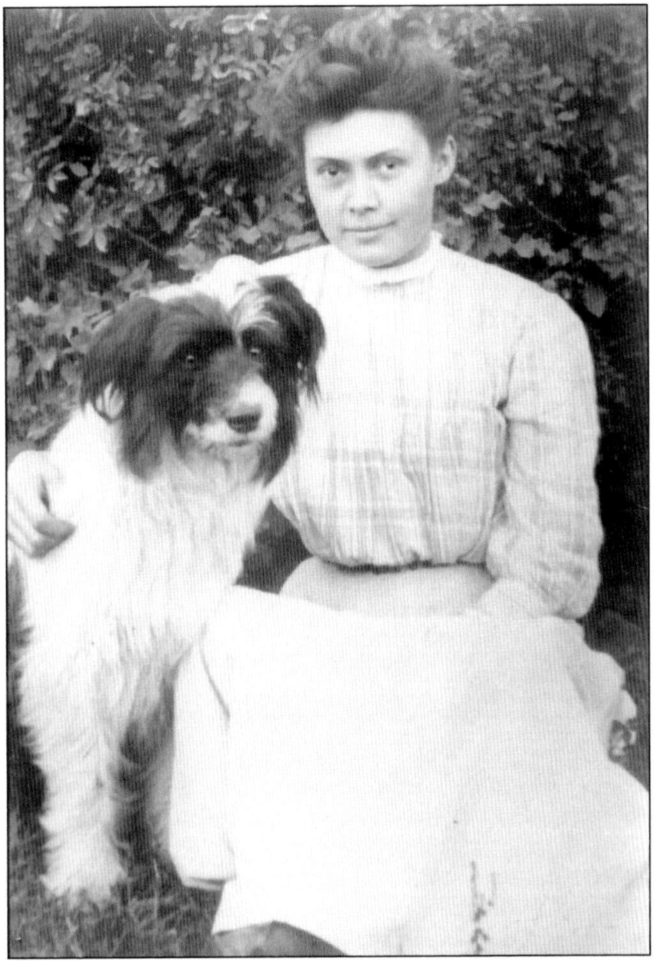

The vines climbing the porch have not leafed out yet, and it is still a little cool outside, but preparations have begun for the upcoming season. Nellie Harris (left) and Pauleen Winchell Crispell relax from household chores on a porch in Slaterville Springs with a friendly pooch. The girls are believed to be about 15 years old in this photograph.

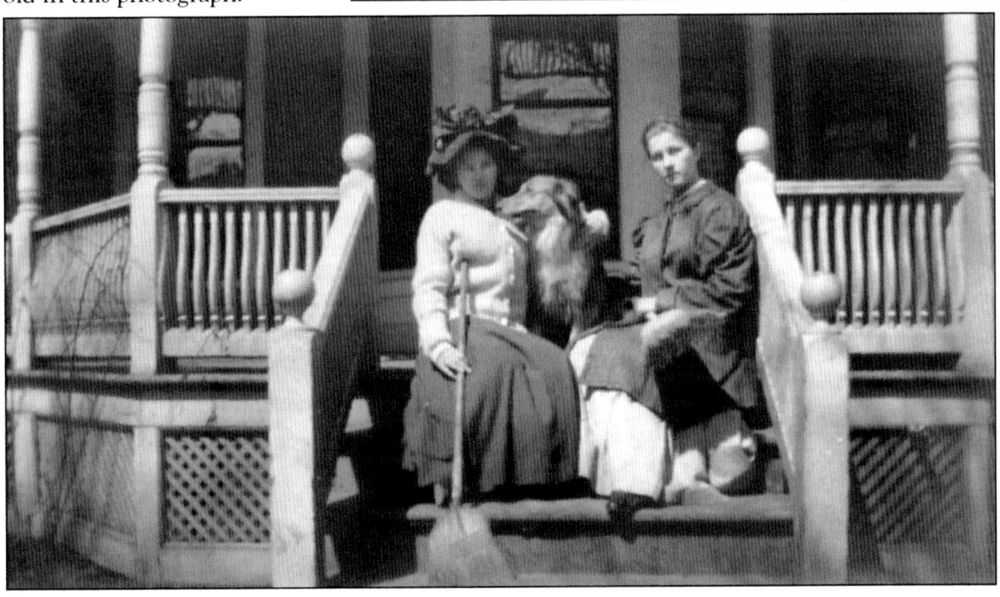

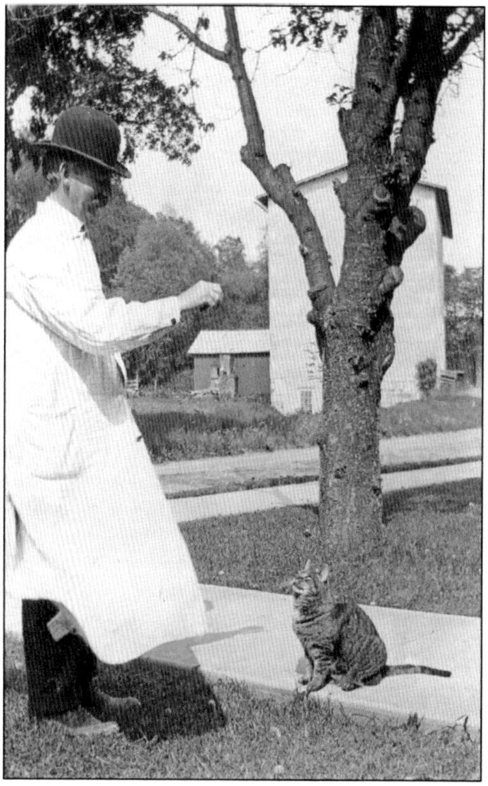

This kitty enjoys the sunshine as she charms the gentleman in the bowler hat. While some cats in rural areas are kept solely as working animals, making sure that the barn is free of rats and the pantry free of mice, this man and cat appear to be good friends.

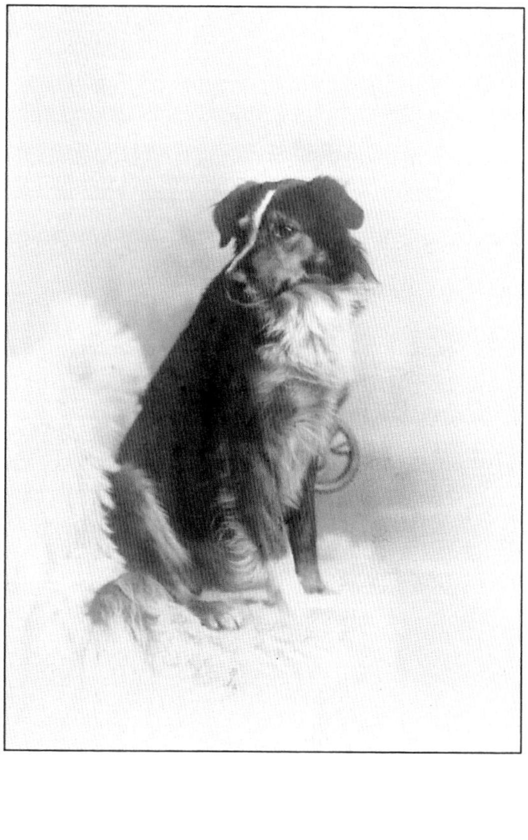

Some animals were so important that they were granted their own formal portrait. This dog may have been a beloved family pet or possibly a working animal, perhaps in charge of a meadow filled with sheep. Whatever the circumstances, he sits quietly and waits for the flash.

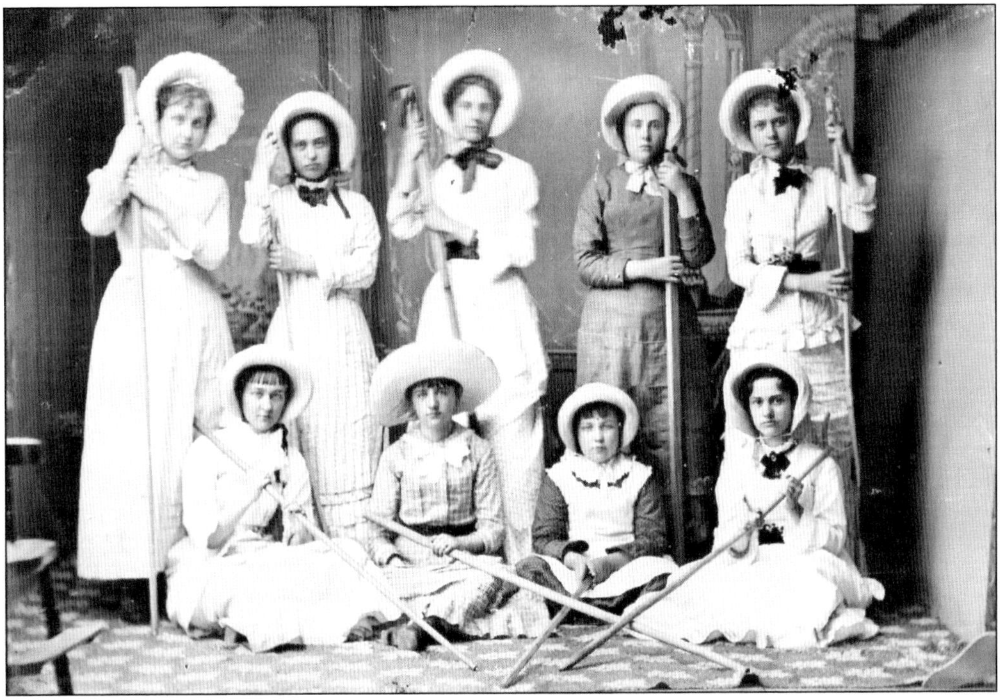

There was more to do in long-ago Caroline than playing with pets. This group of young ladies with theatrical ambitions poses in front of a painted scene. With poles and costumes, it might have been a Gilbert and Sullivan production. The name is lost to time, as are the names of the actresses, but this beautiful photograph remains.

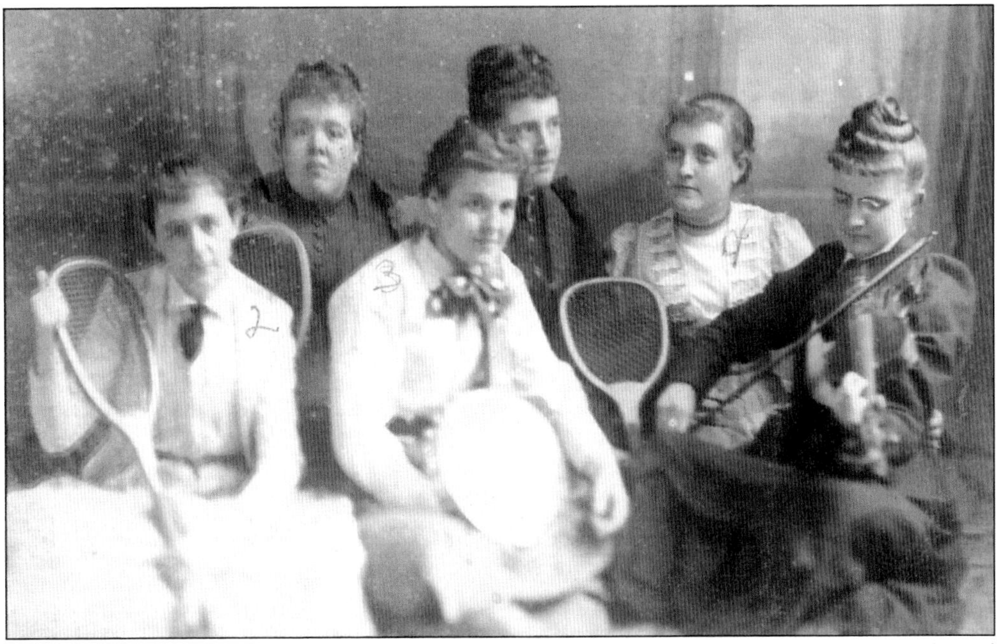

Well-brought-up young ladies played lawn tennis and musical instruments, did needlework, and learned how to run a household, preparing them to be an asset and helpmate to their husband and a good mother to their children. These accomplished friends are well on their way to success.

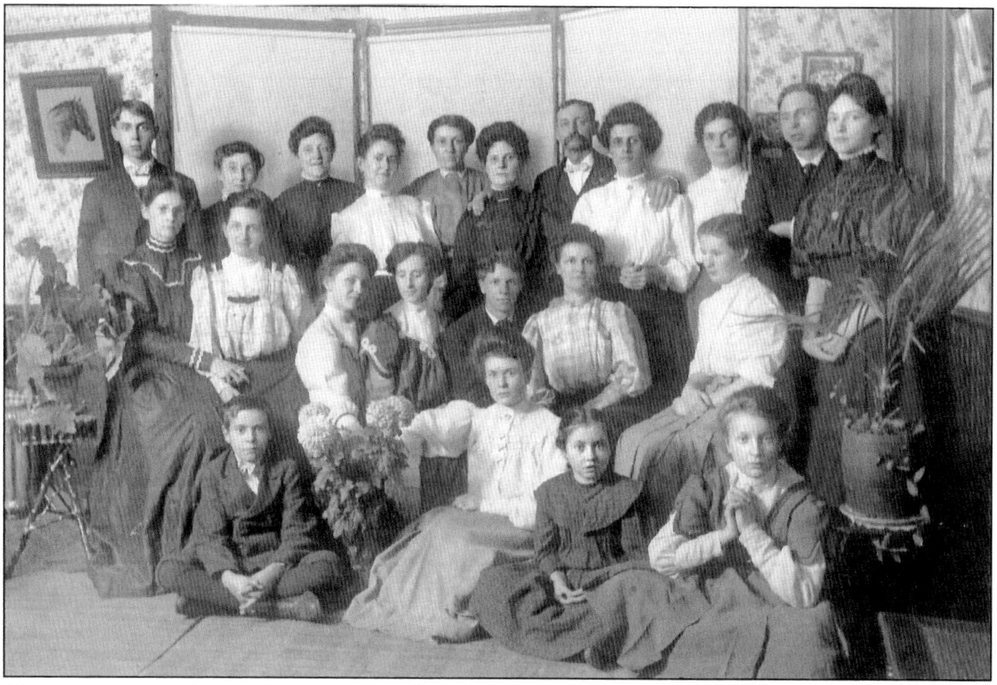

These young people may be part of a 4-H group or Grange League, as there are a great number of plants in the room. On the other hand, they could be rehearsing a theatrical production or part of a church group. Whatever the reason, a gathering of 22 youngsters was sure to make for some fun and interesting times.

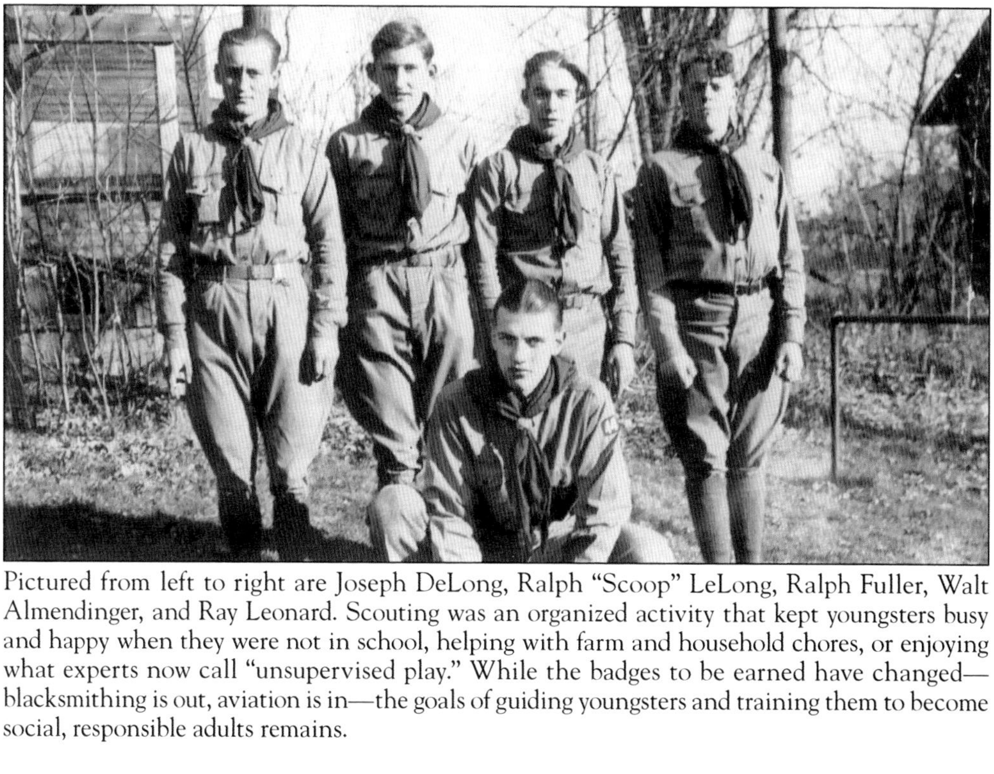

Pictured from left to right are Joseph DeLong, Ralph "Scoop" LeLong, Ralph Fuller, Walt Almendinger, and Ray Leonard. Scouting was an organized activity that kept youngsters busy and happy when they were not in school, helping with farm and household chores, or enjoying what experts now call "unsupervised play." While the badges to be earned have changed—blacksmithing is out, aviation is in—the goals of guiding youngsters and training them to become social, responsible adults remains.

In the past, boys who lived in rural areas were expected to learn how to shoot. Whether it was hunting for food or eliminating animals that were a threat to livestock, they needed to be prepared to know what to do when such a situation might arise. These young men are doing the practical part of their hunter safety course, a good idea for anyone who lives in the country.

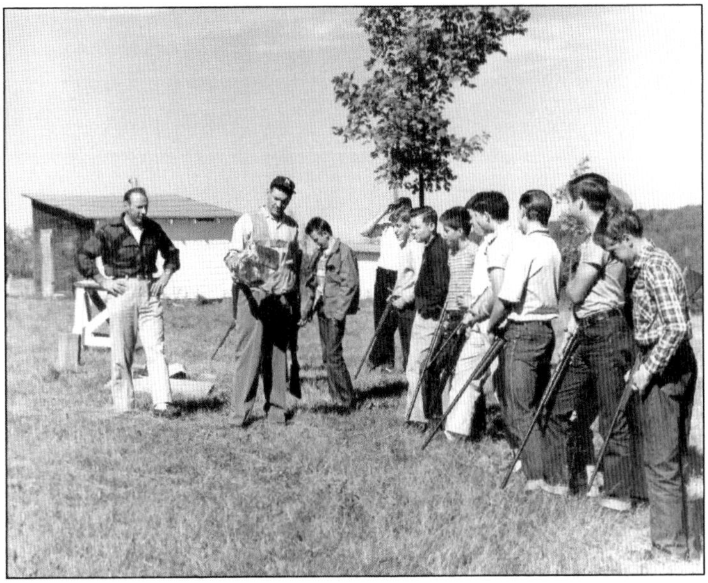

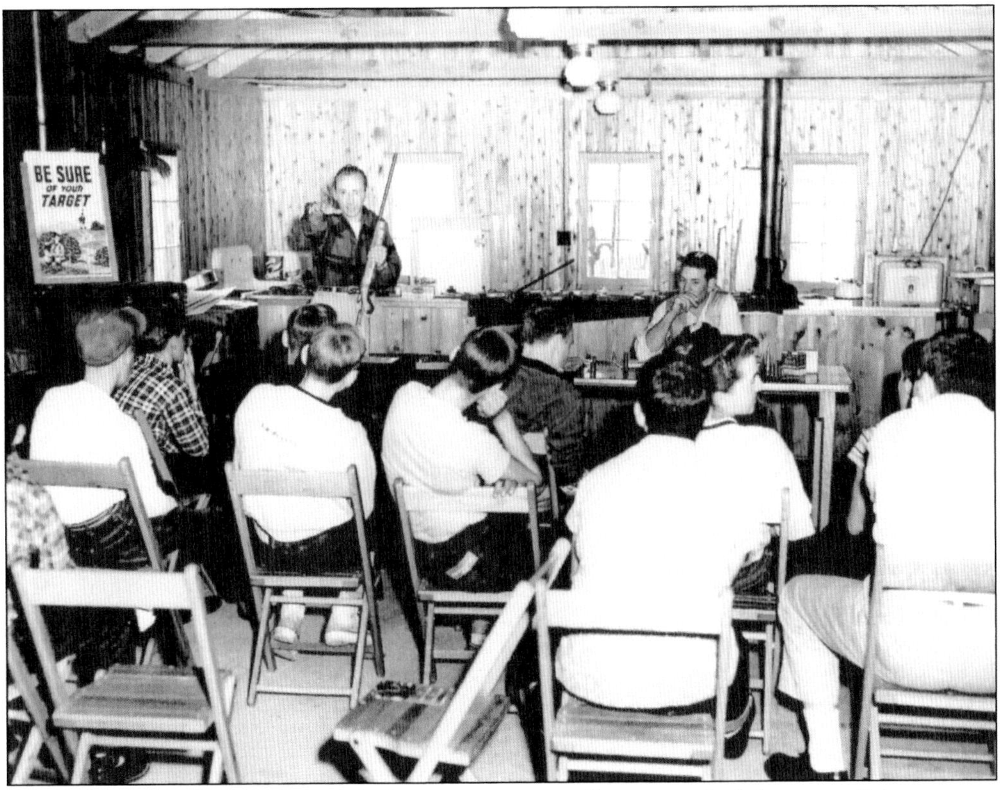

Classroom work was also required of any prospective rifleman, and while some of these young men seem a little bored, what they are learning will keep them and those they encounter in the woods safe, as well as ensure a successful hunt. As Caroline changed from a farming town to a community where many men went to work in Ithaca, it was no longer a given that a boy would learn everything he needed to know about woodcraft skills from his father, hence the reason hunter safety courses were offered.

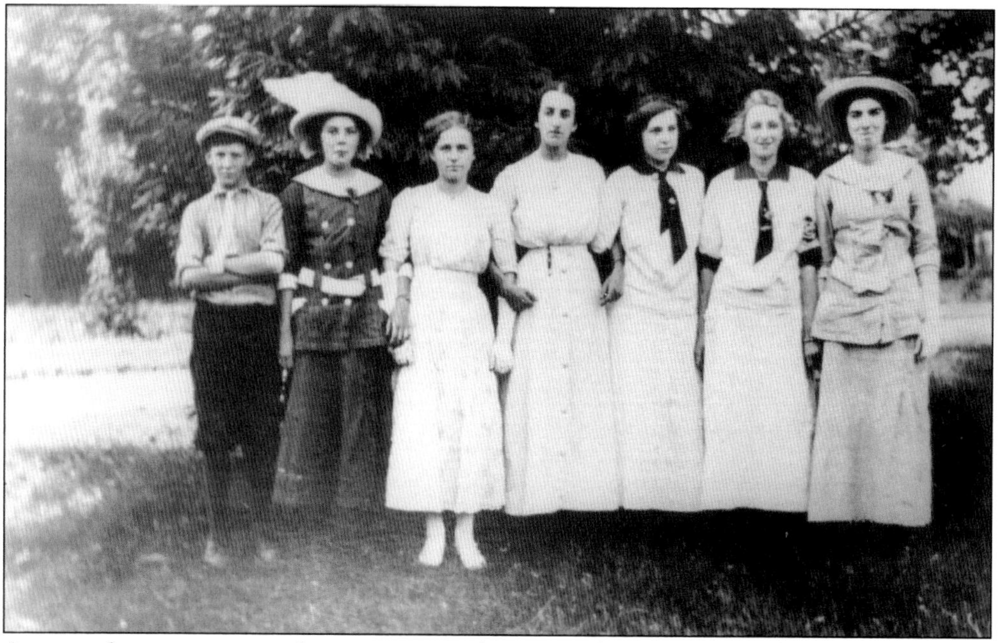

A group of young woman and one young man line up on the lawn. Two of the young ladies have neck scarves, which may tie them to a Girl Scout troop. In rural areas, girls joined Scouts and ladies' aid societies, and took classes at the local grange hall to prepare themselves for a future as mothers and farm wives. As the 20th century progressed, they began training for jobs outside the home.

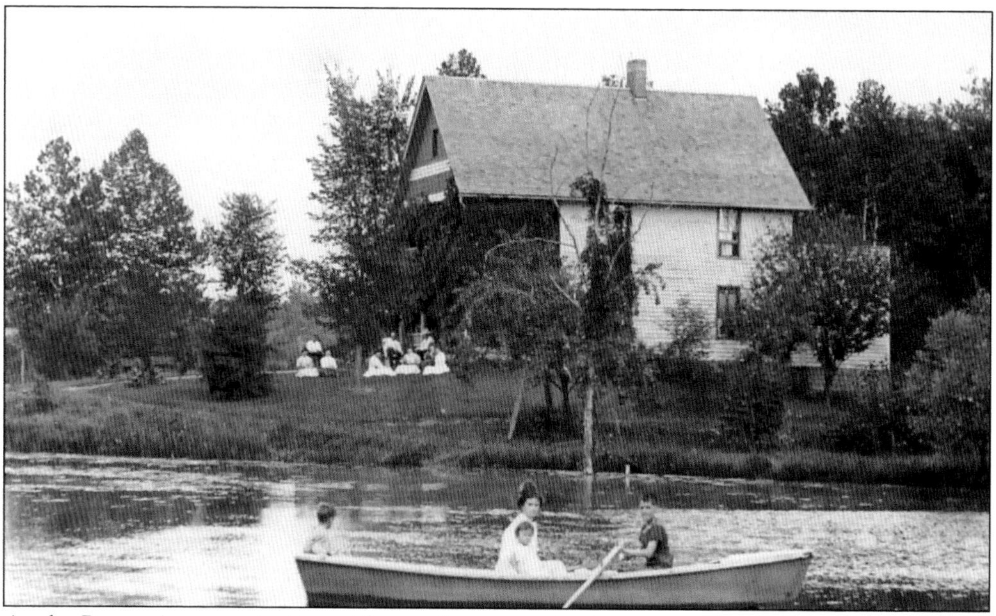

At the Browns' cottage in West Slaterville, rest and relaxation were important too. After a Saturday picking apples or Sunday services, relaxing on a grassy lawn after dinner or a quiet row on the pond (especially if someone else could man the oars) was the perfect way to spend a late summer or early fall afternoon.

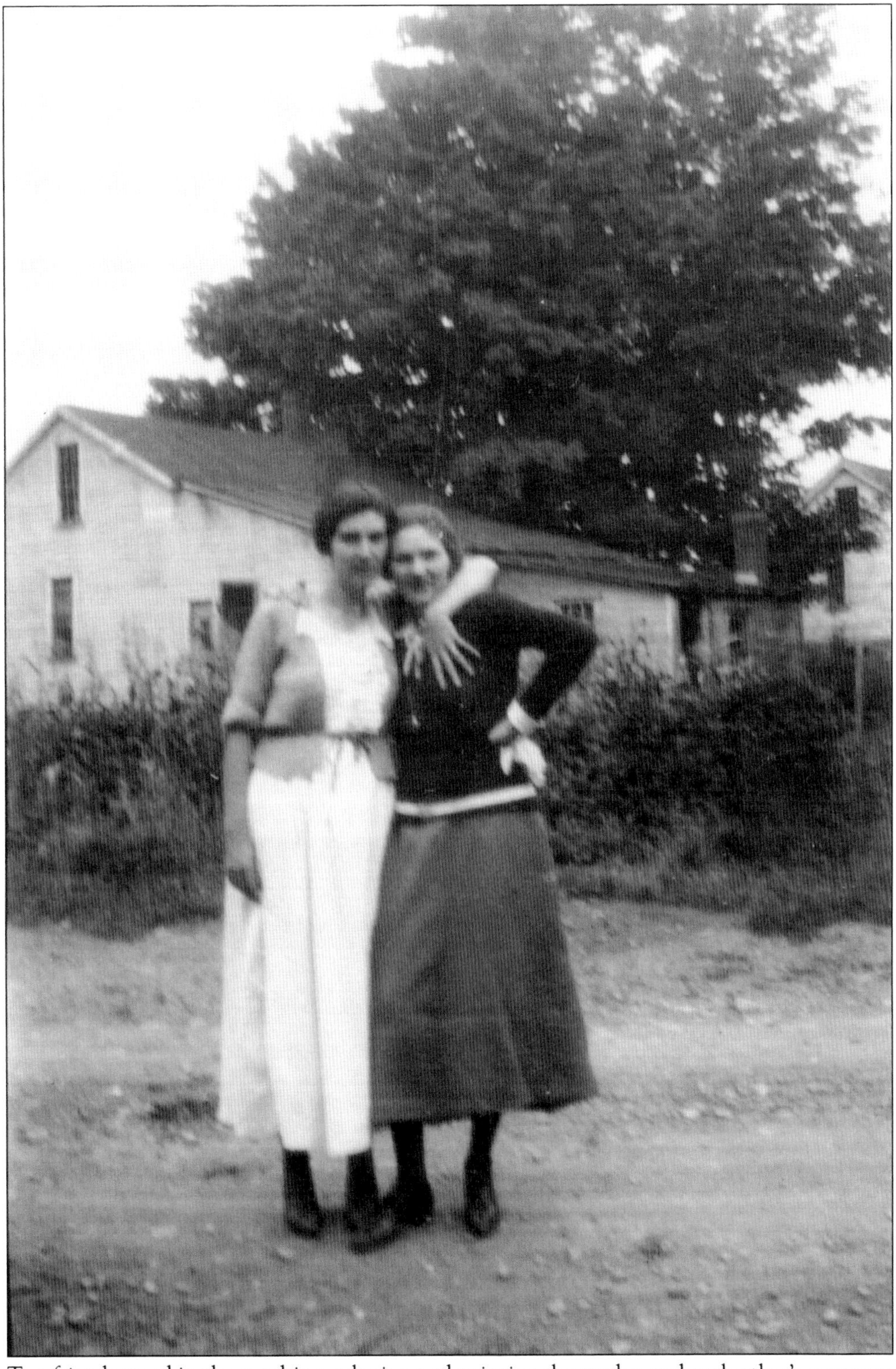

Two friends stand in the sunshine, relaxing and enjoying the garden and each other's company.

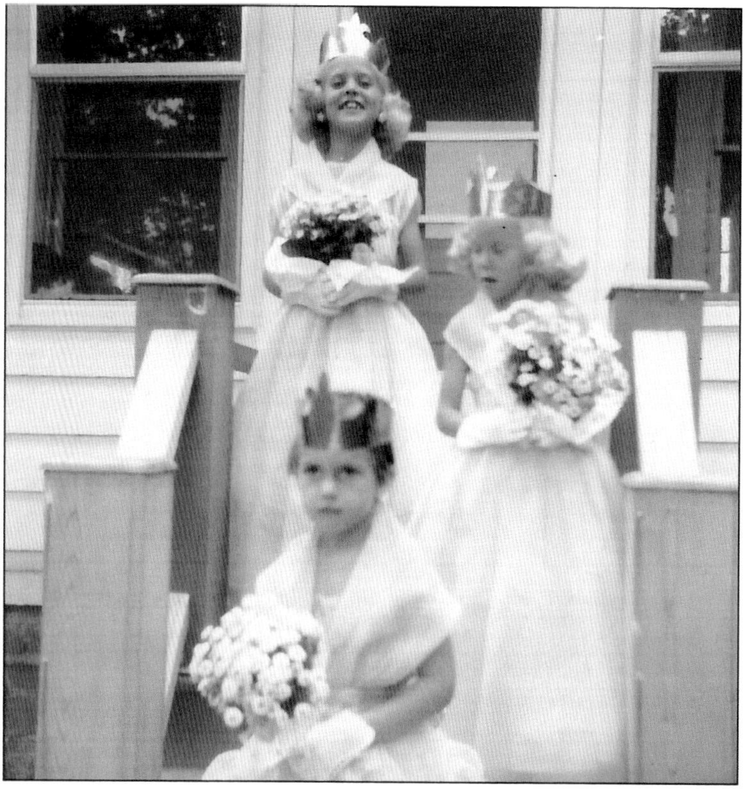

The Slaterville Fire Department sometimes conferred royal titles as part of its celebrations in the 1950s and 1960s. Here, Sandra Brown, Darleen White, and Diane Mix enjoy dressing up and being princesses for a day. In addition to providing fun and games for community members, it may have been a ploy to ensure future fire department or auxiliary members. It often worked, as some former princesses grew up to be loyal volunteers.

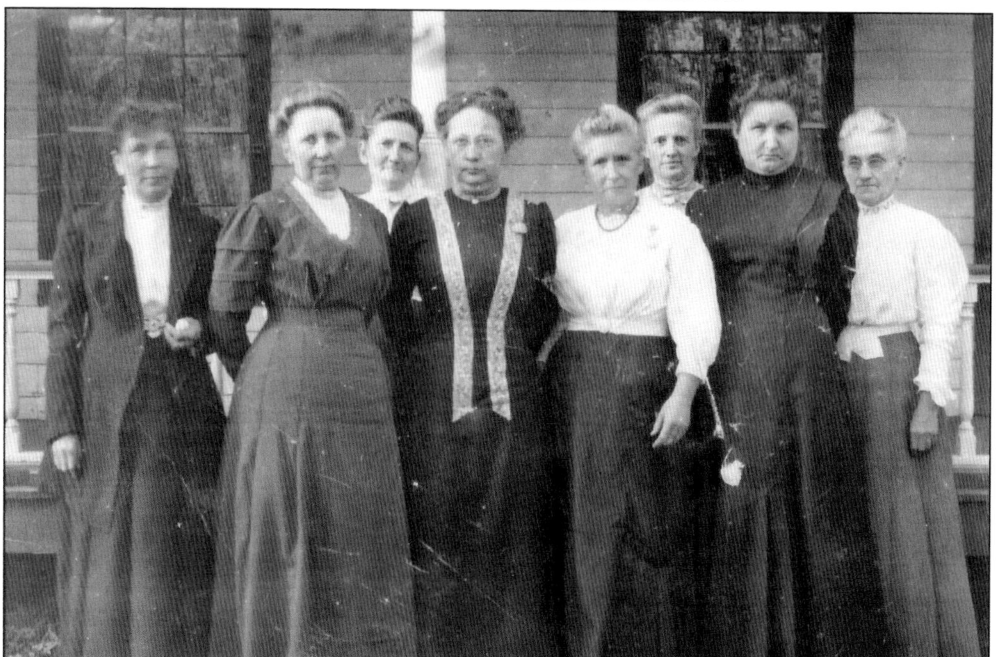

Young or old, the girls stuck together. These women went to school together, raised families in the Caroline community, volunteered for many community projects, and finally—after much laughter and many tears—reached their mature years, still side by side.

Survivors of the Whittaker clan may disagree as to which of their many ancestors this is, but all confirm that this bright and curious youngster is one of them. Before babies could walk, they often wore these long gowns, both to keep them warm in drafty houses and to accustom both boys and girls to the shorter, but still full-skirted, dresses they wore for their first few years.

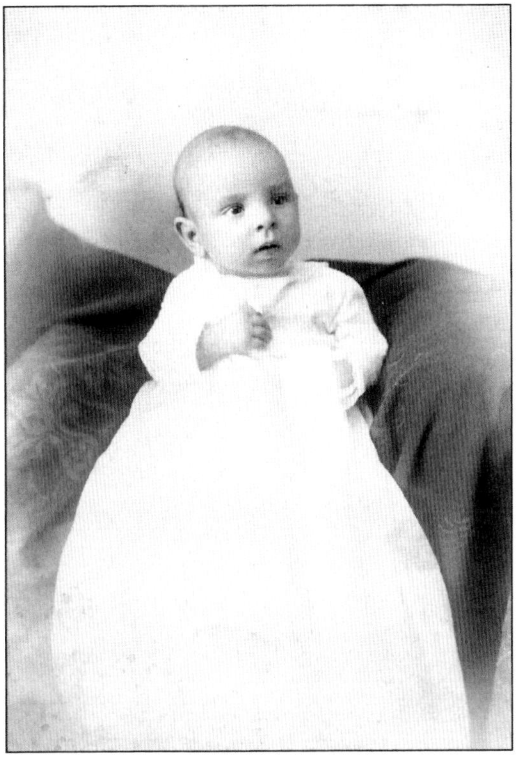

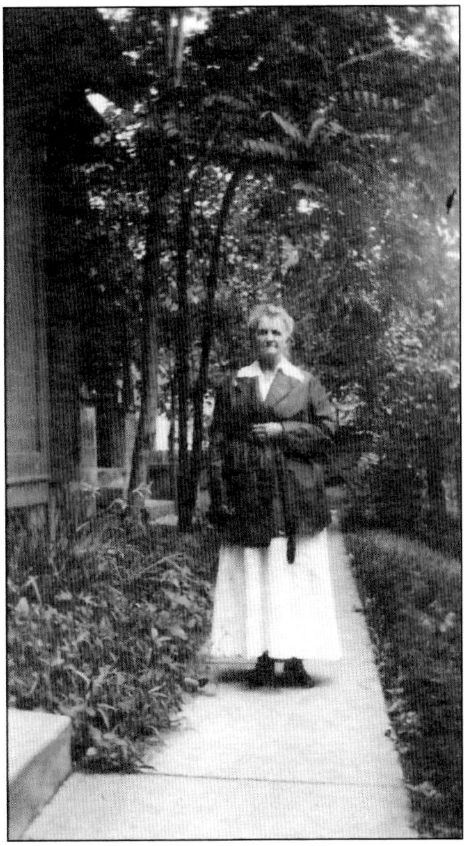

No matter her age, a woman will do what she can to look her best and to beautify her surroundings. This fine figure of a woman stands beside a flower garden she could be justly proud of. There are day lilies growing beside the walkway, but the garden may stretch well beyond the limits of this photograph, with rose bushes out front and vegetables in the backyard.

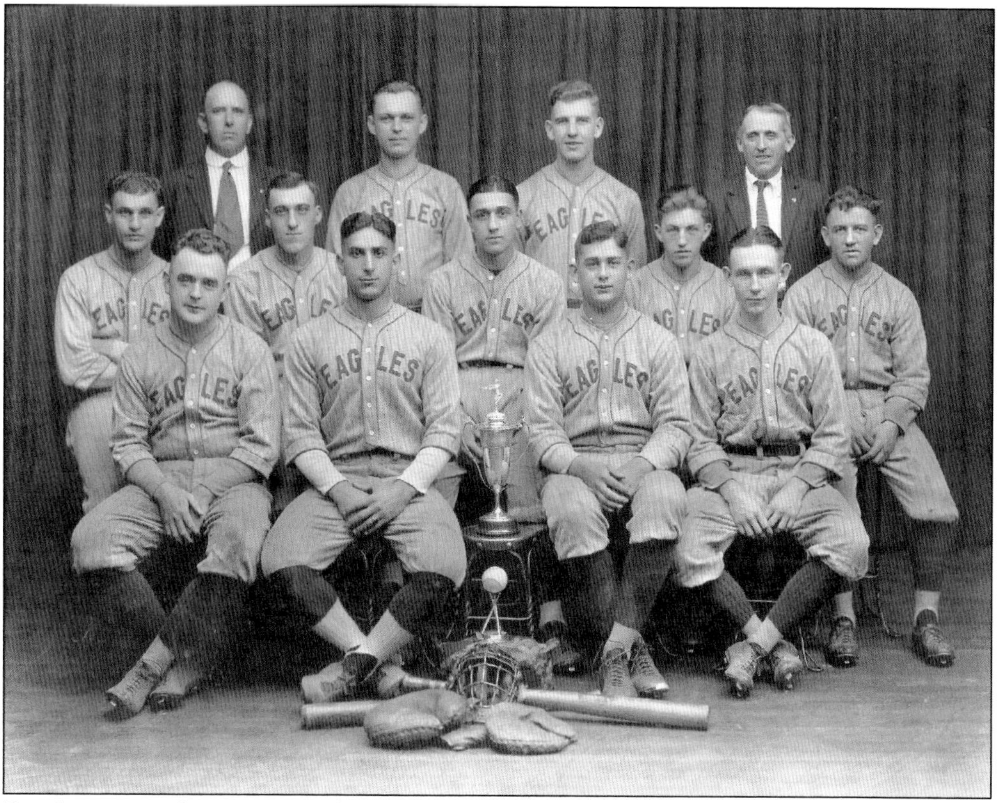

Fire department fetes were not the only regular fun in town. Like many hamlets, residents had baseball. The trophy-winning Eagles played against many local teams. They also had a loyal fan base, and locals were encouraged to come out and cheer them on.

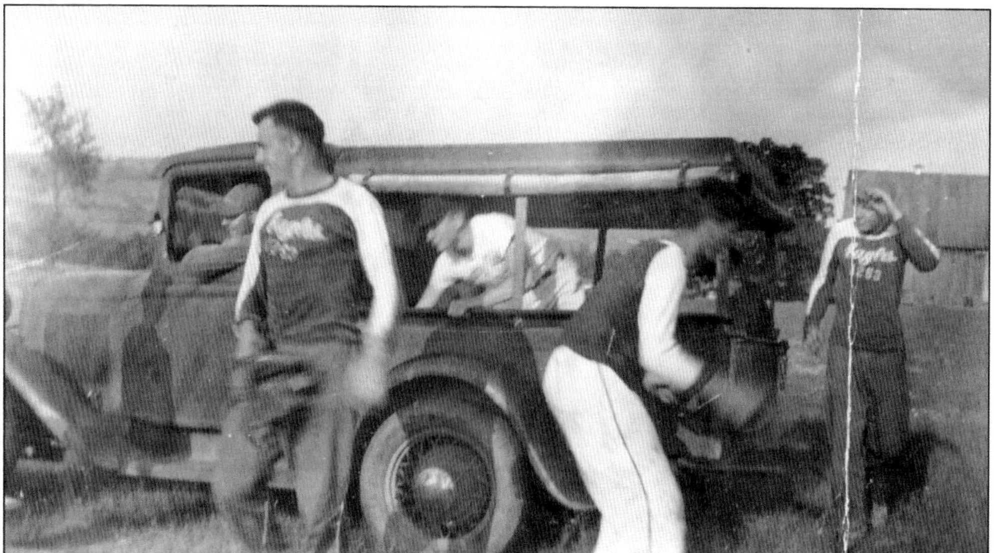

The Eagles unload from their usual accommodations—a truck with side curtains to keep out the dust and rain—for a game or, perhaps, a practice session. These enthusiastic young men look very different from the stiff formal portrait at the top of the page.

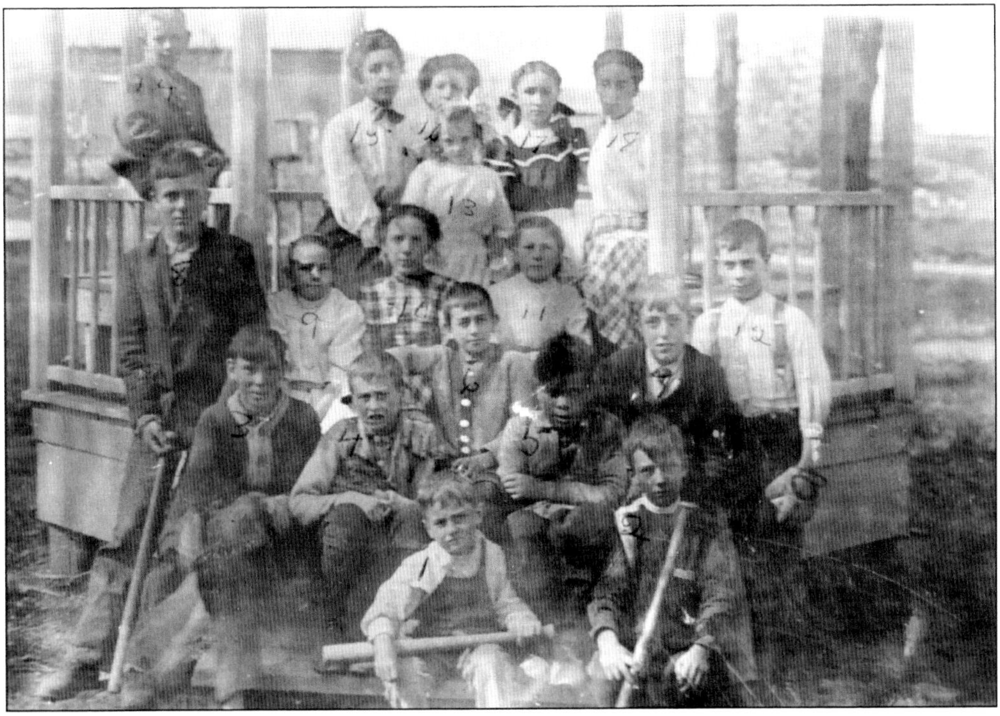

What these youngsters lacked in uniforms, they made up for in sheer enthusiasm. This Speedsville baseball team and their admirers take a break in the town square gazebo. Baseball-playing youngsters in rural areas rarely had the Little League organization considered necessary today, but they had plenty of fun while learning about self direction, negotiation, and compromise, as they often played with far fewer than nine to each side.

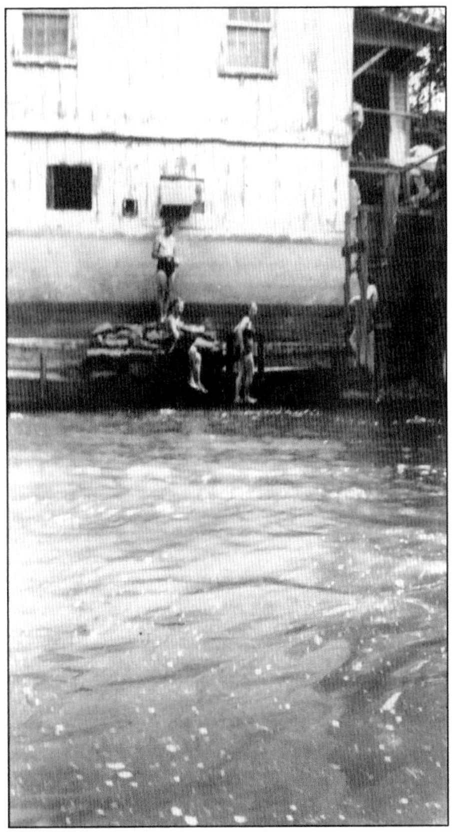

Swimmers leap from the side of the mill into the millpond on a hot summer day. Taking a dip in the millpond was a great way to beat the heat before air conditioning and video games provided youngsters with entertainment. These millponds, though much altered, are still in use by local kids and adults.

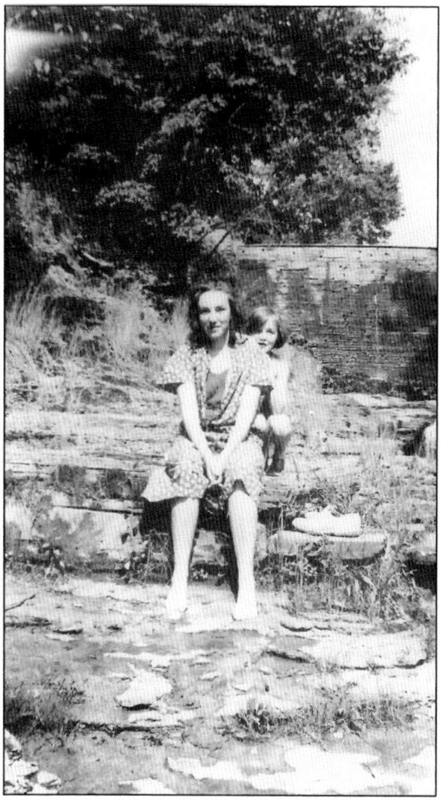

Two locals dip their toes in the cool water of Six Mile Creek. Perhaps their mothers forbid swimming, or maybe the water is just too cold for total immersion.

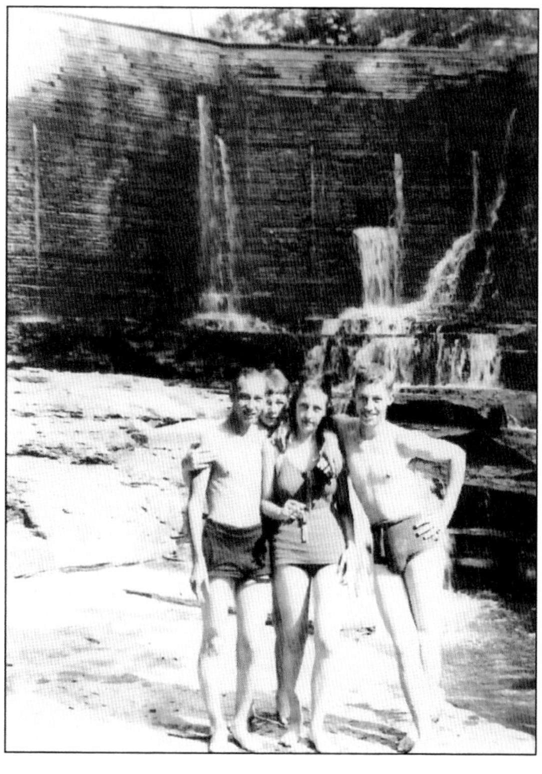

These youngsters pose below the milldam. The dam is gone for the most part, but adults, children, and even dogs still swim there all summer long. It is also a great place for trout fishing. Spring floods change the topography of the bottom every year, so caution is necessary until the depth is redetermined before diving can begin.

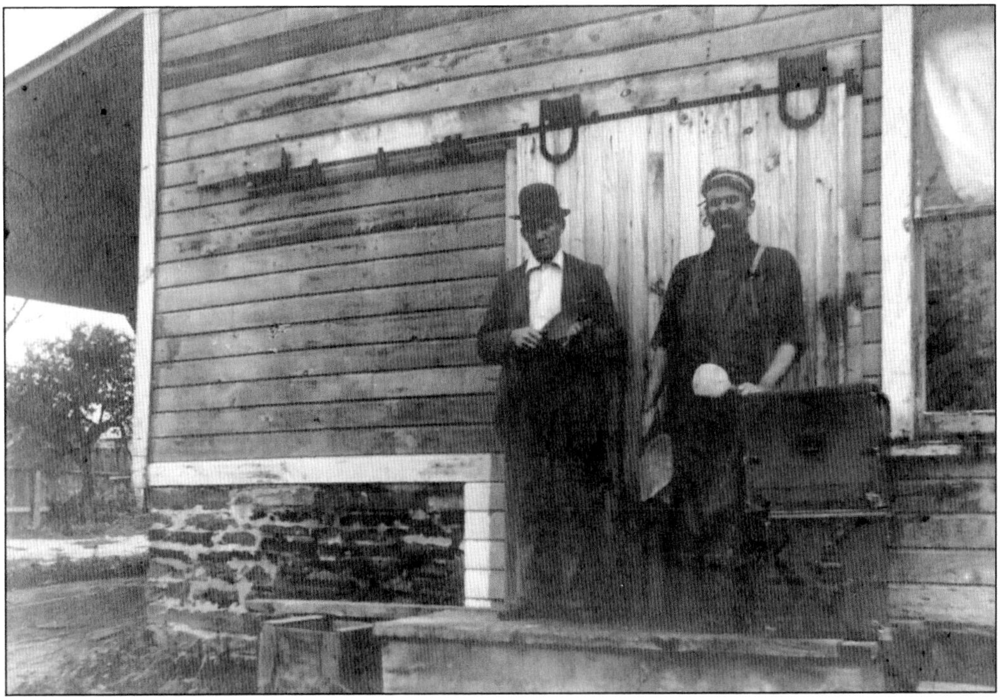

The Butter Factory in Caroline took advantage of the many regional dairy farms, exporting these tasty delights throughout the area. The man on the right holds a butter paddle, used to stir and press the butter into molds.

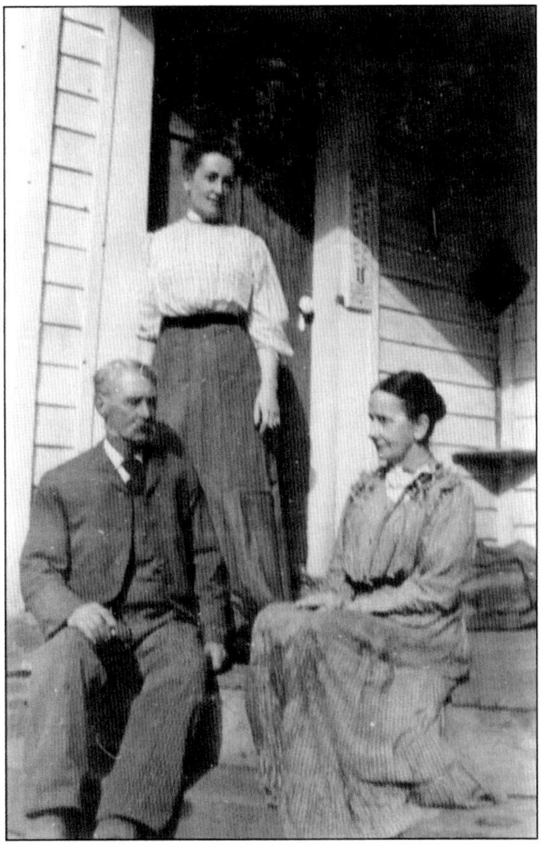

The children were not the only ones who liked to get away from the hard work that rural living could entail. These adults take a break on the back steps, perhaps after a long day spent getting fruits and vegetables ready for canning, drying, or storing in the root cellar. During the late summer and fall, this was a frequent task, but one that reaped rewards for months to come.

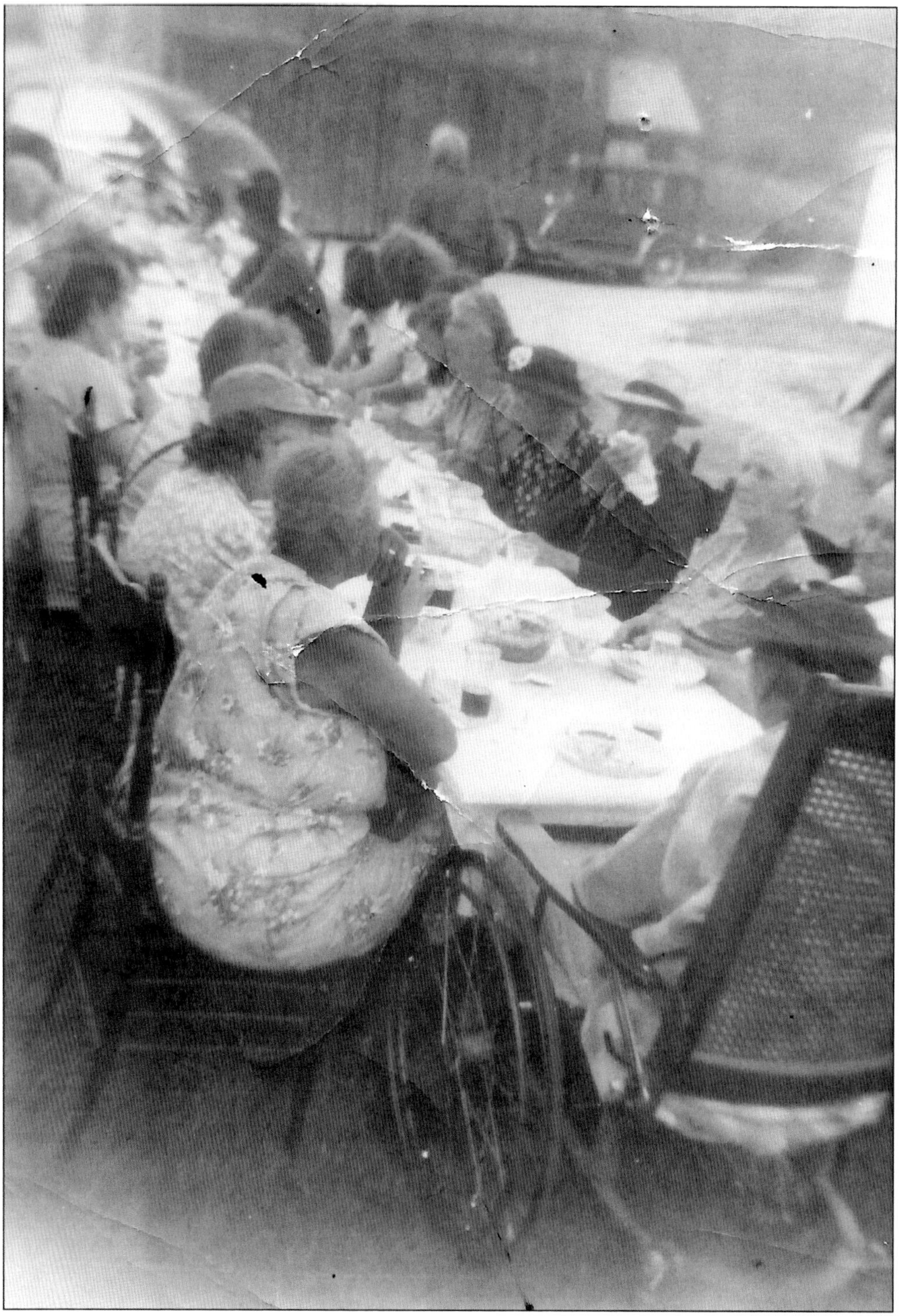

Summer also meant family reunions so that people might gather from miles around to enjoy a meal, meet the new babies, and pay homage to the elder relatives. As families were often large, the reunions could be very well attended.

Other people found it more fun to be active. Fishing was one of those things a person could do that, with the possibility of bringing home some dinner, seemed almost virtuous. This fellow is happy to show off his catch.

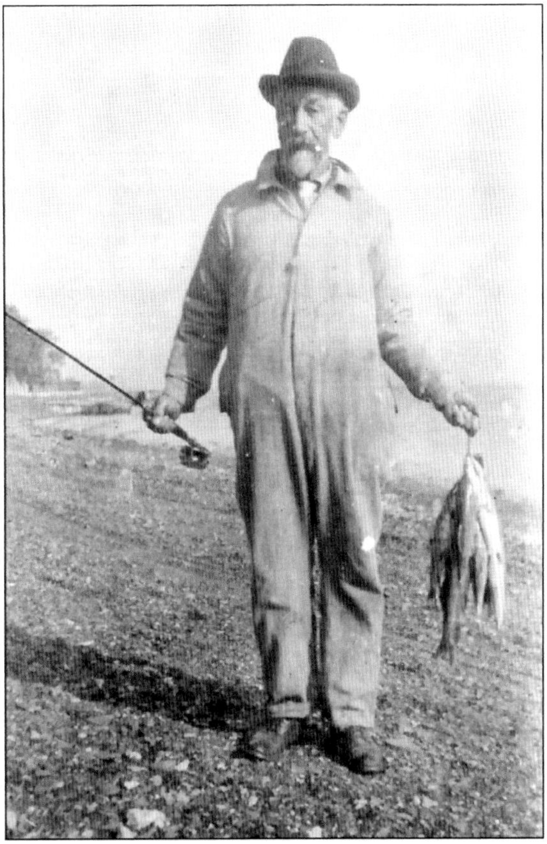

The Dusenbury girls relax on the grass at the Ward farm. Sisters, cousins, and friends enjoy the warm weather and companionship, exchanging stories, gossip, information on how to grow up, the secrets of dealing with boys, and perhaps, the best way of getting around the parents to secure a few extra treats or privileges. (Courtesy of the Ward collection.)

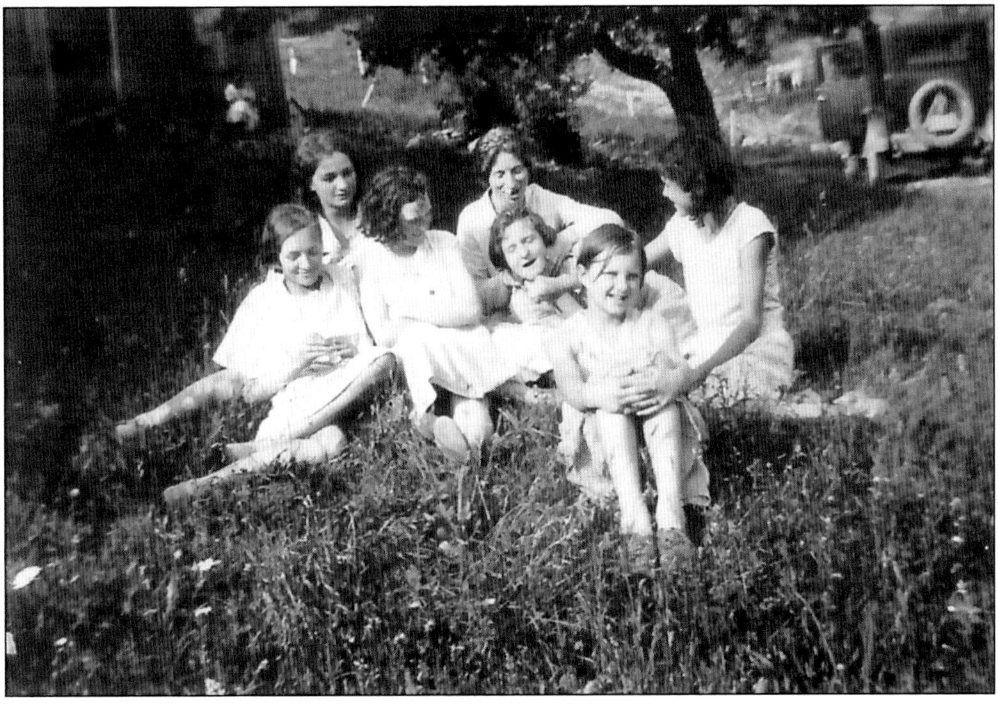

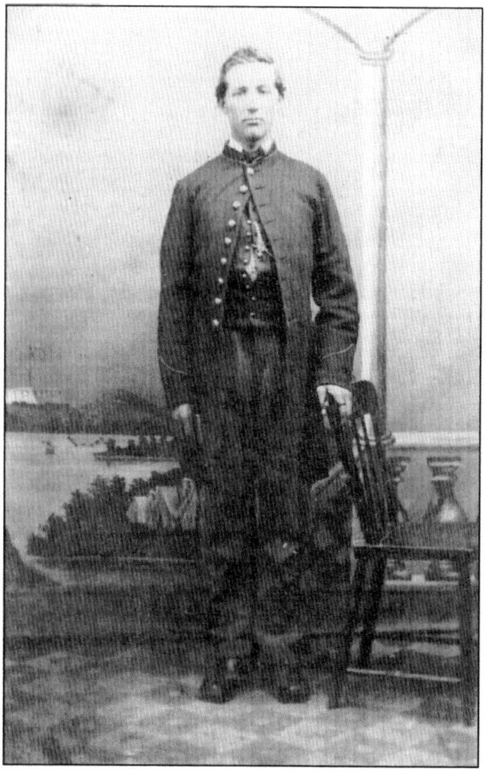

Leonard Reed poses for his going-away portrait before joining the 109th Regiment Company, New York. Whole families were affected by war. An anxious mother would carefully follow the news and visit the post office or newspaper office after every battle, where lists of the injured and missing were posted, seeking information about her loved ones. Sometimes the only thing left to the grieving mother was one last portrait.

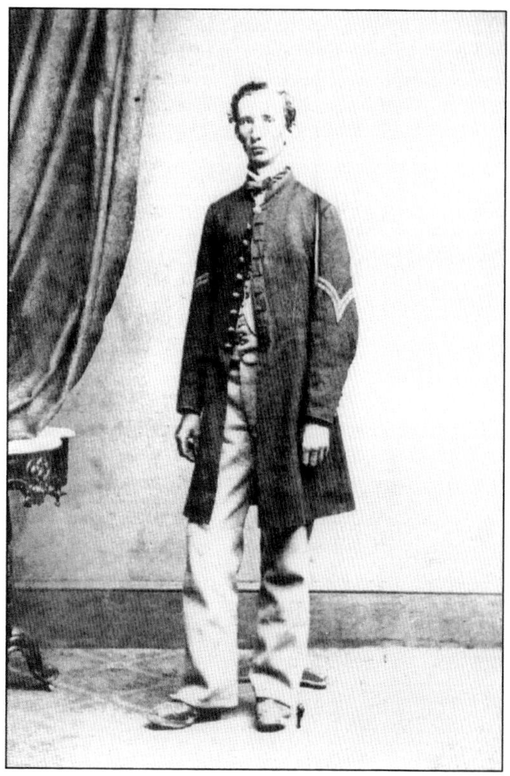

Like his cousin, James Benton Reed was in the 109th Regiment Company, New York. He survived the Civil War and came home to Caroline, where he died on September 18, 1875. His diary can be found on the Caroline Town Hall website.

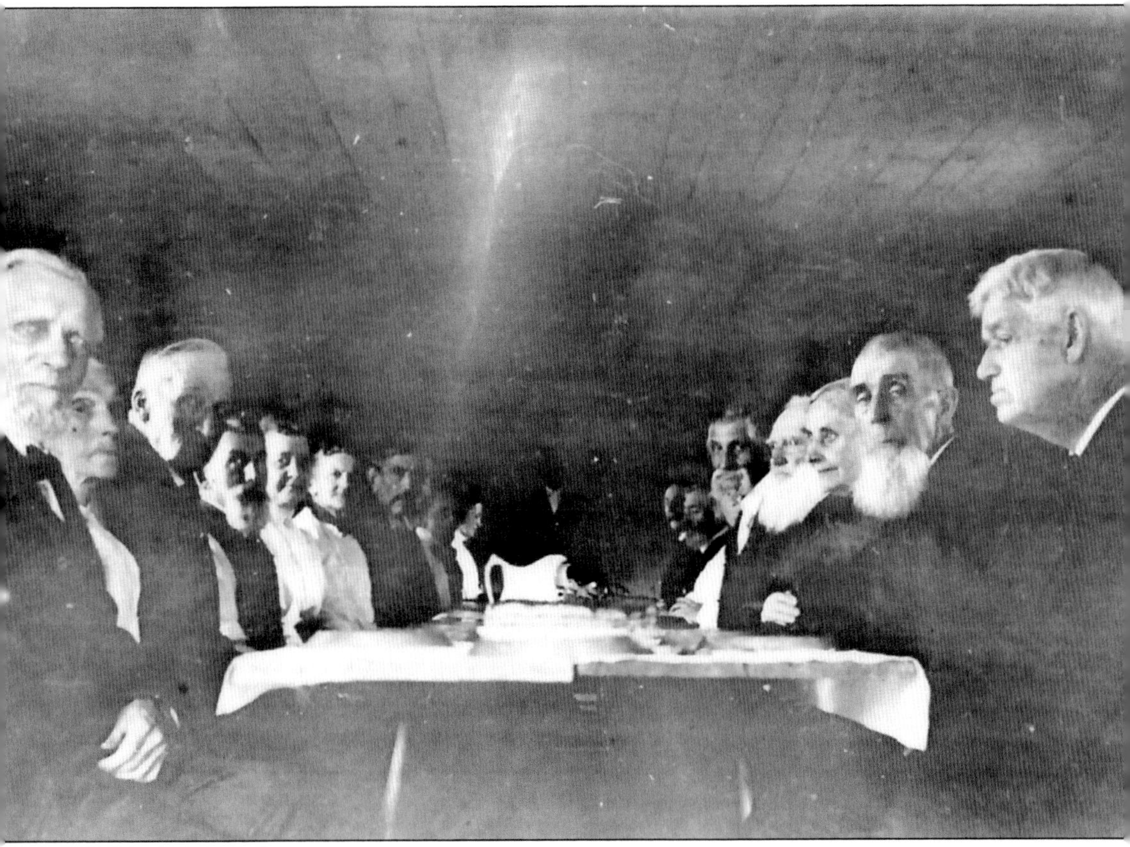

The Caroline members of the Grand Army of the Republic, men who had in their youth fought for the Union army in the Civil War, sit at table with their wives for a meal and conversation. For the rest of their lives, these men shared a bond that outsiders could not understand.

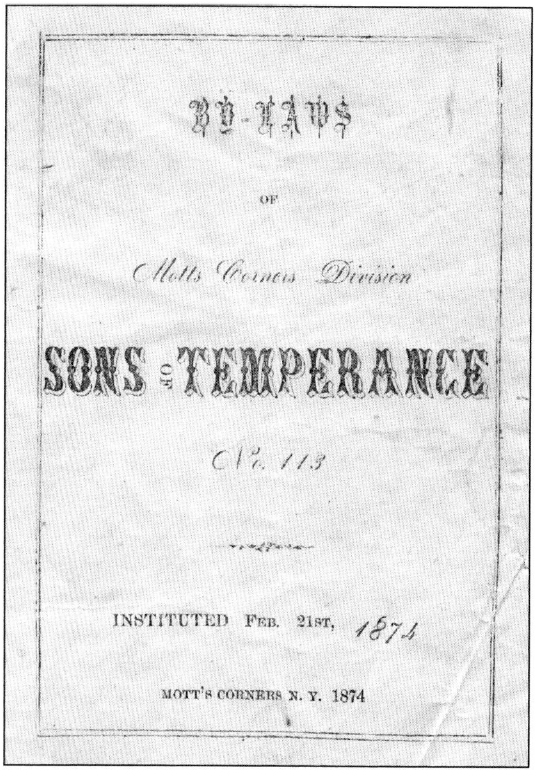

BY-LAWS

OF

Motts Corners Division

SONS OF TEMPERANCE

No. 113

INSTITUTED FEB. 21ST, 1874

MOTT'S CORNERS N. Y. 1874

The Sons of Temperance was an organization whose members pledged to abstain from intoxicating drinks, tobacco in every form, and profanity. The Caroline chapter started in Motts Corners (now Brooktondale) in 1874. Members also promised to help their fellow members if sick, and some chapters even helped with burial expenses.

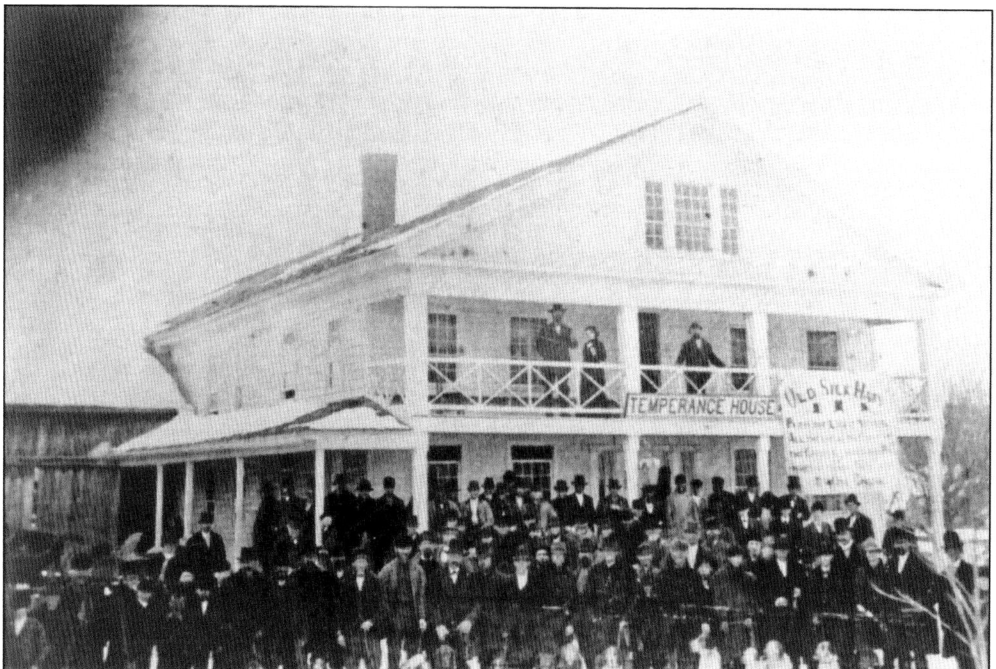

Temperance organizations were popular during the decades leading up to Prohibition, and some went well beyond helping men refrain from drink. Here is a group gathered for fox hunting at the Speedsville Temperance House.

Two

CHURCHES AND SCHOOLS

In the wilderness that was upstate New York, a community was greatly aided by having a place of worship. God was more than just someone to pay lip service to on Sunday morning; he was a protector and a moral guide through life. Many of the early settlers came west for religious freedom, including the people who built and maintained the Dutch Reformed Church in West Slaterville. Methodists, especially the Wesleyans, organized their lives around the church. Ministers and others were strictly admonished to "not lay abed until the scandalous hour of six a.m.," which no doubt aided them in becoming successful farmers. The church served as a place to seek comfort in a world where crops could fail and the death of family or close friends was never far away. Church was often held twice each Sunday, and families sometimes brought a picnic lunch in good weather or warming pans for the ladies' feet during long, cold winter sermons. Horses' comfort was also considered; most churches had a shed out back where a horse could get out of the weather and have a bite to eat before the long pull home.

A town was not complete without a school, and an education was something much sought after by most families. Until consolidation in 1959, up to 19 one- and two-room schools graced the hills and valleys of Caroline. The Slaterville Springs two-story school has become the town hall, and the Brooktondale two-room school became a teen center, the Skip and Joe Club, named after local teens Skip Lattin and Joe English, who were killed one Easter Sunday when out for a joyride. When that building succumbed to a fire caused by an electric short, the Brooktondale Fire Department, which owned it at the time, donated the land and the insurance settlement to start the community-owned and -run Brooktondale Community Center. In 2004, the fire department moved to a modern station about a mile up the road and sold its original building to provide the center with a much-needed expansion.

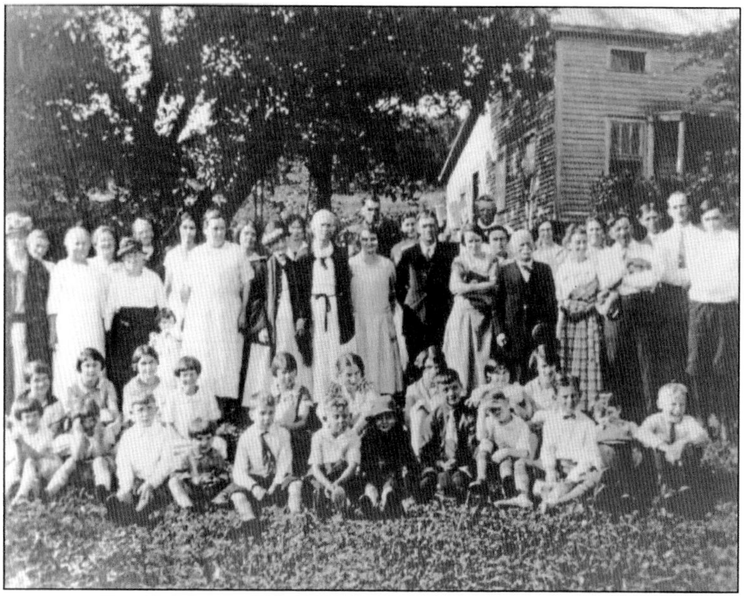

The Brooktondale Baptist Church is still active, though it has moved out of downtown Brooktondale and into a newer building on Route 79. The structure of the old church, which hosted this picnic for its members in 1925 or 1926, was turned into an apartment building.

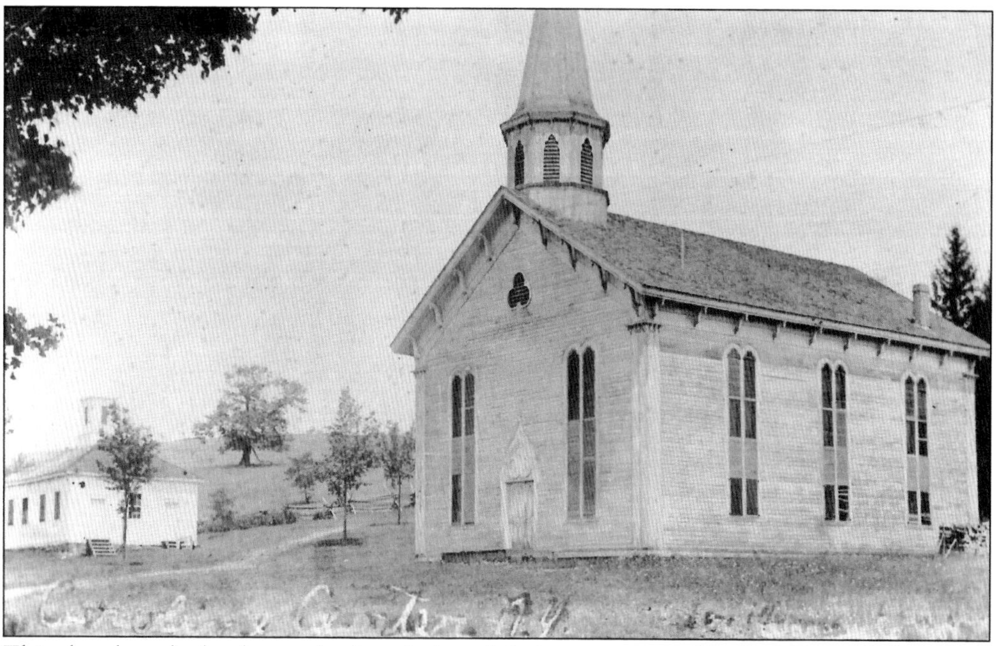

This church and school were the foundation of their community, Caroline Center. The school closed in 1957 and the children are now bused to Caroline Elementary or the Ithaca middle and high school. The look of the church has changed a lot over the years; however, the Caroline Center Church, built in 1825, still maintains its role of pulling people together and helping community members.

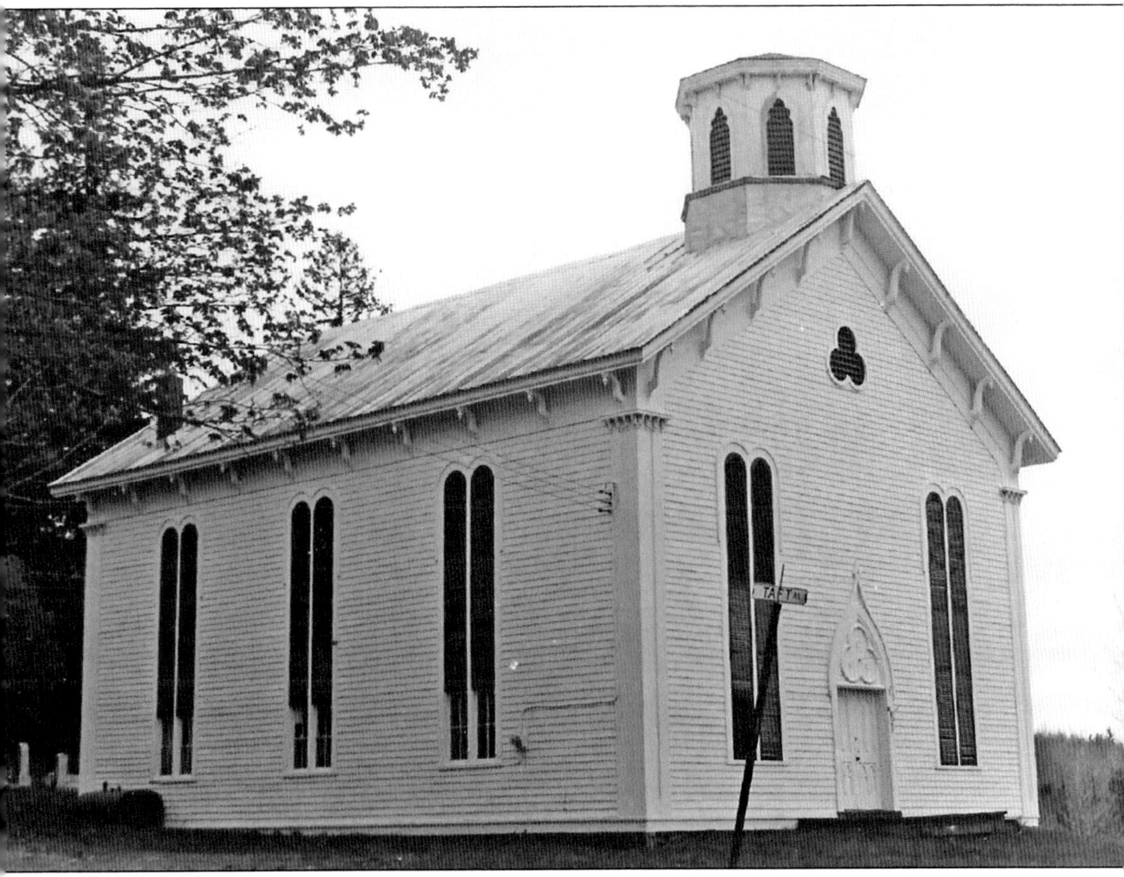

In this photograph are the Caroline Center Church and its associated cemetery. The cemetery is the final resting place of Revolutionary War soldiers Samuel Stevens and George Vandemark and War of 1812 soldiers John Lynch, Ephriam Personius, William Perry, and Jonathan Taft. The church was built, like most in town, with light airy windows and high ceilings. The Caroline Center Church is still a vibrant part of the community. While the steeple is gone, it now has a basement kitchen and meeting room—a place to host a monthly fish fry fundraiser and other events. The fish fry is widely attended both for the excellent food and the chance to visit with friends and neighbors. Proceeds help to pay the heating bills and also allow the church to donate money to other local nonprofits, including the food pantry. Free dinners are held one Sunday a month and at Christmas, offering another way for the church members and the local community to relax together and enjoy one another's company.

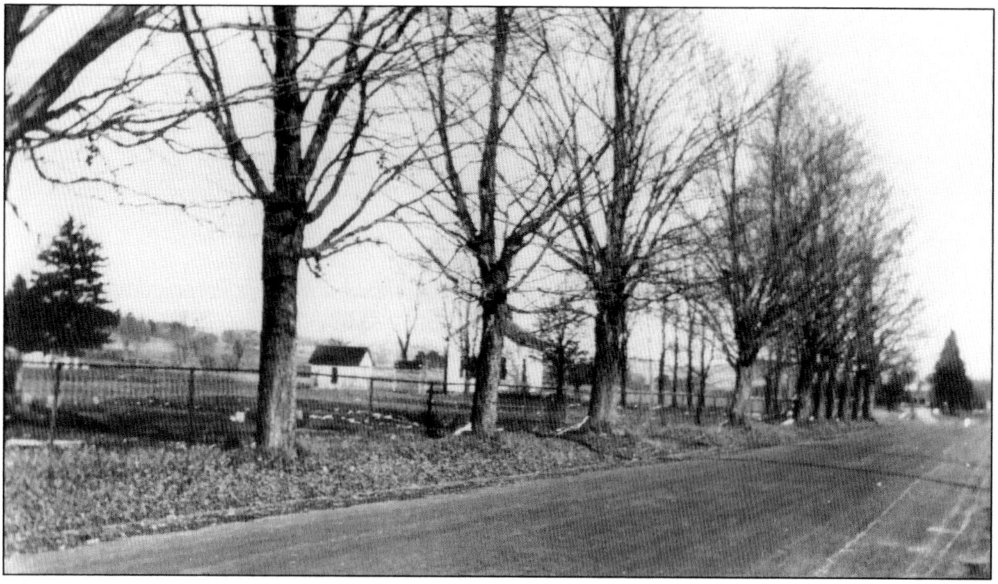

The site of the former Dutch Reformed Church and its cemetery has also changed. The church, built in 1820, was torn down, and the lumber recycled. The cemetery, called the Garret Mandeville Cemetery in honor of the first minister to settle the area (in 1810) and serve as minister for the next 25 years, contains the remains of four Revolutionary War soldiers and five veterans of the War of 1812.

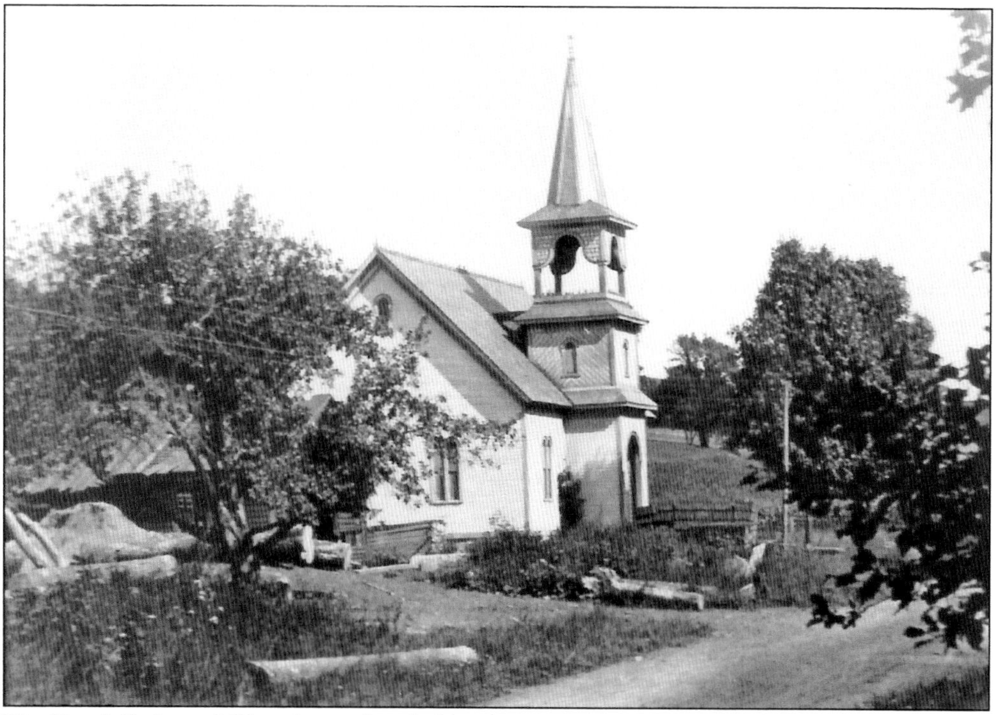

The Dutch Reformed Church was founded by those moving west to avoid religious persecution. It conformed to the times by having a set of steps in the back that led to a second-floor balcony where local slaves were allowed to worship.

Now called the Caroline Community Church, the Federated Church in Brooktondale has sheltered a variety of Protestant congregations. Years ago, the church lost its steeple but not its mission. It helps support the food pantry and provides practical assistance and spiritual guidance to church members and the community, participates in the Brooktondale Apple Fest, and holds its own annual craft fair, the Christmas Country Store, to help provide funding for various missions.

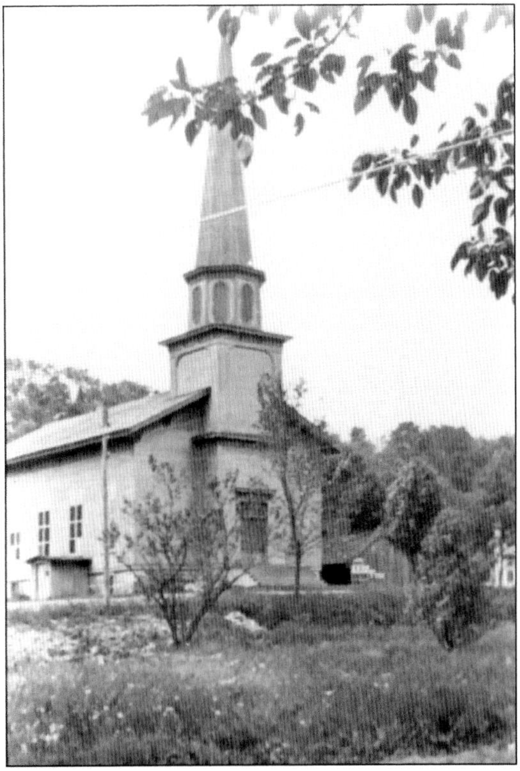

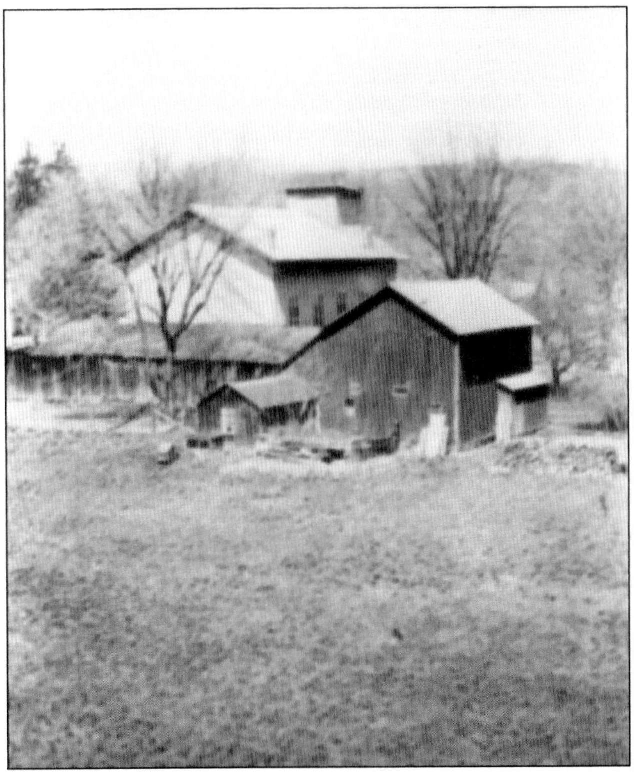

Before the automobile, accommodations had to be made for horses during those long—sometimes multiple—Sunday sermons. Built behind the Federated Church, this livery stable for the horses was decommissioned and dismantled some time ago; now, only the barn remains, but it is still remembered fondly by older church members.

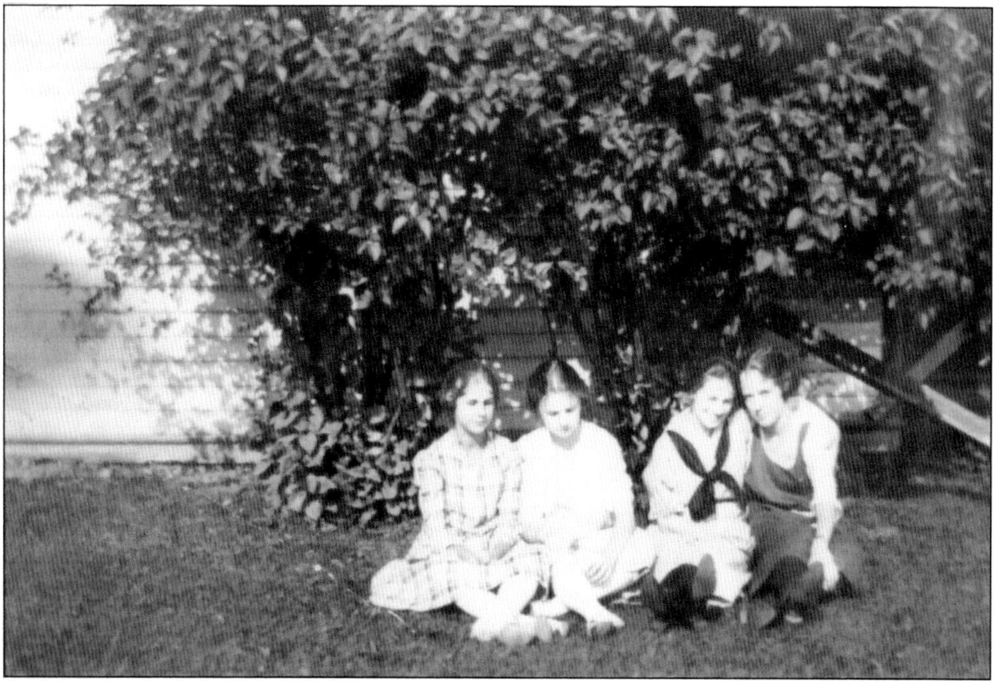

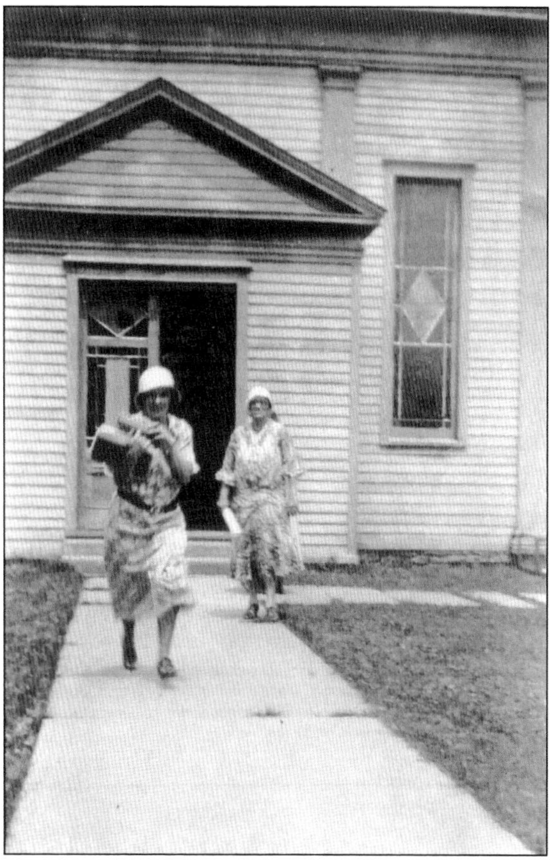

Four girls enjoy a Sunday school class held in the midst of green splendor in the hamlet of Brookton. A number of the elder congregation members remember Sunday school classes and picnics with the sound of Six Mill Creek as the background music and occasional excursions to gather flowers for the church for memorial services.

The Methodist Episcopal Church, built in 1834 at the cost of $1,000, eventually lost its congregation and was turned into a community center where teen activities, dances, and even blood drives were held. In 1957, it succumbed to a fire, and this site is now part of the road leading to the subdivision behind the convenience store in Slaterville Springs.

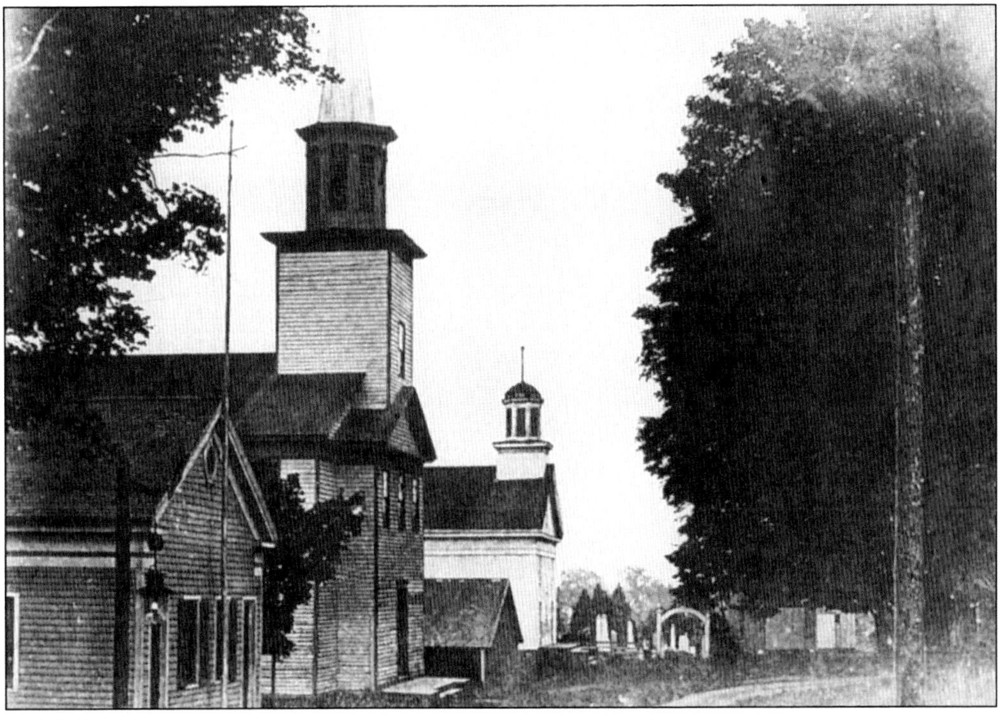

This school and two churches are located on one side of the Commons in the hamlet of Speedsville and shown with the Speedsville Cemetery in the background. The first church was built in 1828 by the Universalists and Methodists together. The second was erected in 1851 by the Methodists when they decided that they needed a church of their own. After that, each church operated independently until a dwindling population closed the Methodist church. It was torn down in 1945, and the lumber was used to build three houses.

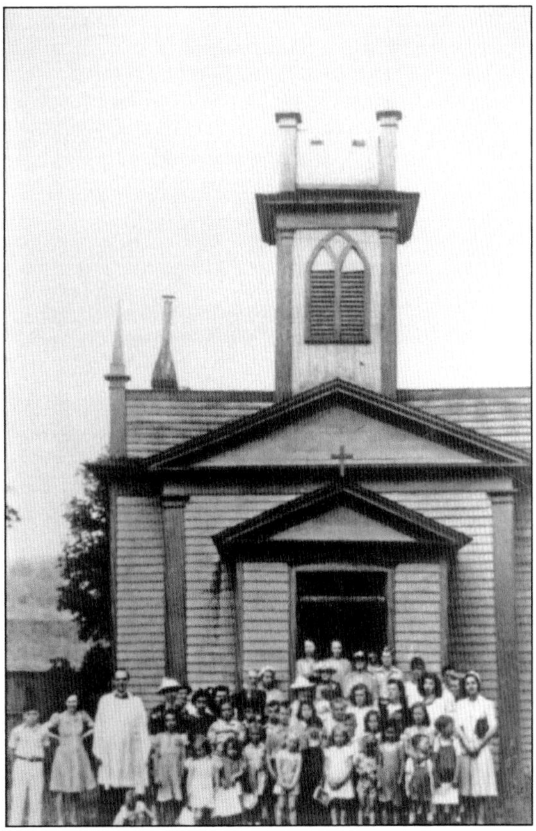

St. Johns Church, just off the Commons and a short distance from the above buildings, was erected in Richford, about six miles away, in 1835, but moved to Speedsville in 1842. As the story goes, the bell rang all the way there. This is one of three buildings in town listed in the National Register of Historic Places. Except for the installation of electricity, it is virtually unchanged.

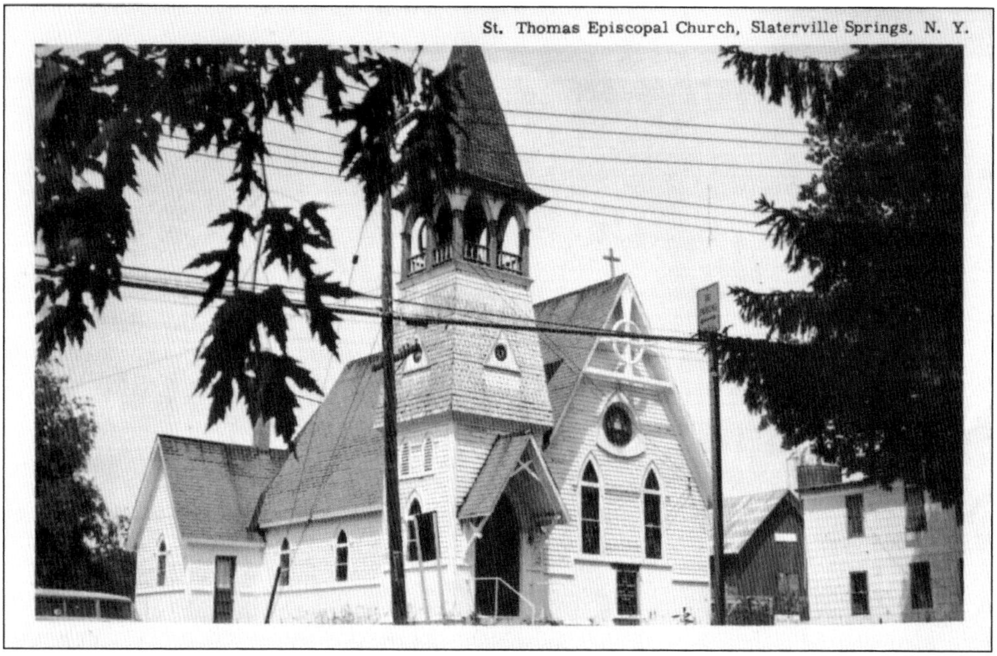

St. Thomas Episcopal Church, built in 1894 at Slaterville Springs, is the second National Register church in Caroline. It was repainted in its original Victorian era colors, with shades of olive green on the outside and bright blue and yellow on the interior. The stained-glass windows have been restored to their original beauty. The additions of a handicap accessible ramp, pipe organ, and modern conveniences have not altered its character or the amazing acoustics.

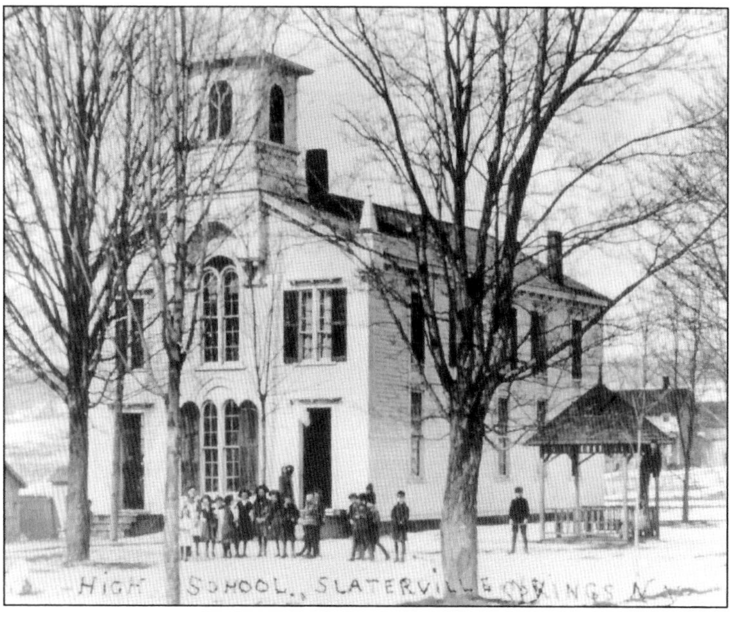

The third building in Caroline to be listed in the National Register of Historic Places is the former high school building in Slaterville Springs, which now houses the town court and meeting space on the first floor and the Caroline Town History Room, with its display, research, and storage space, on the second floor. There is now a one-story building next door that holds town offices and the library.

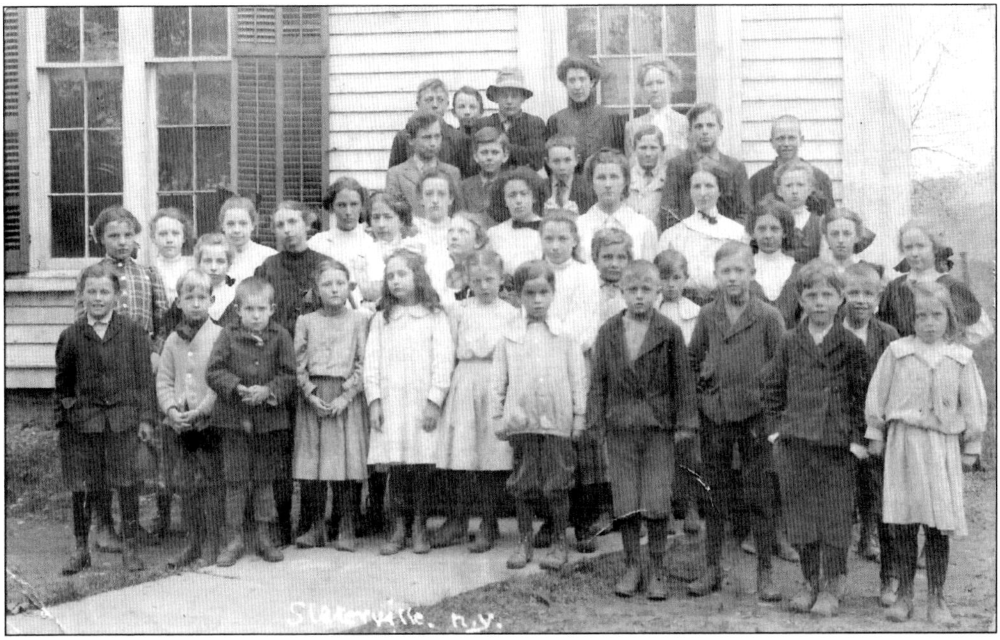

Students and teachers gather on the steps of the two-story Slaterville Springs School. Built to be the most impressive school in the area, it once held eight grades on one floor and high school classes on the other.

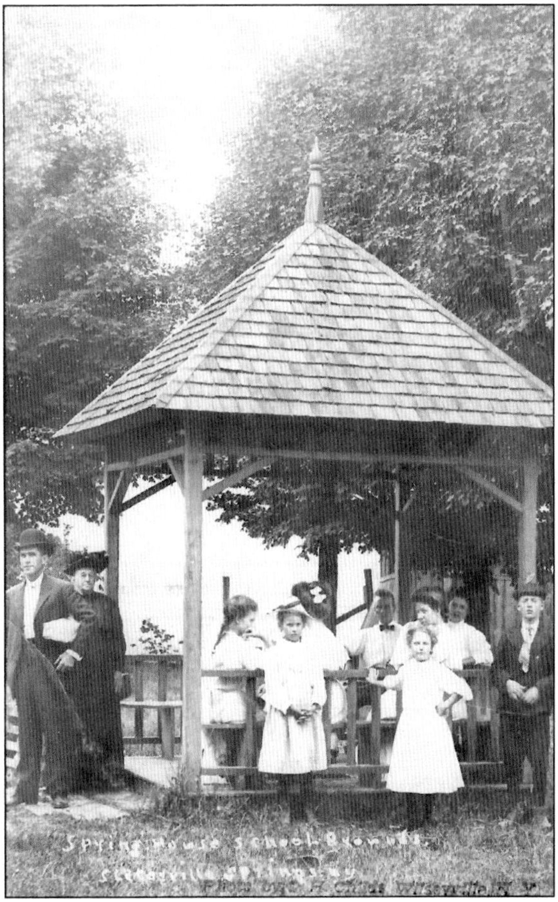

While this wonderful gazebo was torn down long ago, the artesian well that was such a draw for men, woman, and children on a summer afternoon still flows and is a great attraction. Some locals insist that the water is not only healthy, but also health restoring, just as was claimed in the 1800s. One local chicken owner insists that his hens lay better with Slaterville water.

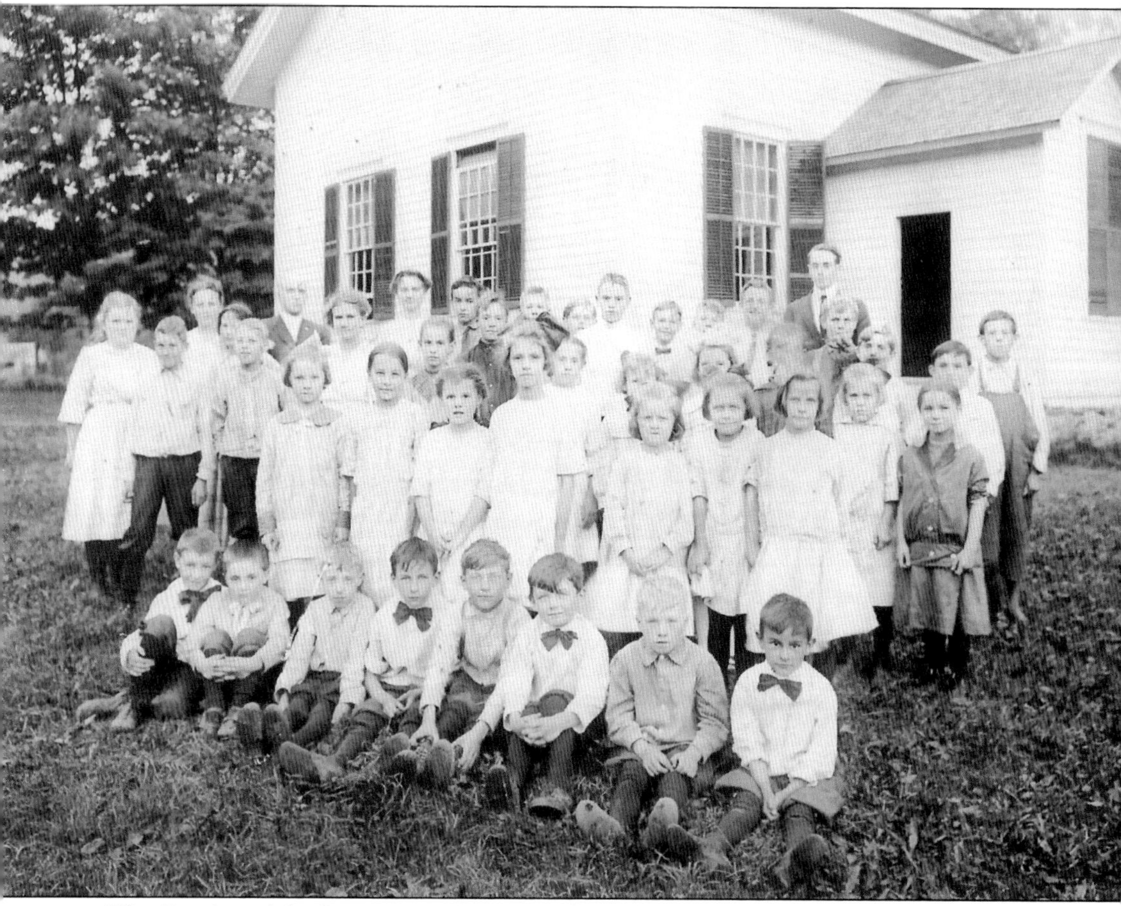

The Brooktondale Community Center and its playground now stand where this two-room schoolhouse once kept these youngsters busy with their "reading, writing, and 'rithmatic." Though the building closed when schools were consolidated in 1959, the surviving students still gather each August for a reunion where they share a dish to pass along with stories. They also continue to pose for a photographer, although there are fewer people in the picture and many are no longer able to sit on the grass.

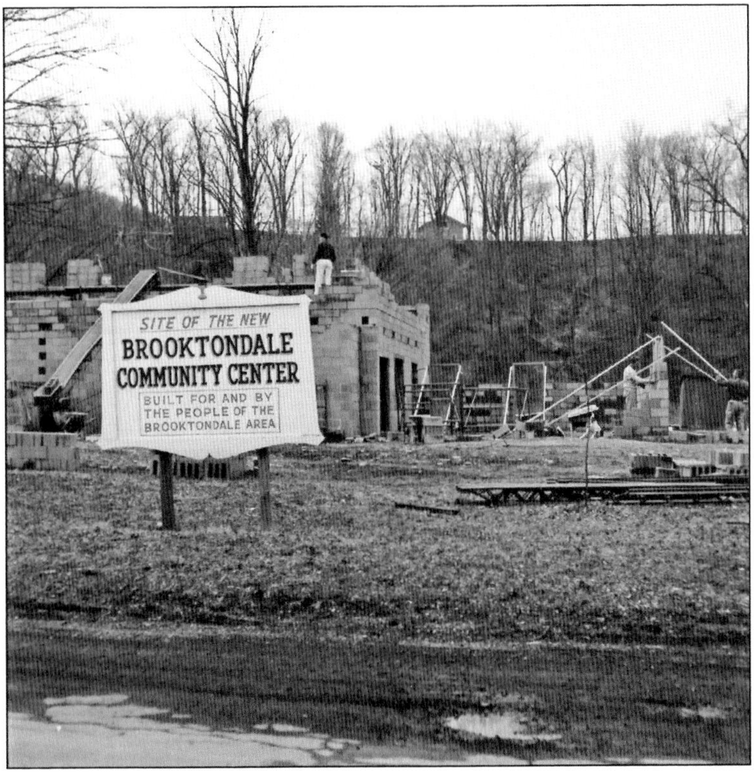

The Brooktondale two-room schoolhouse went through several changes before it became the victim of modernization and the children were sent to Ithaca schools. It was sold to the fire department and was used as a teen center until an electrical fire claimed it in 1962. Since 1964, the site was dedicated to the Brooktondale Community Center, developed to serve the recreational and educational needs of the entire community.

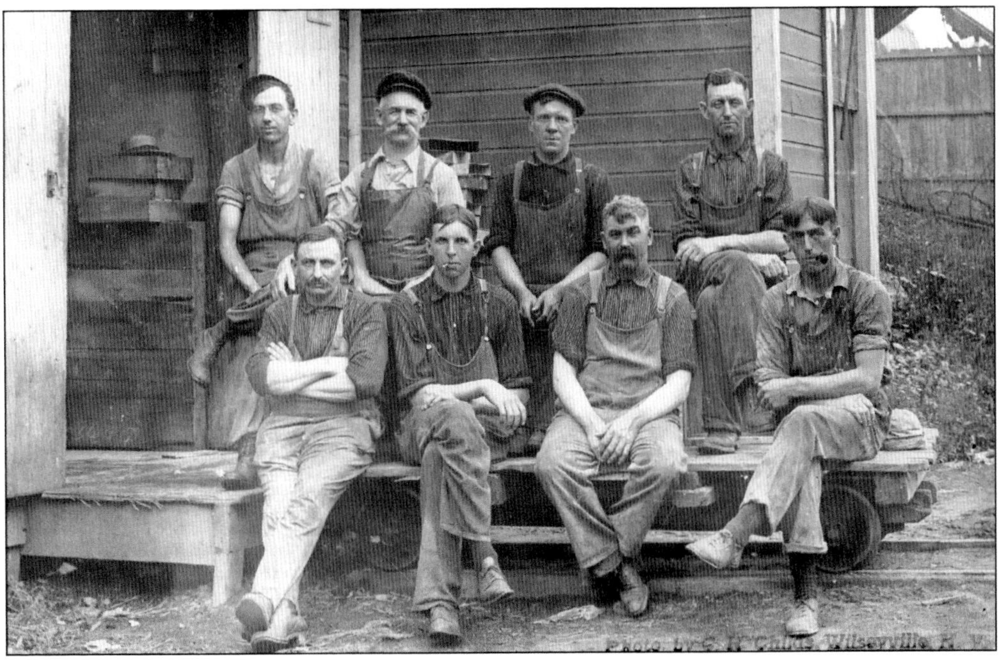

This 1907 photograph shows workers for the Crystal Fountain Creamery, a business that took advantage of the Slaterville Springs reputation as a resort town.

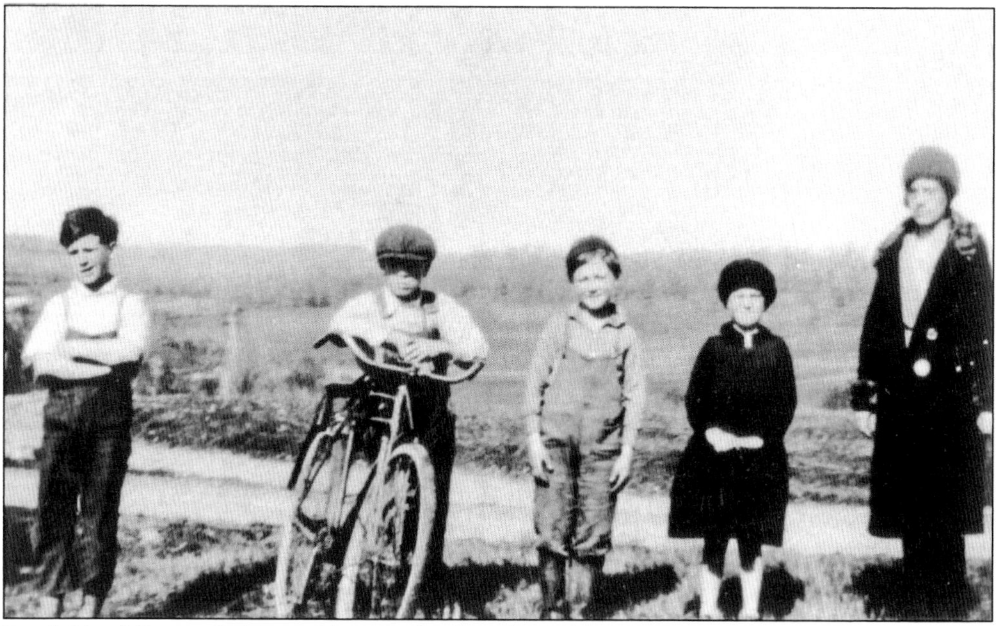

Pupils Lloyd George Robbins, Glenn Lasby, Douglas Robbins, Lillian Robbins, and their teacher, a Mrs. Wright, members of the Caroline District School first class of 1930–1931, pose in this picture taken in the schoolyard by Norman Robbins.

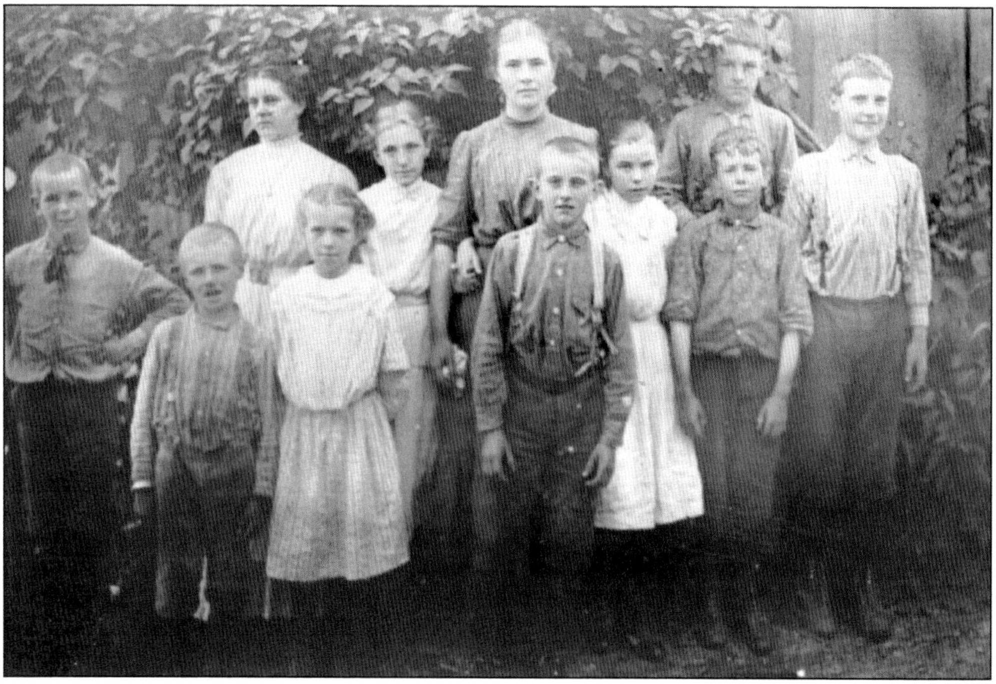

The children of Patch School No. 9 on 76 Road stand with their teacher, Lilliam Waite. From left to right are (first row) Robert Rowe, Clifford Maynard, Hattie Jordan, Eugene Barnum, and Bill Northrup; (second row) Waite, Rena Jordan, Grace Barnum, Susie Jones, Maurice Rowe, and Arthur Maynard. It is somewhat unusual for all of the children in these older photographs to be identified.

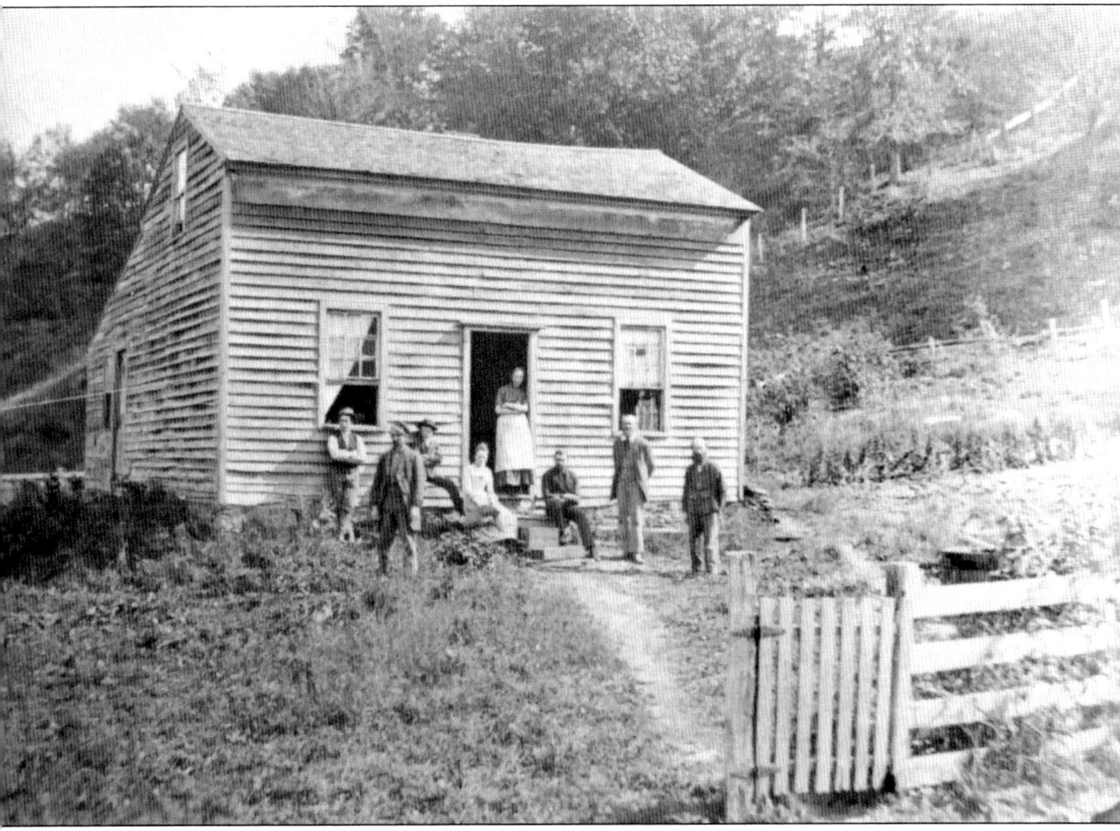

Phyllis Whittaker was the teacher of the Brearley Hill School, one of the many one- and two-room schools that dotted the hills of Caroline. Here, she poses with school board members. Parents and school board members often took a hands-on approach, which may have helped ensure a quality education in even the smallest schools.

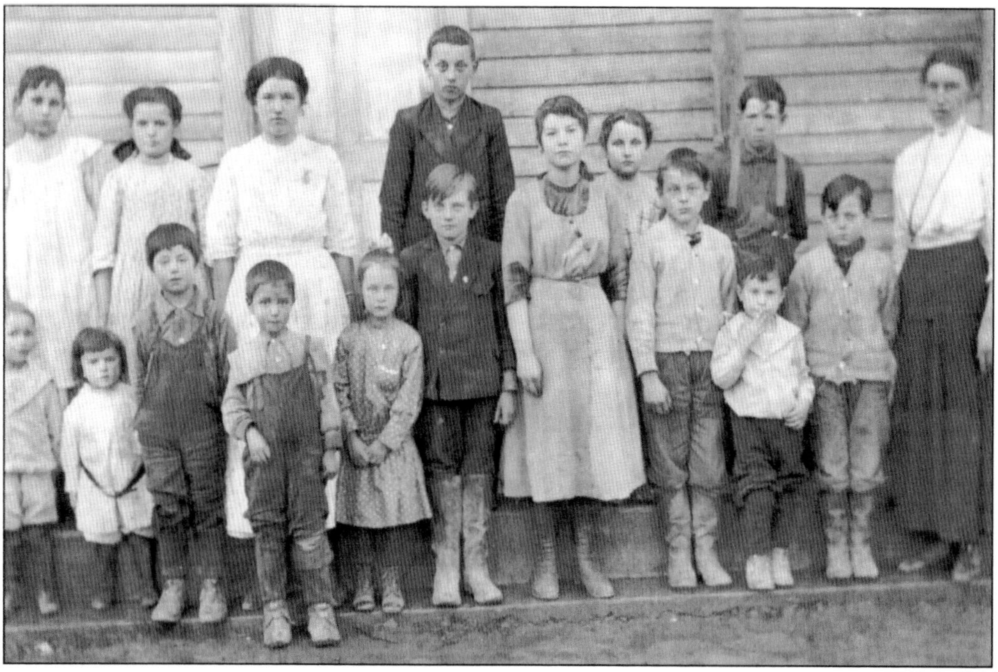

It is spring, and the children attending Rawson Hollow School have muddy boots, especially the farmers' youngsters, who may have mud nearly up to their waist. The group poses for their school picture with all of the solemnity they can muster.

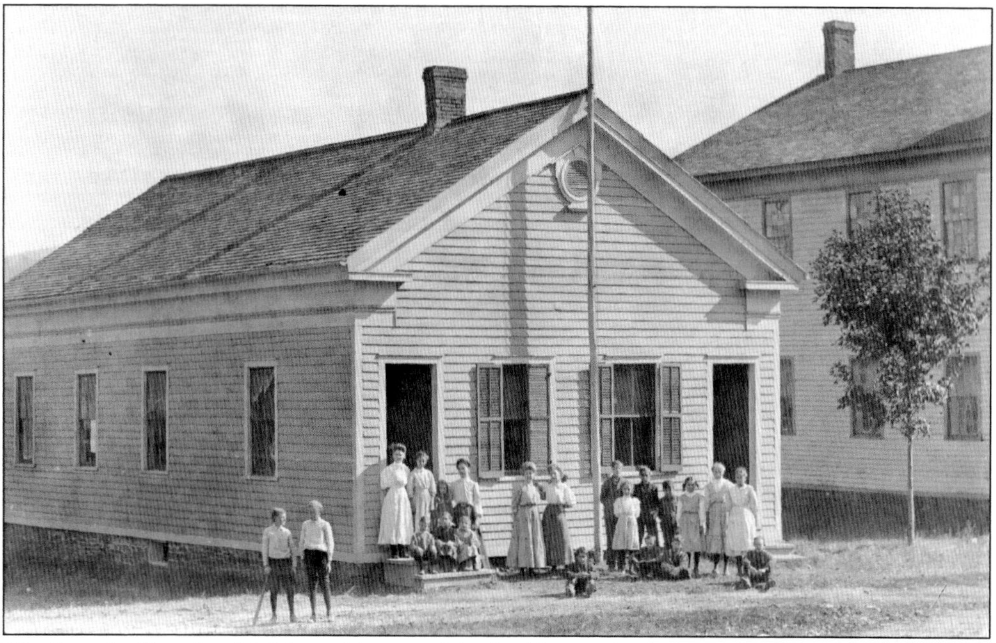

The Speedsville schoolchildren skip out of the building at high noon. Some may have mothers waiting outside, while others will run home to a good meal, and those who live too far away for an easy walk will settle indoors or outside to enjoy their noon repast. One former pupil recalls eating a lot of bean sandwiches and other leftovers, as his mother had neither time nor money for anything more elaborate.

Three

Farming Feeds All

Like most rural areas in upstate New York, agriculture has been important here from the very beginning. Farming meant survival to the first settlers, and from almost the beginning, Caroline growers provided—and continue to provide—food, not just for themselves and for locals, but also to export. There are several farms that have remained in the same family for over 100 years, and a few have continually operated for almost 200 years. Recently, new families have moved in to begin or expand farm operations on revitalized or new land, and in addition to the milk picked up daily by the big truck, a variety of vegetables, including beans and grains, both raw and processed into flour, are sold as far away as New York City.

A look through old scrapbooks reveals photographs of crops flourishing and critters from chickens to horses playing important parts in everyday life. Farming also created a need for additional businesses, such as creameries, to provide a way to turn very perishable milk into more easily stored and transported butter and cheese.

There was a need to transport these dairy products, as well as vegetable crops, eggs, and meat, to Ithaca and beyond, and every method from horse and wagon to train boxcar was employed. Almost every hamlet had a train station where goods were loaded and passengers could catch a ride to the big city of Ithaca or beyond. Crispell Trucking grew rapidly in the 1930s with a contract to provide eggs to markets in New York City. At one time, Crispell provided bus service in the area, even taking schoolchildren to Ithaca for advanced education, more than the education available in area one-room schools.

Most housewives kept a few hens and used the income from excess eggs as pin money for the extras in life. However, several area farmers went beyond that to ride out the Depression, paying their taxes with profits from their chicken coops.

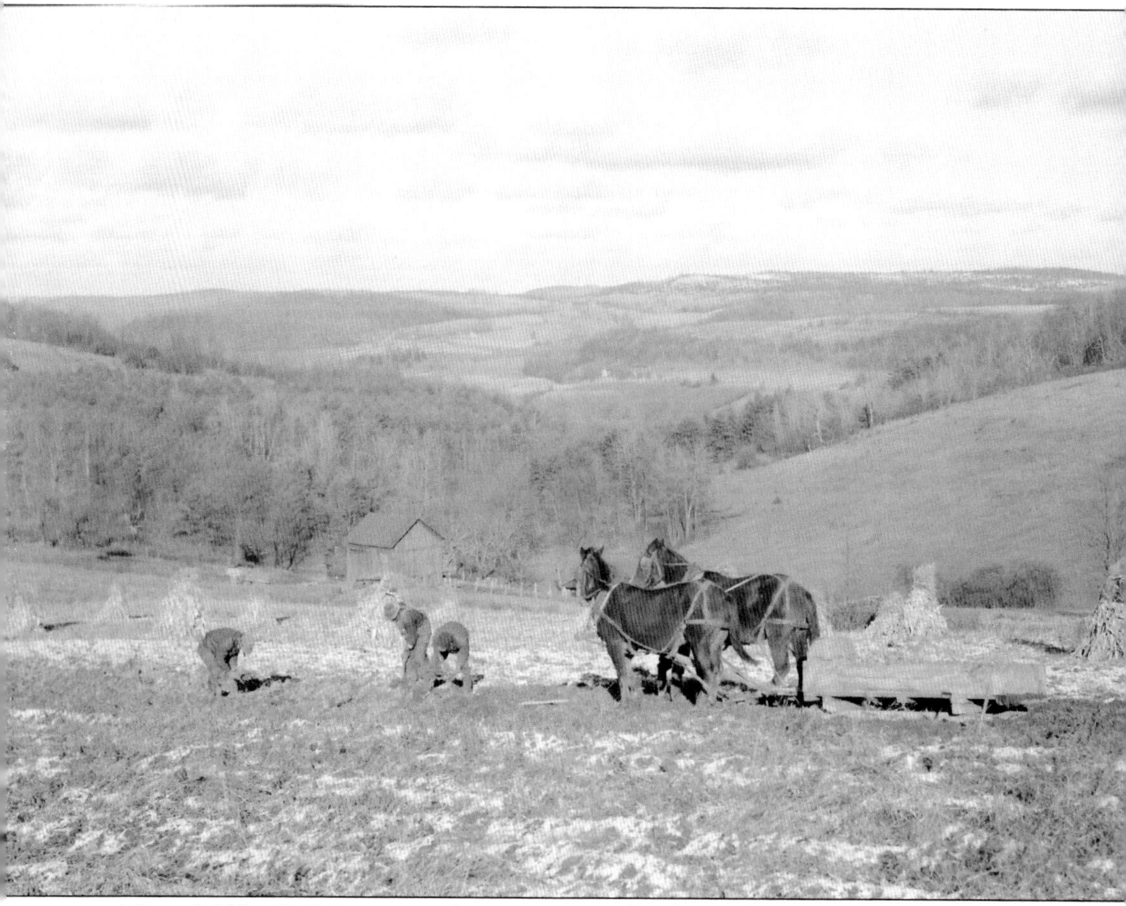

After a field has had the trees and stumps removed and a rough plowing is done, the larger rocks need to be removed. A low, wooden sled called a stoneboat is prepared and, in pre-tractor days, was pulled by a horse, mule, or oxen. Plowing and planting is easier and faster once the rocks are removed, and tillers or planters are less likely to be broken.

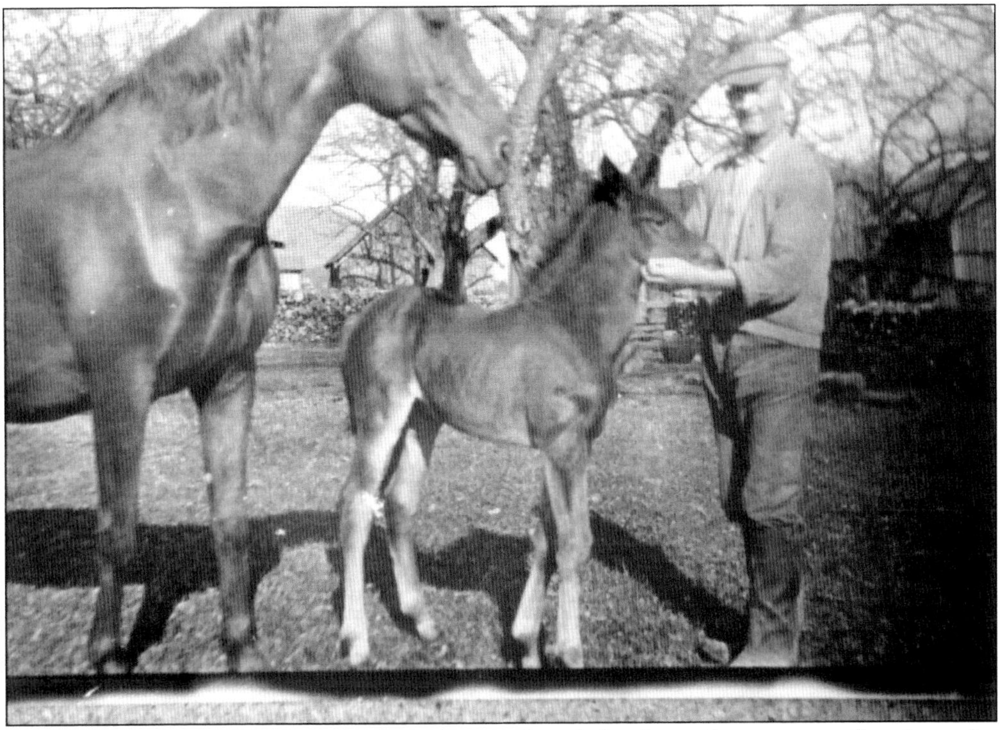

A well-run farm has a good supply of wood cut and ready for the cook stove, as well as the parlor stove that keeps everyone warm in the winter. The owner also makes sure that future plowing and transportation needs are taken care of by breeding the newest model. This farmer and his baby enjoy a friendly moment while the proud mother looks on.

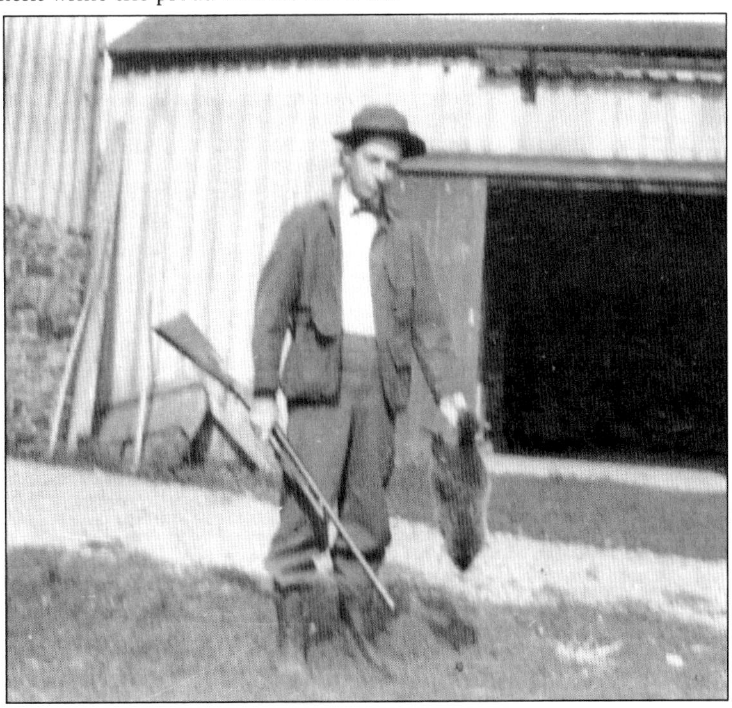

Plowing, planting, fertilizing, and harvesting are not the only things that happen on a farm, especially when all work was done with horses that might break a leg in an unnoticed hole; therefore, woodchuck, or groundhog, hunting was considered an aid to the community. Varmint hunting was done alone or with a friend on a sunny afternoon in the spring or fall, when the other chores were done.

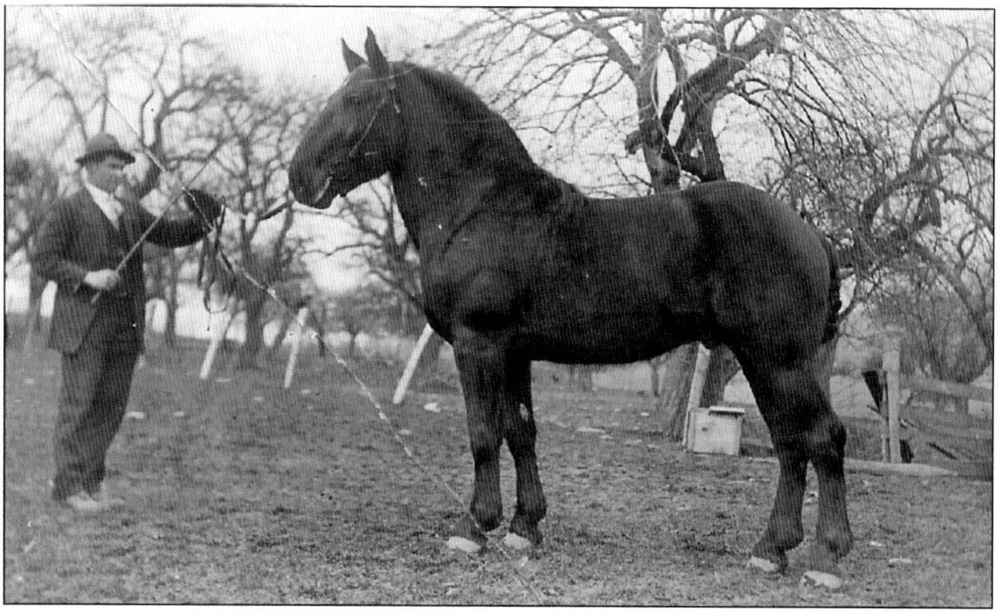

A horse to be proud of, Fremont was known for racing and fathering colts who not only worked hard, but could also run. His owner is demonstrating Fremont's great size, form, and good manners.

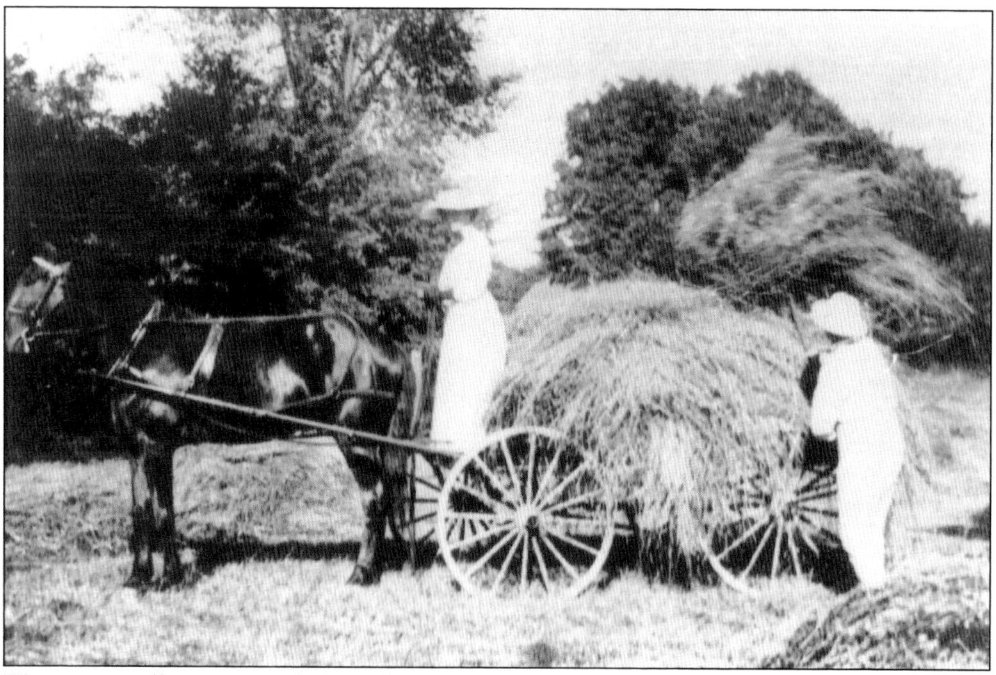

Women, as well as men, might be called upon to help. This woman drives the wagon while the men pitch hay. Once the wagon is back at the barn, the hay might be loaded loosely into the hay loft or put in a hand bailing machine and compacted into more easily stacked and stored bails one at a time. It was hard, dusty work, and everyone came home itching and in need of a bath.

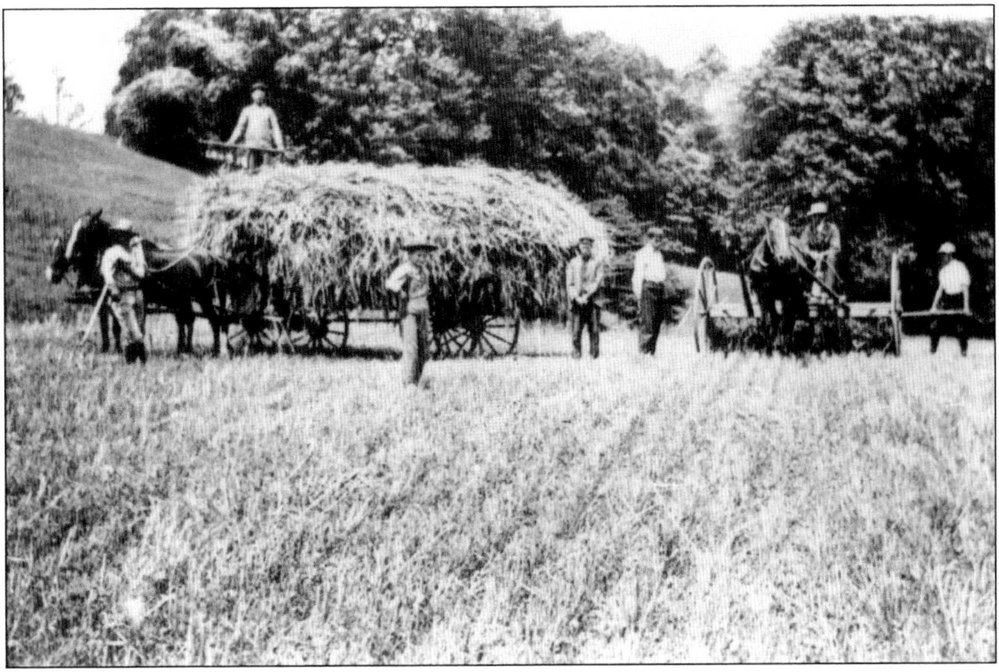

This larger crew is cutting, raking, and loading hay as it goes through the field. Hay must be made while the sun shines, cut, dried, and put under cover or it will be ruined by mold, so farmers often gathered together or hired extra men at haying to make sure that it was done quickly. When this happened, the women became more valuable in the kitchen, cooking for the crew.

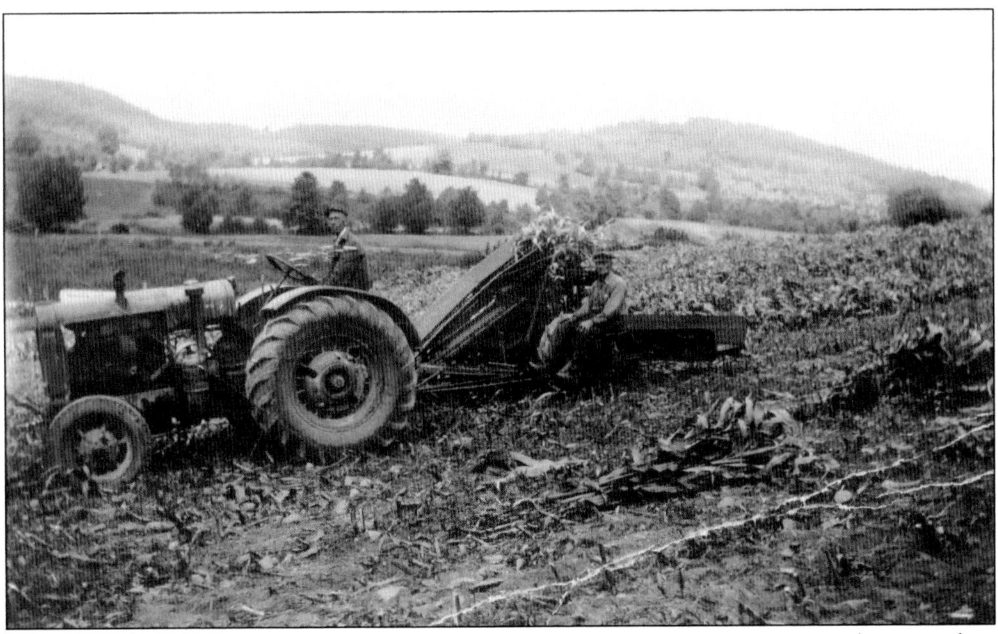

Like making hay, cutting corn for silage used to be a big job, requiring many men working together. This tractor with its attachment is making the work a little easier, though riding a tractor across a bumpy field is not nearly as comfortable and easy as taking one's car to the store for groceries. Even the big modern tractors are no picnic to pilot.

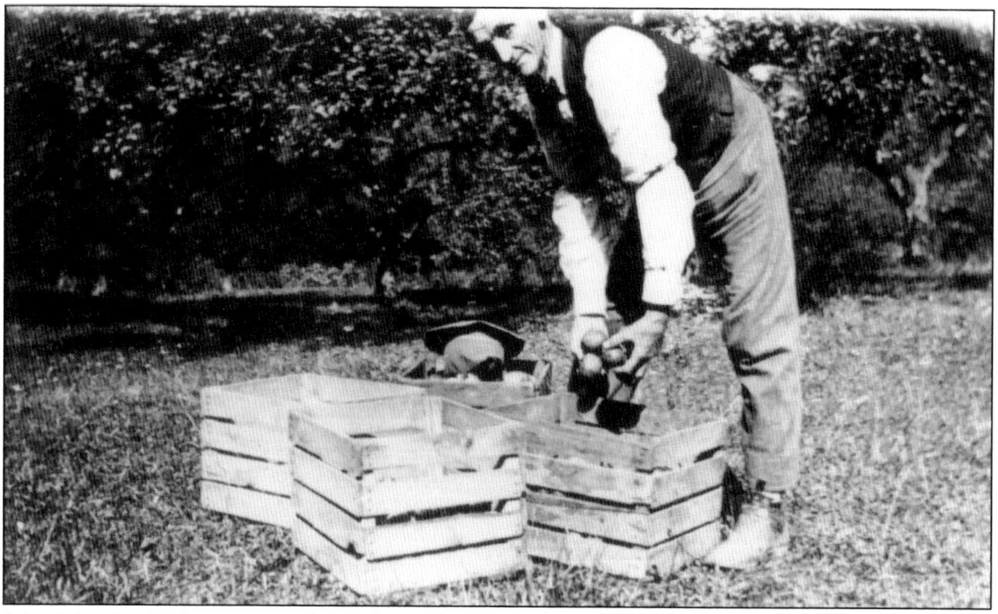

John Mandeville harvests apples in his orchard and packs them carefully into boxes. Vegetables and fruits from Caroline were loaded onto the trains that stopped at several stations and sent around New York, as far away as the Big Apple.

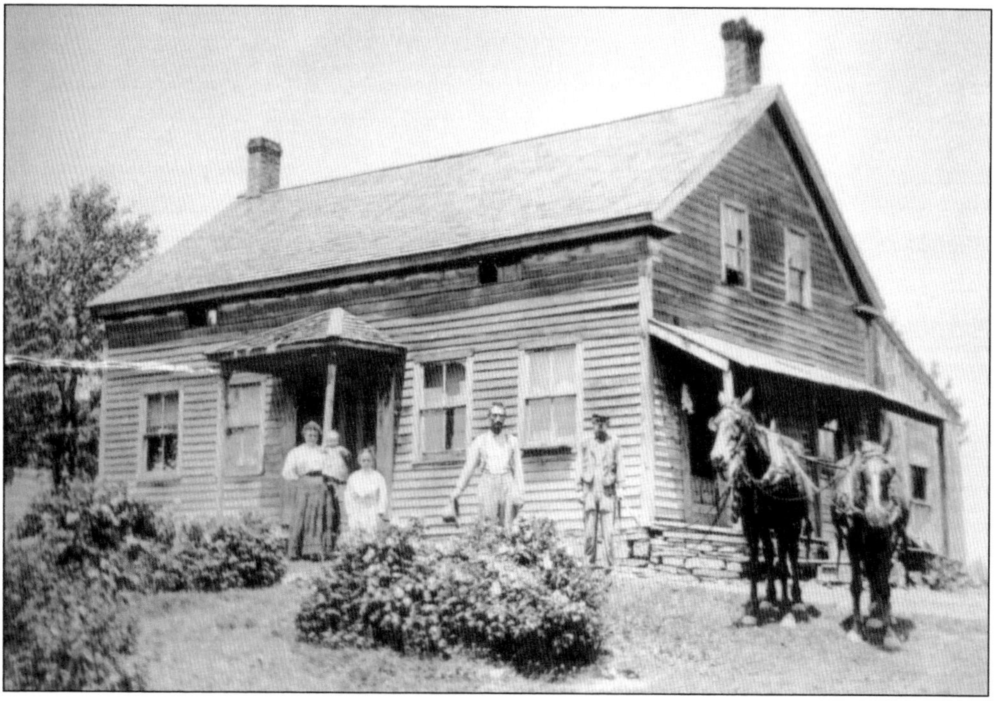

Sam Onan and his family show off a good harvest and the horses that helped make it possible. The house may not look pretty, but it is snug and roomy. Farmers by necessity concentrated more on their crops and animals than their homes. The wife might plant some flowers and bushes, but with children and a husband to care for, along with cooking, cleaning, preserving food for winter, and sewing, it was not easy to keep up.

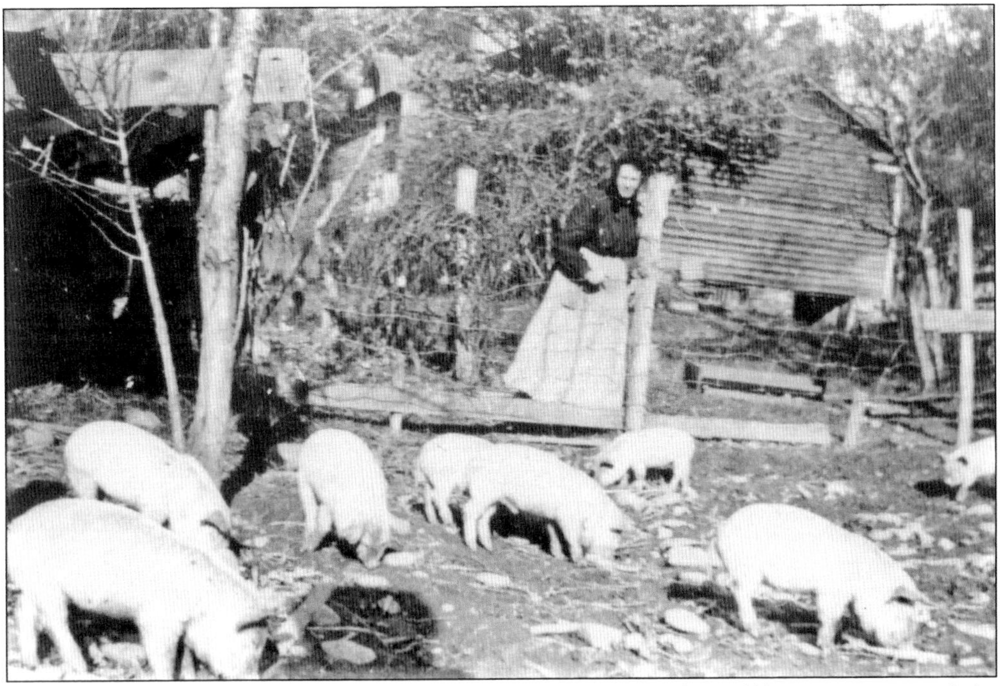

Mrs. Menzies takes care of her herd of pigs, feeding and talking to what will become many meals for the family larder. Meat was an important part of the diet, and protein was much welcomed by people who worked hard from sunrise to sunset and occasionally even earlier and later than that.

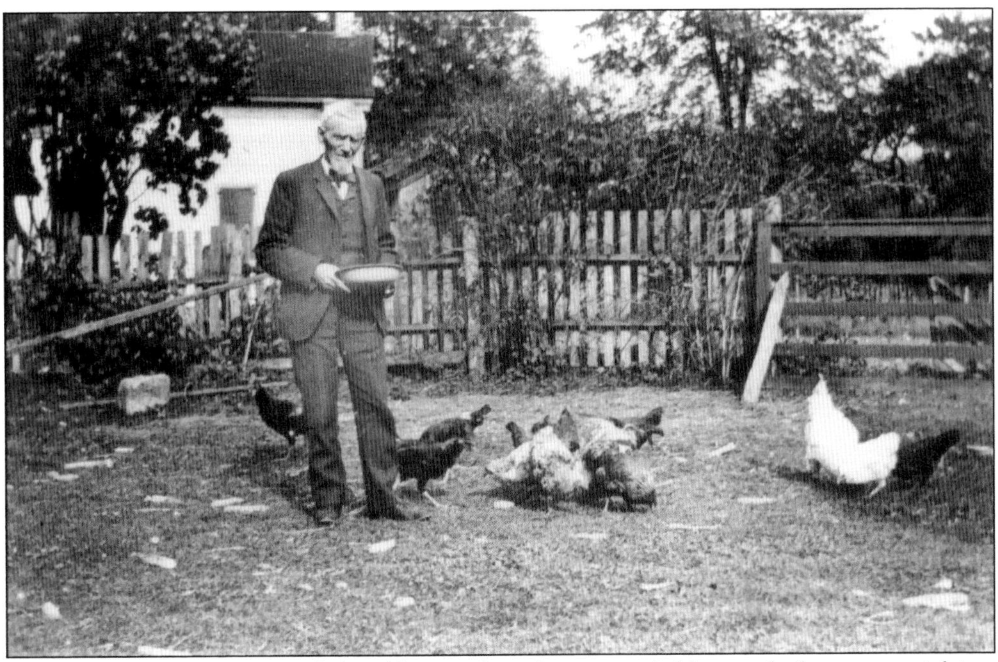

Feeding the chickens was work for older people and younger children and often very satisfying. A pet chicken or a flock brought not only eggs and Sunday dinner, but also much amusement to their owners.

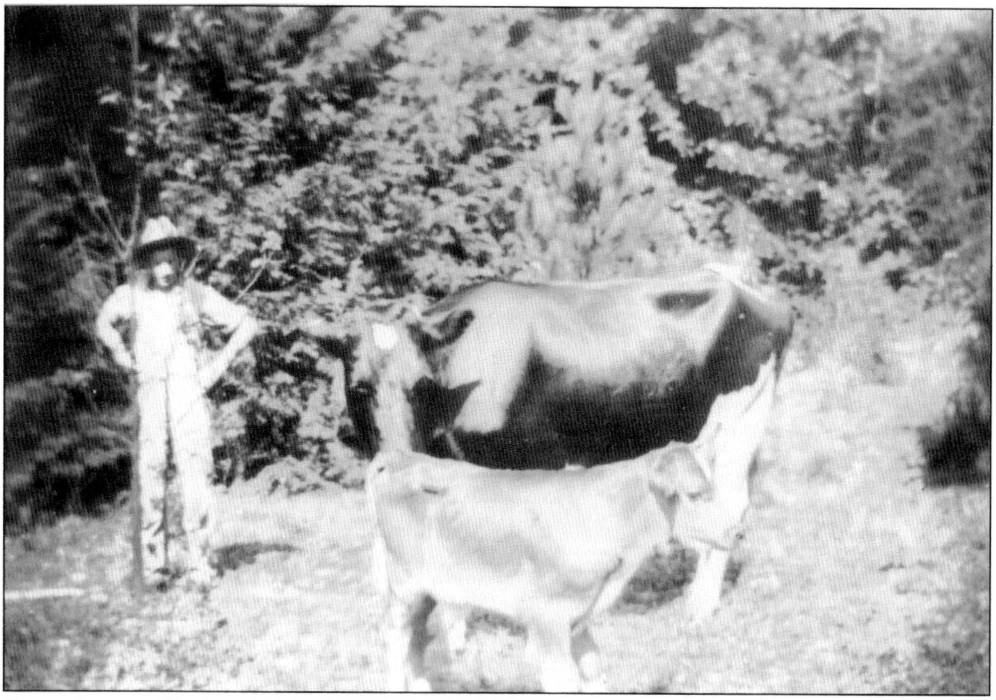

Young George Ward stands with Star and her calf. No doubt he was excited by all the events in their country home and proud to be of help on this Depression-era farm.

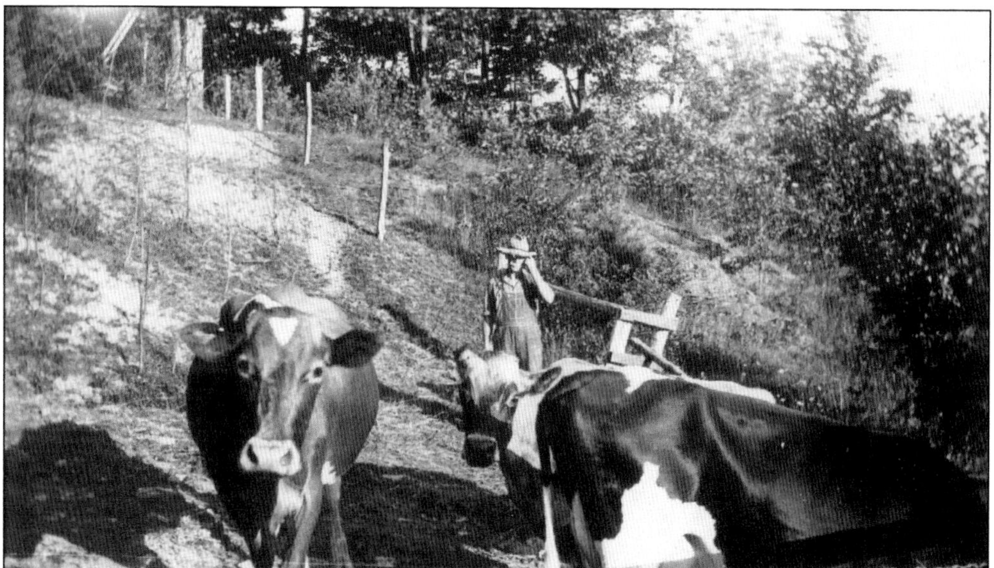

Cow herding was a common farm chore, often performed by the youngsters and sometimes with the help of a dog or two. The trick was to keep the cows happy so that they would yield good and plentiful milk while getting them efficiently to the barn. Sometimes it took several family members to accomplish this, but on such a well-appointed farm, the outcome was almost certainly good.

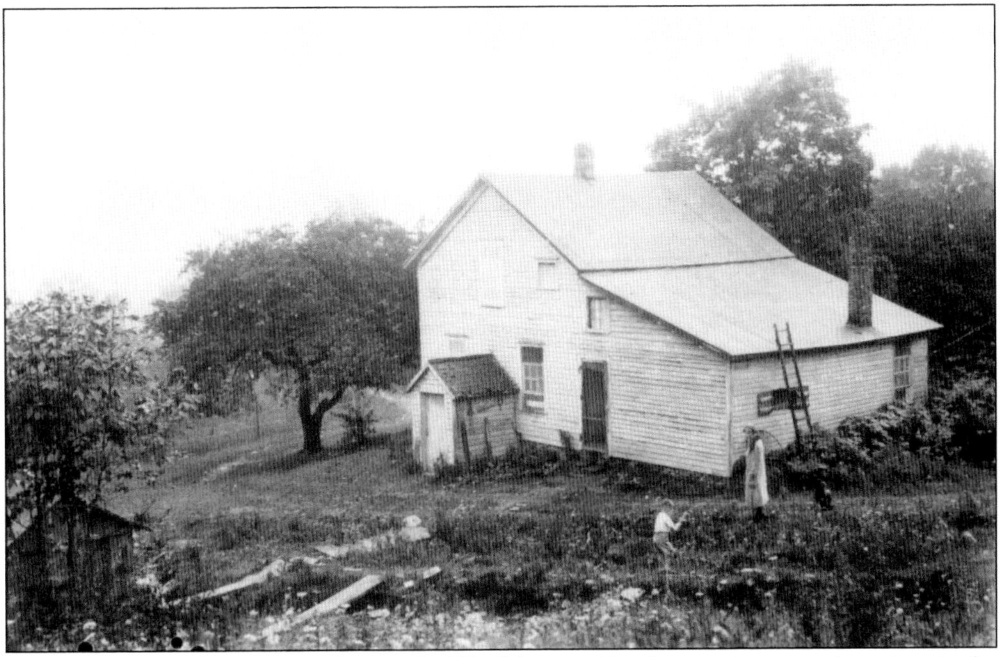

It is an autumn or late summer day on the Ward farm in Caroline, and a young boy plays in the side yard while his mother looks on.

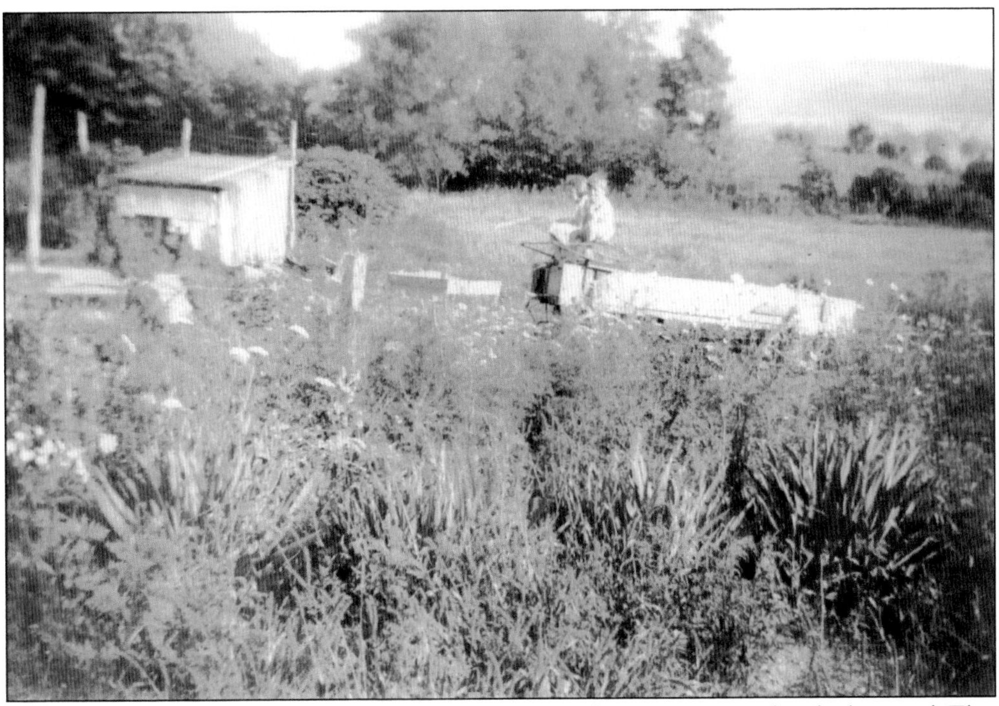

Two youngsters relax on a farm wagon while observing the goings-on in the chicken yard. This might have been their first year on the farm, as they are thoroughly entranced by the show the hens are putting on.

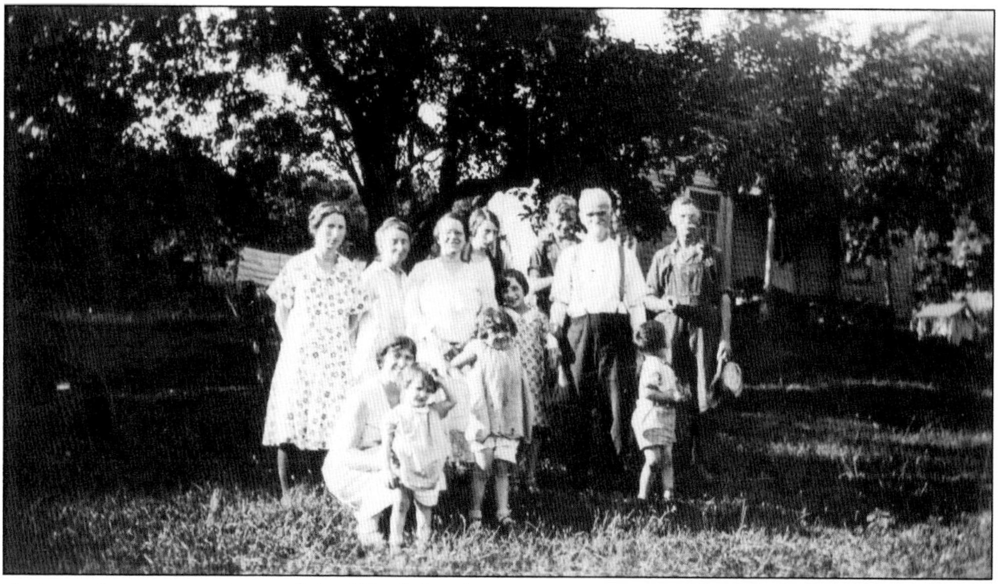

At least three generations of the Ward family enjoy a reunion on the front lawn of the family farm in August 1931.

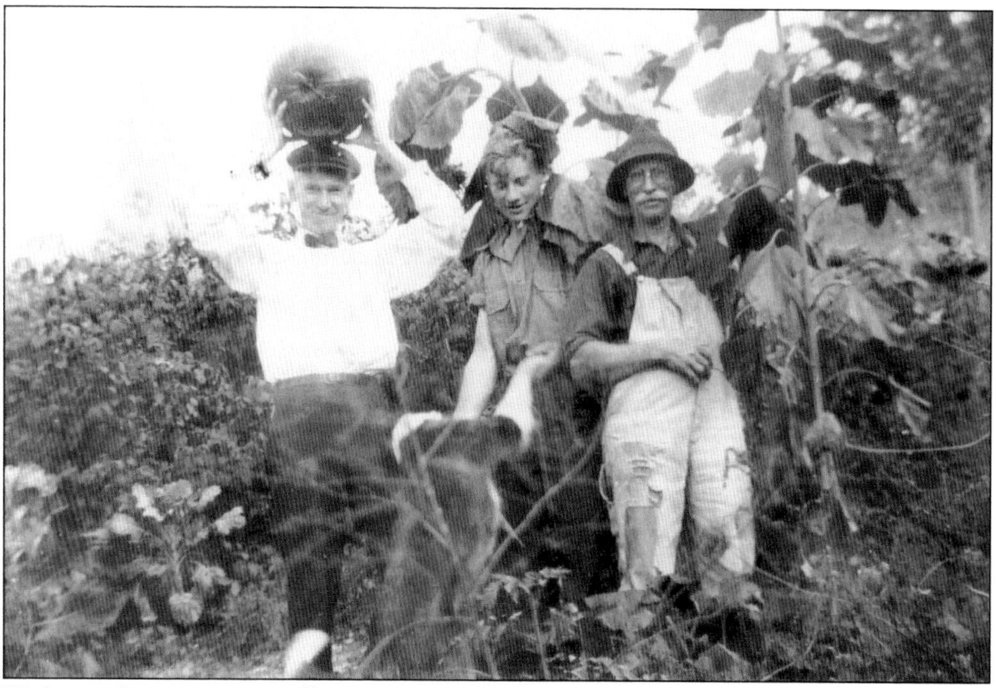

With pumpkins, turnips, sunflowers, and other crops harvested, the Ward men, young George, and even Major the dog get a chance to show off and celebrate the results of their hard work. Life in the country seems to have been a good decision for father George Ward.

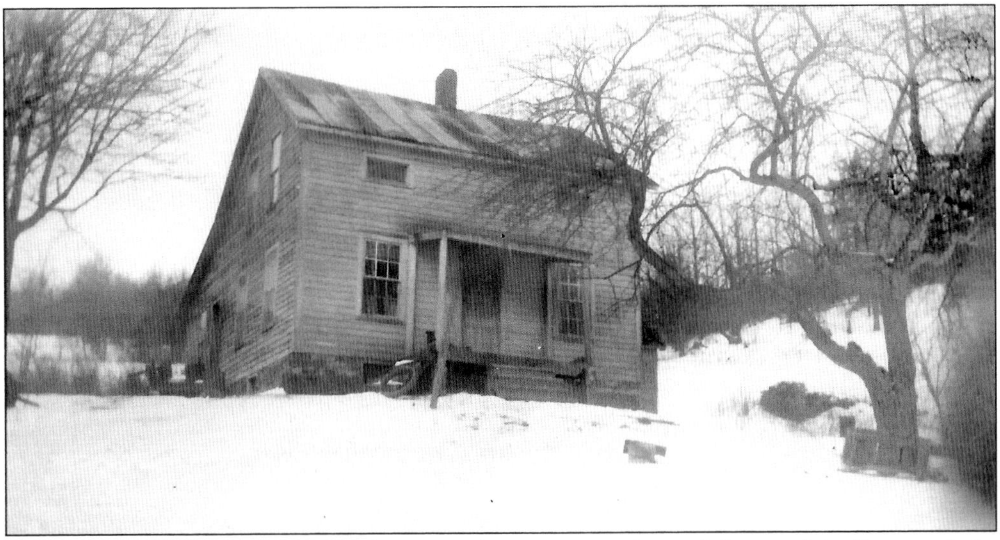

Winter is a time for quiet contemplation in the country, at least if the wood is all cut and the tools and equipment have been mended. It is a time for enjoying last year's bounty and planning for the year ahead. Seed catalogs come in the mail, and soon enough, signs of spring will gather force with the lengthening of the days.

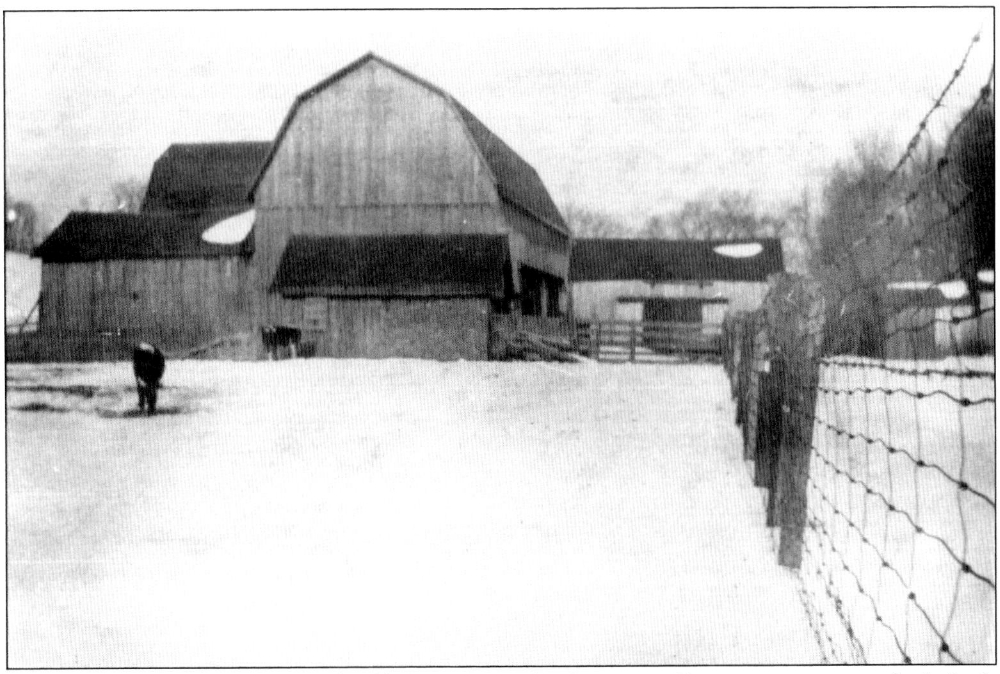

The cows seen here at the Mandeville Farm, now the Greenway Farm, are enjoying a little fresh air on a late winter day. There is not much grass to be found under the snow, but getting out for a bit is always a welcome change.

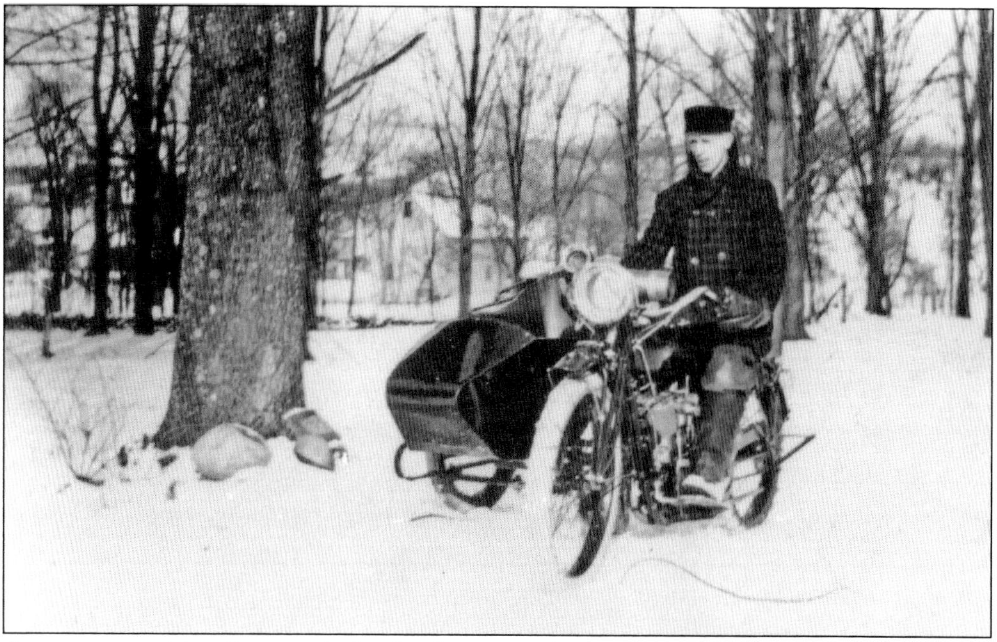

A young man with miles to go before he sleeps stops his motorcycle and sidecar to contemplate the scenery near the Menzies farm. While a motorcycle may seem dangerous on the snow and ice, the sidecar added enough stability that getting through the winter was not considered especially hazardous, and it was certainly cheaper to operate than an automobile.

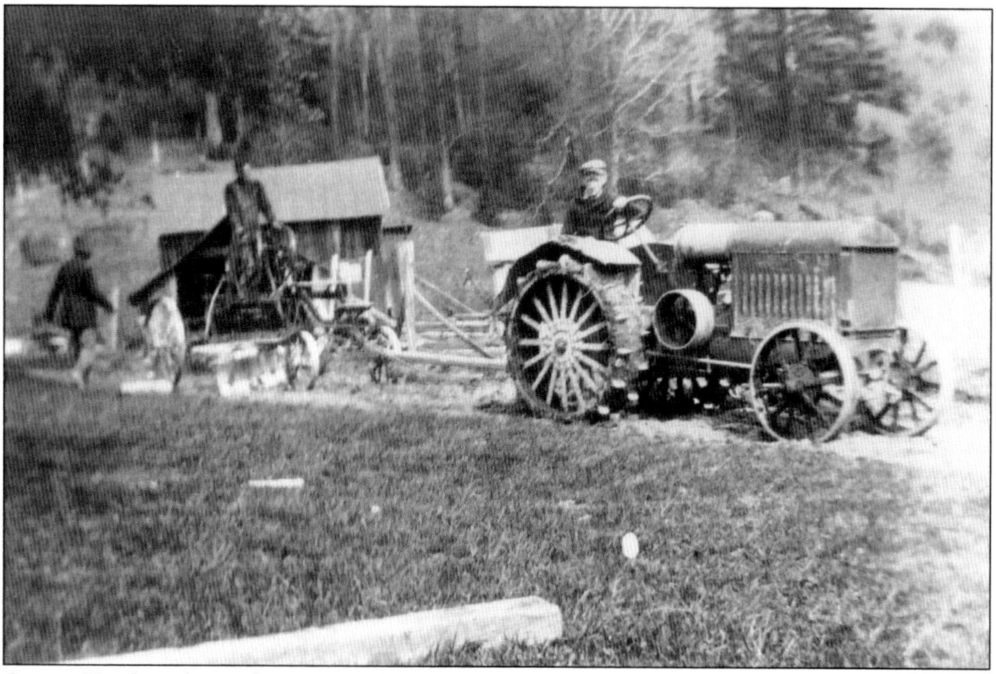

George Hawkins drives the tractor while another man rides on what looks like a scraper to repair farm roads. Note the handkerchief over George's face to protect against dust. The tractor, with big steel wheels and a small power take-off wheel, was an important piece of machinery, as a farmer could run a small sawmill, grain thresher, or other implement using the same power source.

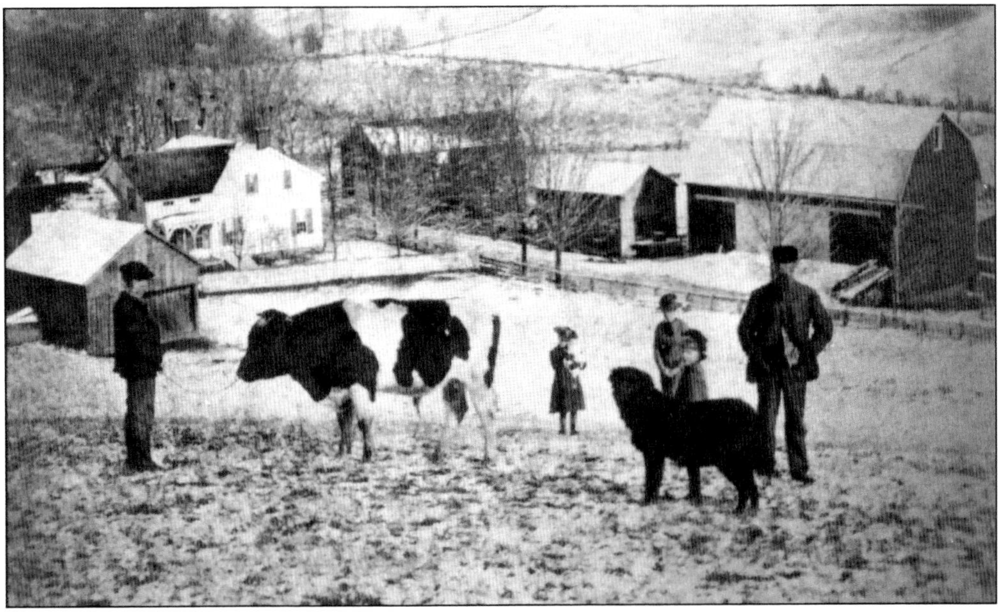

Cows are notorious escape artists and will wander off, searching for patches of grass, even when the snow is still on the ground. Occasionally, they will find a hole in the fence and have to be herded back toward the barn. It might require several family members and the dog to convince a particularly reluctant cow or, more likely, bull to head in the right direction.

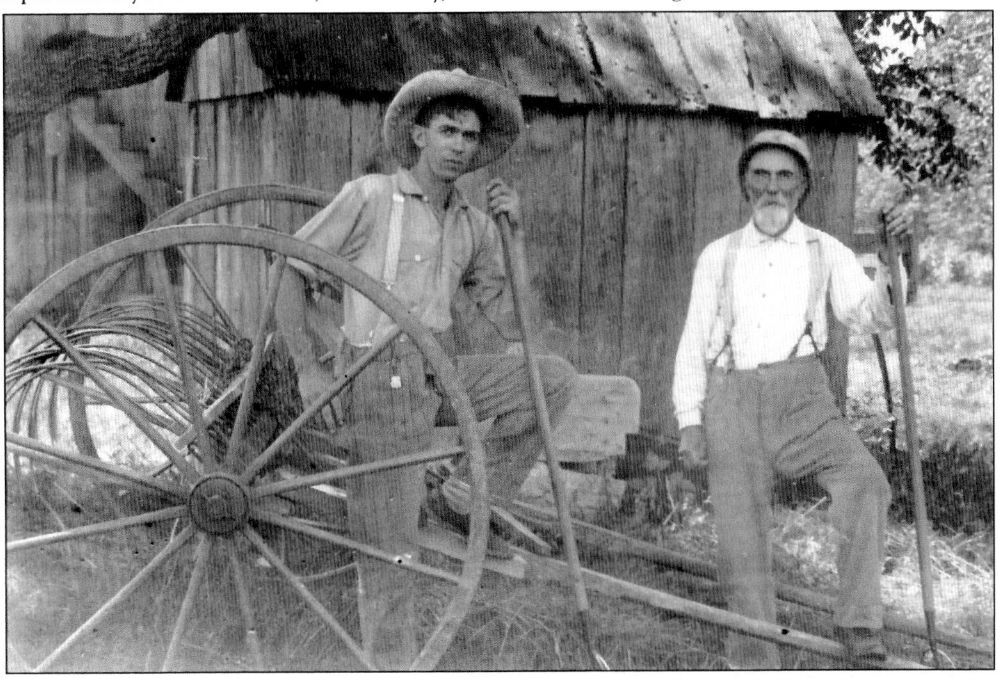

George Hawkins (left) and George Legge lean on their pitchforks, taking a break from raking and piling hay. Even when the cows do not escape, producing milk is still hard work. There is the growing of food, feeding them twice or more each day, taking care of mothers and calves and, until artificial insemination became practical, maintaining a bull. Milking must be done at least twice a day, and then there's barn cleaning to be done.

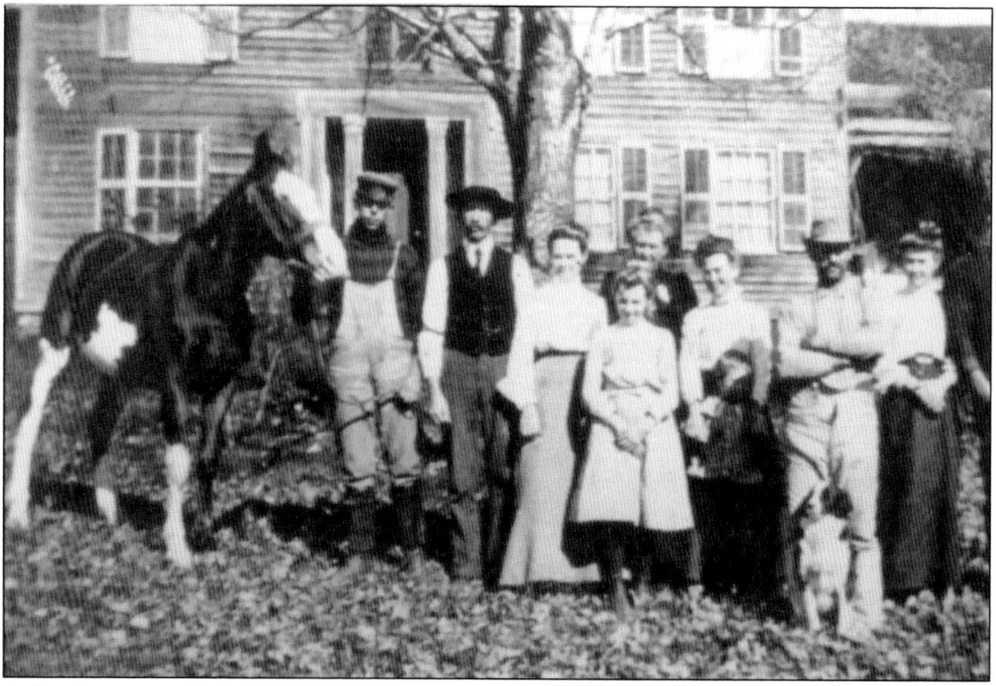

A family poses with their horse and dog, animals that were considered best friends and helpers on many a farm.

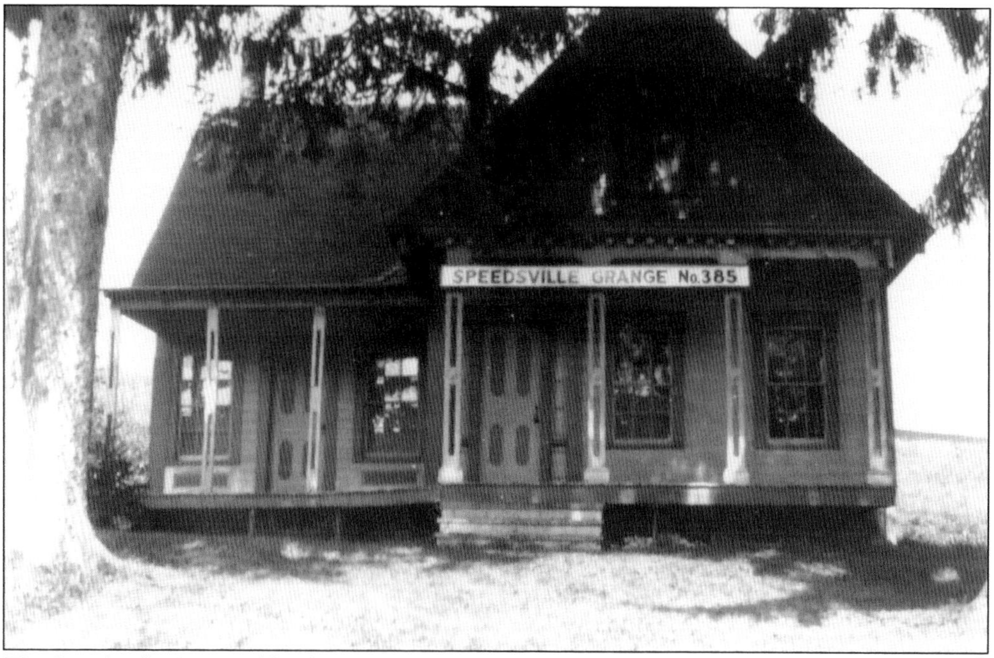

The Speedsville Grange, like those in the other hamlets of Caroline and rural areas in the United States, was an important gathering place for farmers and farm families. The grange passed out information on the most modern farming techniques and safe ways to store the harvest; it was also a social club where dances, poetry readings, and dish-to-pass suppers allowed rural families entertainment and a break from hard work and isolation.

Four

Businesses Thrive

Nowadays, people who live in Caroline may shop online or drive to Ithaca for most goods and services, but they still use local stores for part of their needs. Years ago, each hamlet had a store or two, a barber, a blacksmith, and other people to tend their needs. Small grocery stores still exist in Brooktondale, Slaterville Springs, and Speedsville, with a produce stand on Hartford Road, and seasonal markets throughout the area. Many still keep their business local as much as practical, buying stock from the neighbors or growing extra produce or eggs to sell. Items not obtainable locally were acquired by shipments from the city or the offerings of traveling salesmen. In the past, everything from fox traps to spools of thread were to be found on the shelves or stashed in barrels or boxes on the premises. Penny candy counters were a fascinating place for youngsters with a hard-earned coin burning a hole in their pocket, and they might spend many minutes perched on a box, staring into the glass case. With bubble gum at two pieces for a penny or licorice at 1¢ per foot-long rope, it might take quite a while to reach such an important decision.

The local store was and is a place to catch up on the news, swap stories, and post notices about free kittens, community activities, and upcoming farm sales. Older men might have gathered for a game of checkers, laid out on the cracker barrel, and treated themselves to a pickled egg or dill pickle. It was the place where polite strangers could stop and ask for directions and where the less polite were sometimes playfully told "you can't get there from here."

A recent remodel at Brookton's Market revealed that chickens were kept in wooden cages in the basement. There is little doubt a sign on the sales floor above advertised fresh eggs and poultry.

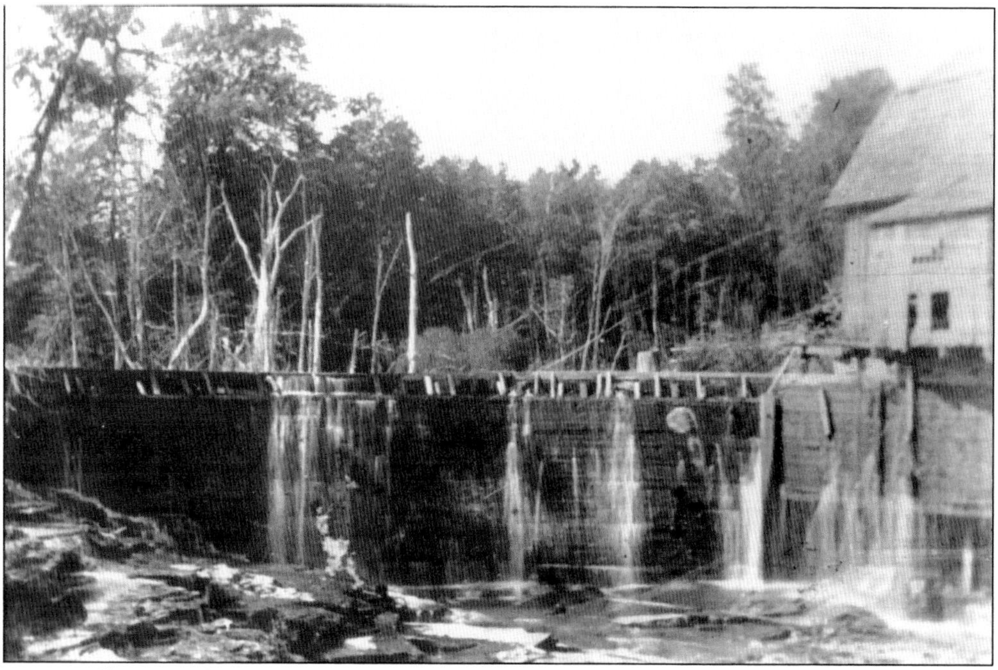

Annis Falls, created by the large timber dam in Six Mile Creek, was the scene of many picnics and swimming hole experiences. The water spills from the various portals and makes its way down to other mills, until eventually ending up in Cayuga Lake. There was a path built into the top of the dam, which improved access for the hamlet of Brooktondale.

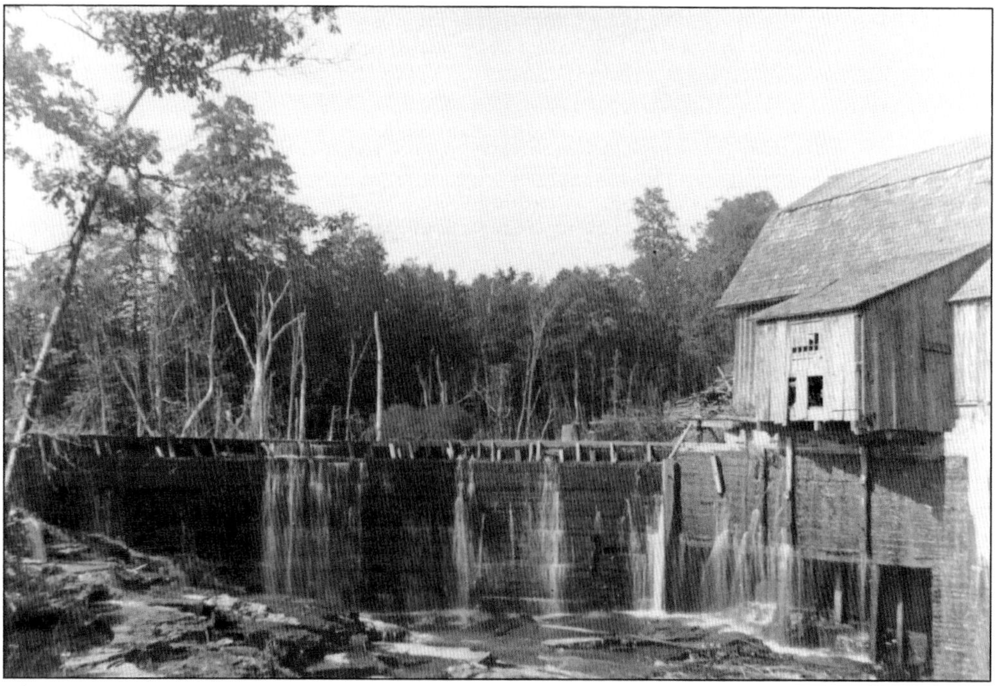

The Annis family, like many who lived in the Caroline hamlet of Brooktondale before them, prospered because of the power of Six Mile Creek, which they used for this mill.

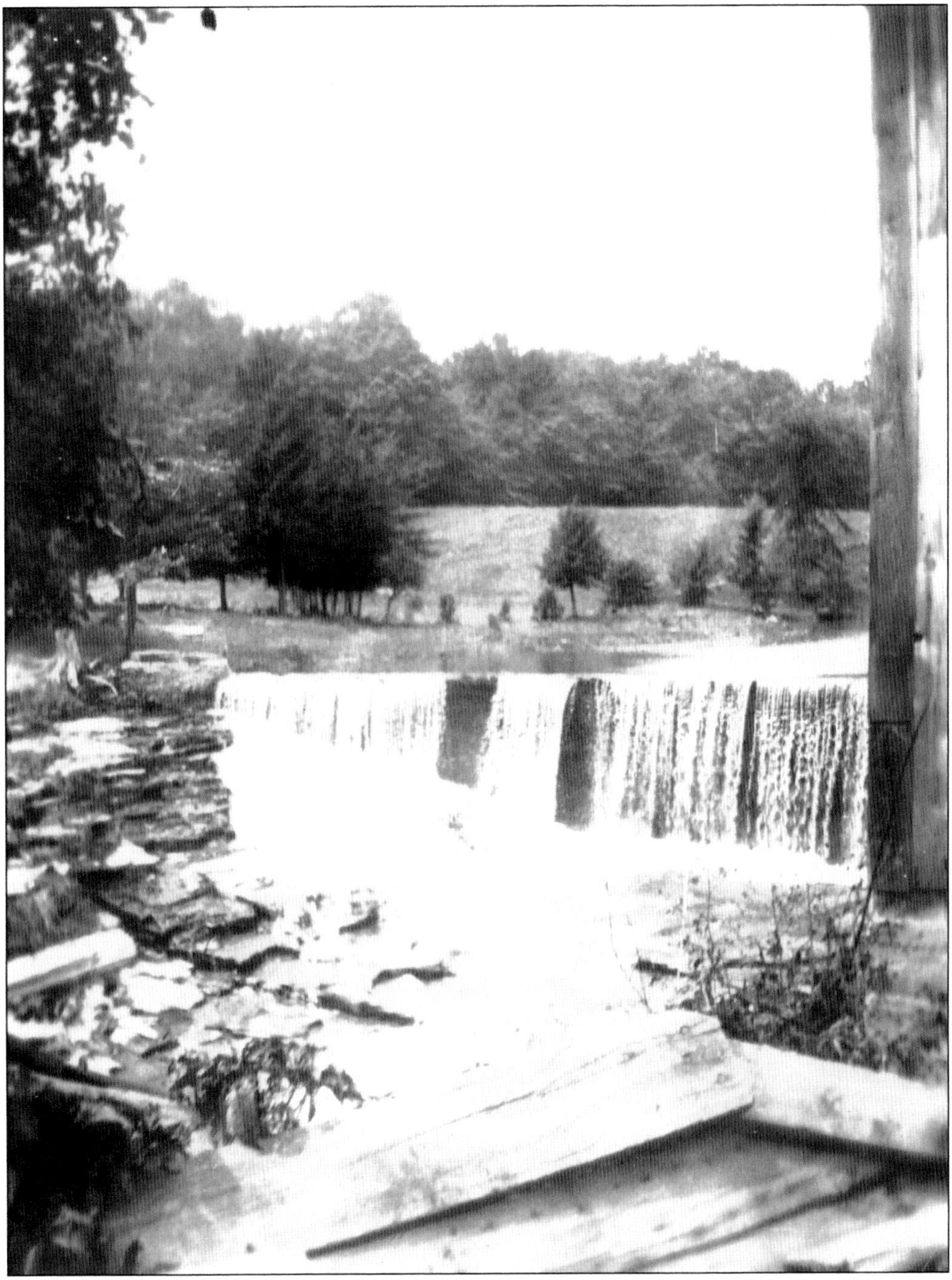

Farther down Six Mile Creek, the Schlobohn family dam varied quite a bit from the Annis Dam. Dam builders had to take into account the local topography and what use would be made of the power created. Each dam was constructed of local materials as much as possible.

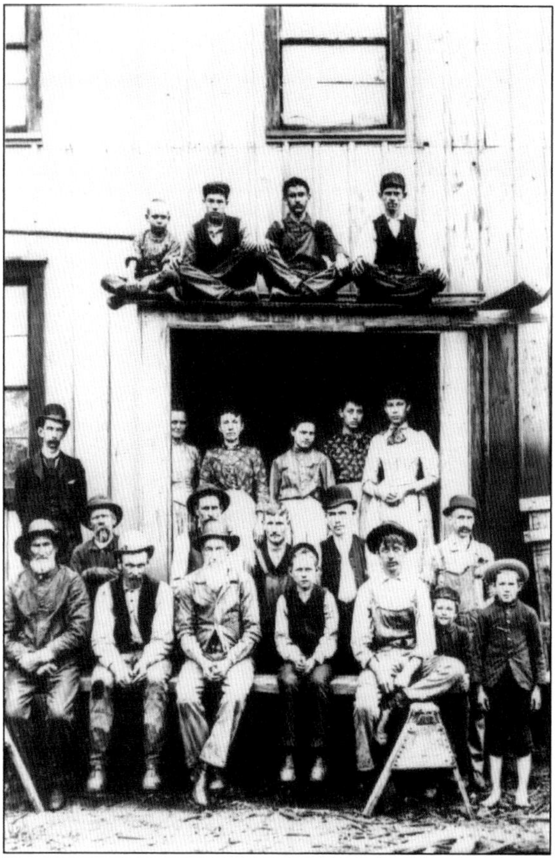

Before unions were formed and child labor laws were passed, not every child went to school, even part time. There were nine mills along Six Mile Creek in Brooktondale at one time, with some making gloves, rifle stocks, and other consumer goods and others grinding flour and mixing animal feeds. At one point, flour dust covered the bushes along the creek.

This is a close-up of the millworkers sitting on the porch roof, including one young boy. Is it the serious business of having their photograph taken or sheer exhaustion that is seen in their eyes?

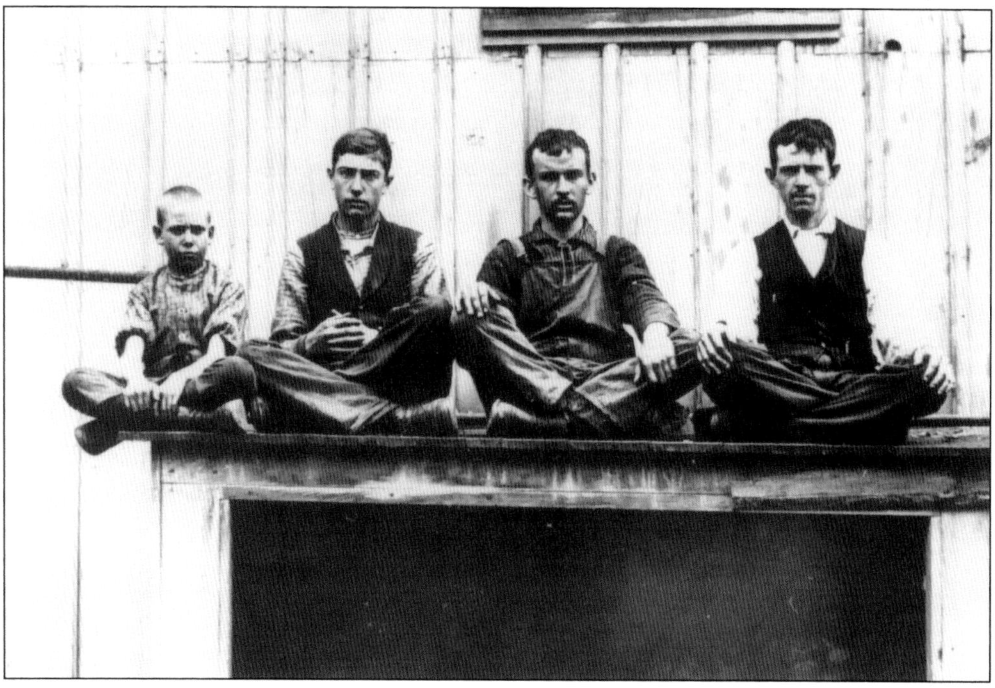

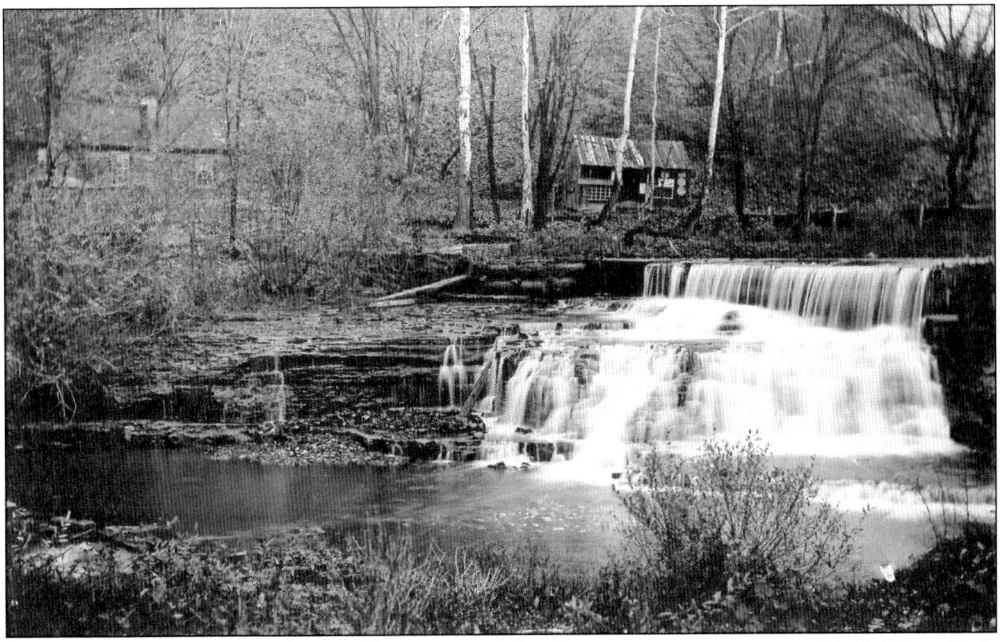

With the mills gone, Six Mile Creek has returned, for the most part, to its original bed. These little falls lead to a swimming hole that is used by neighbors young and old and even the occasional dog. There are also trout hiding in the depths for those wishing to match wits with the fish.

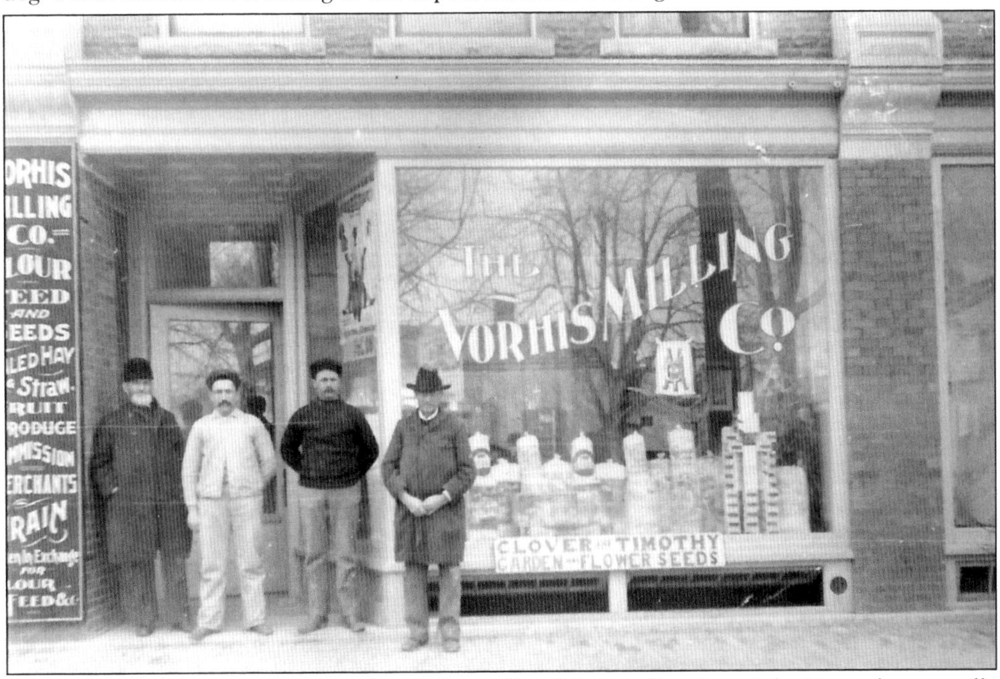

Descendants of the proprietors of the Vorhis Mill still live in Brooktondale. Here, they proudly display their many offerings. The mill offered flour, feed, seeds, baled hay, straw, grain, and fruit and would often grind flour on shares, keeping part of what they ground for the farmers to sell to other customers instead of asking for payment for their work. At one point, flour dust covered the bushes along the creek.

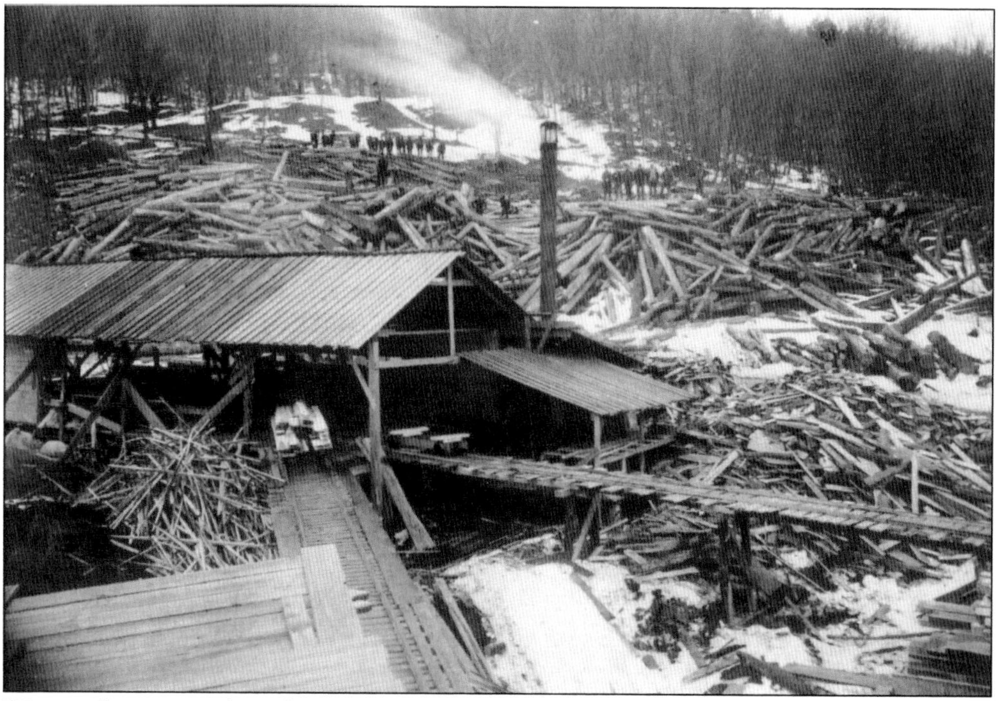

Water mills were not the only mills in the town of Caroline. Lumber was extremely important for building new homes and businesses in town and far away. Many of the rolling hills were stripped nearly bare of trees as the country grew and the need for raw materials increased.

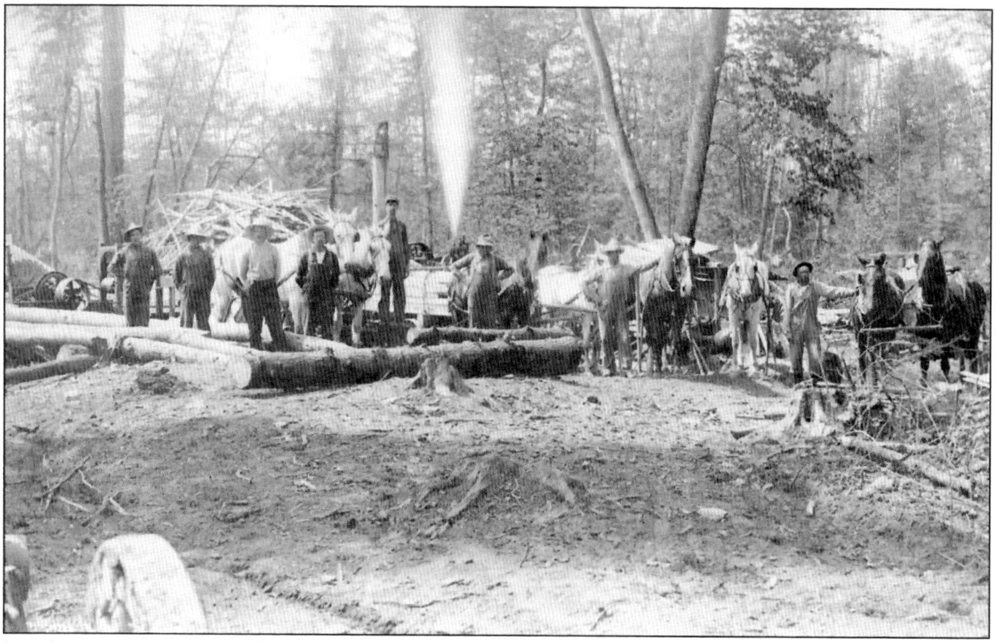

Lumbermen were a proud, hardworking bunch. It took a lot of manpower and horsepower to cut down trees, chop off the limbs, pull the logs out of the woods, and get them cut into boards. In the early days, it took men with a two-handled pit saw; later, steam and then gasoline engines were used, and trunks were fed lengthwise into the spinning saw blades.

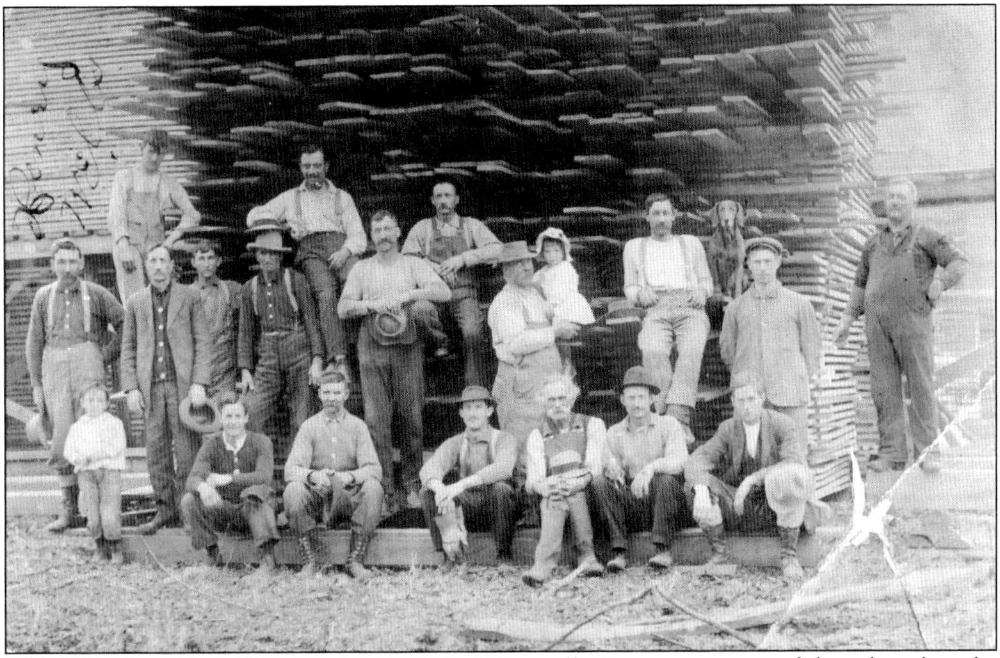

The Wells sawmill, on 600 Road, just west of Slaterville Springs, was one of those kept busy by the building boom. Henry Wells stands on the left in this group of workers, family members, and one attentive dog, displaying huge stacks of finished lumber ready for sale.

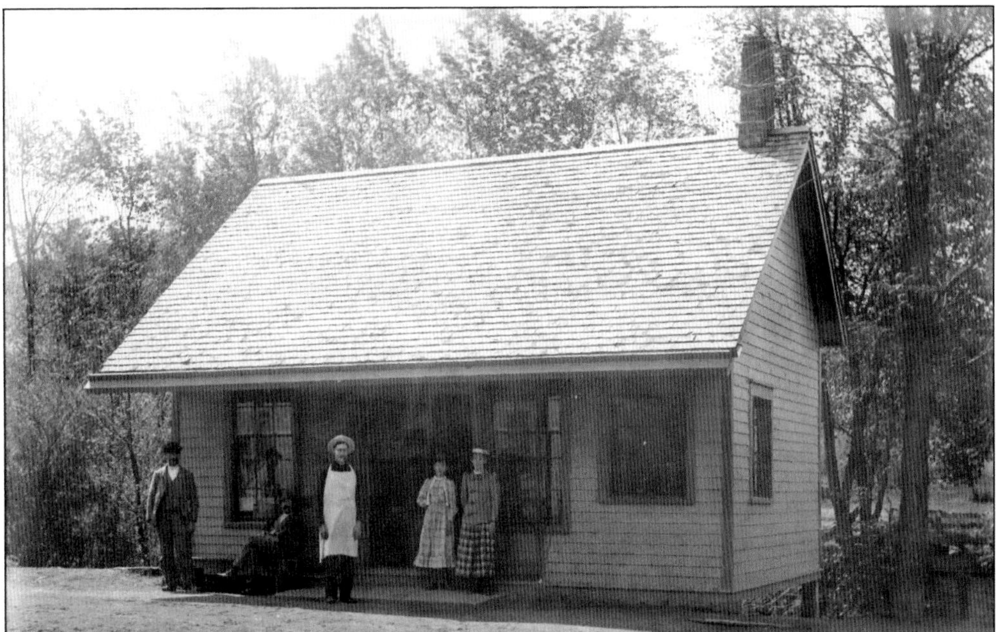

Men and women working the mills needed places to buy the essentials and some of the luxuries of life, and several stores were there to serve them. This bakery, with proprietor and patrons out front, was on the same street as the mills along Six Mile Creek. This was no doubt a handy spot for refreshments before and after work.

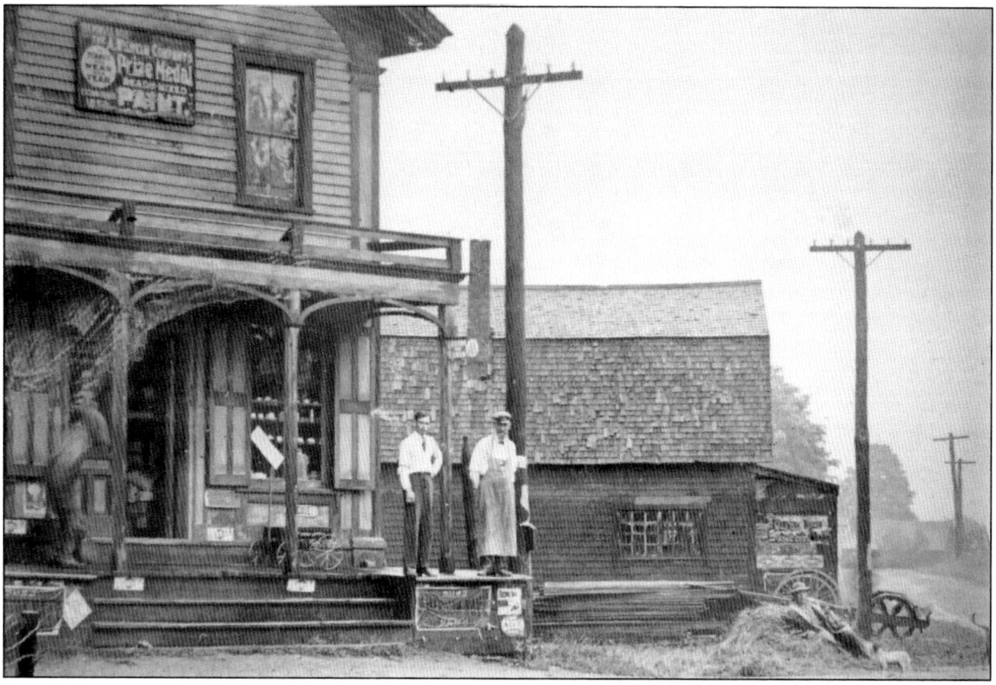

Brinks Store in Caroline Center offered a wide variety of goods and services to the people of that community. Everything from butter to paint could be purchased, and many times, excess farm produce could be sold or traded for items that locals couldn't provide for themselves.

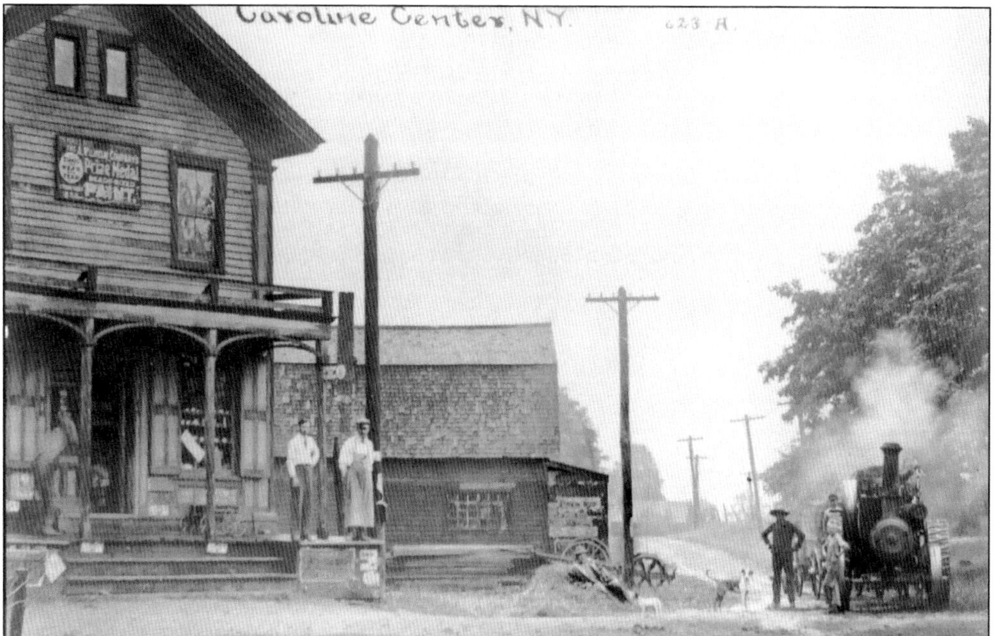

Another view of Brinks Store shows a steam engine chugging up the road. It was not unusual to see, puffing up the road, steam-powered tractors with power take-off to allow the use of a hay thrasher, grain mill, sawmill, and other attachments. The owner would travel from one farm to the next, hiring himself and his machine out for cash or a share of the crop.

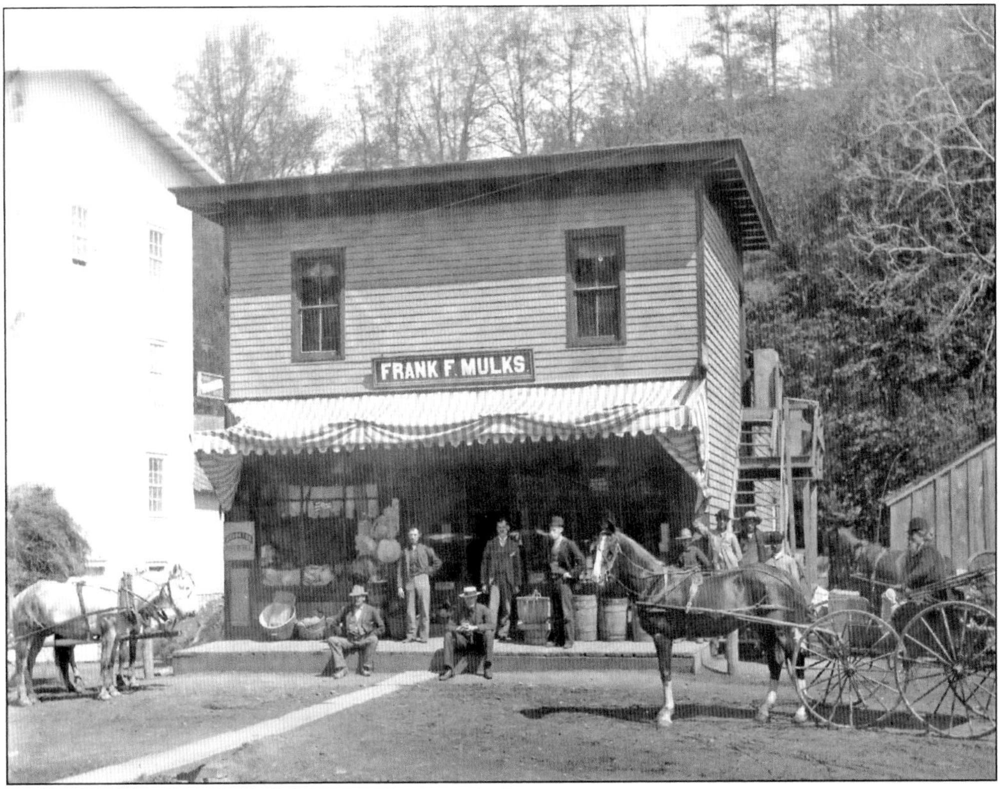

Mulks Store in Brooktondale enjoys a lively variety of customers, including the doctor in his buggy. It no longer serves as the post office but is still very much the heart of this community. The store, now called Brookton's Market, is still in business, offering a wide variety of groceries, deli items, books by local authors, handicrafts, and locally sourced meats, fruits, and vegetables.

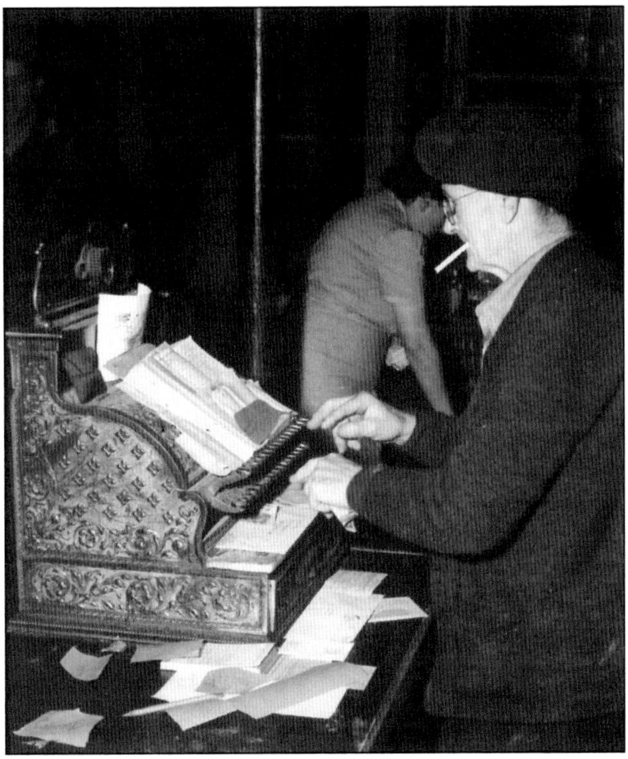

Frank Brink was supposedly quite the character, almost always with a cigarette hanging out of his mouth. He had his own unique system of keeping track of bills, his customers' credit slips, and accounts receivable, but it always worked out in the end.

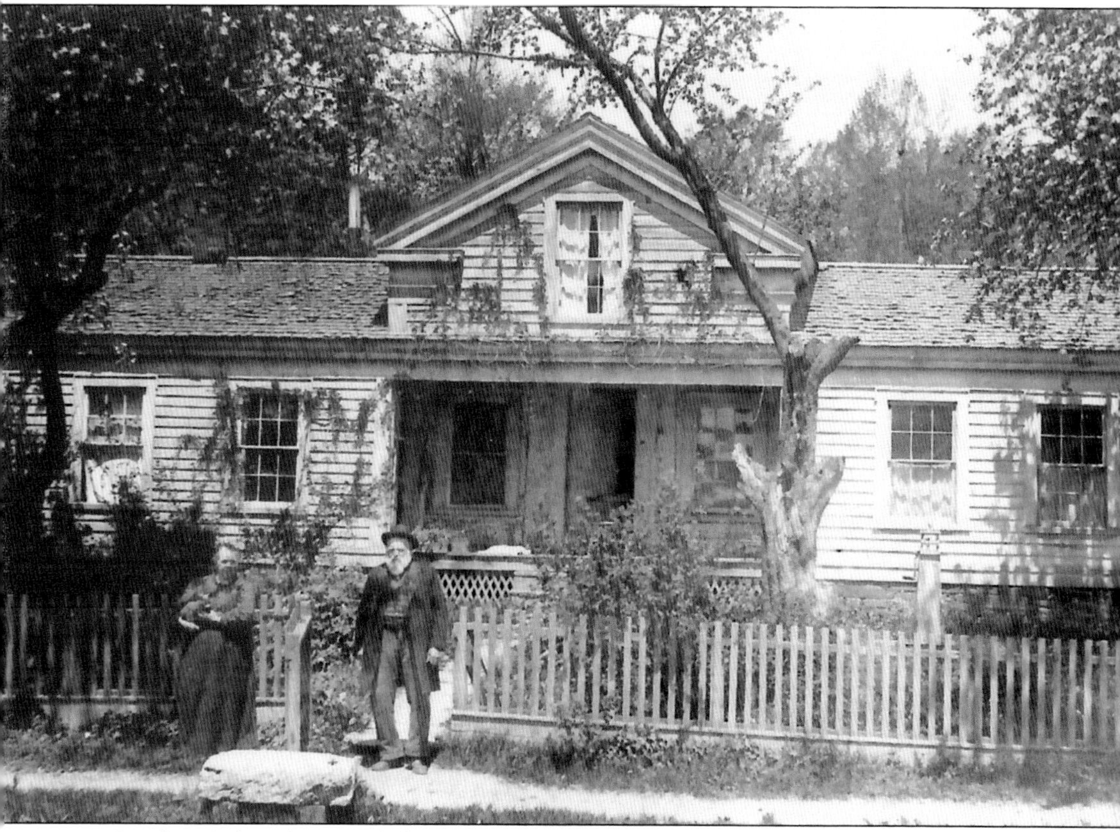

Caroline Aults, who ran a bakery in Slaterville Springs and was known for her pastries, stands by a carriage step. The well in the front yard is also visible. Most of Slaterville Springs has artesian well water or very shallow wells, so big well casing is not required.

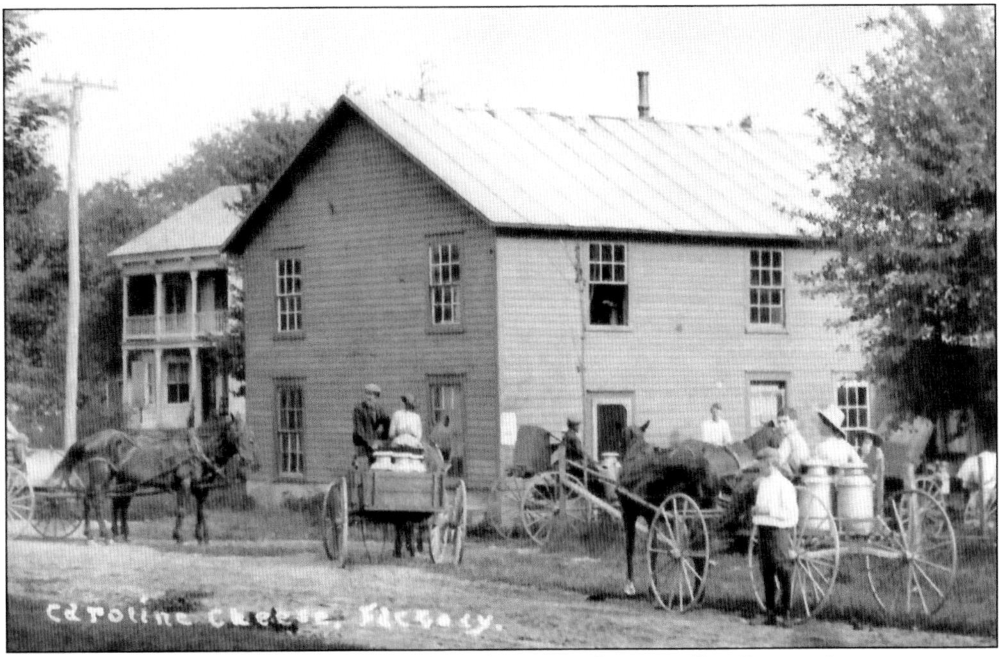

The Caroline Cheese Factory provided these farmers a place to sell milk or make arrangements to be paid in cheese or butter for a portion of what their cows produced. In the days when an icehouse or springhouse was the only way to keep things cool, regular trips to the cheese factory were necessary to keep the milk from spoiling.

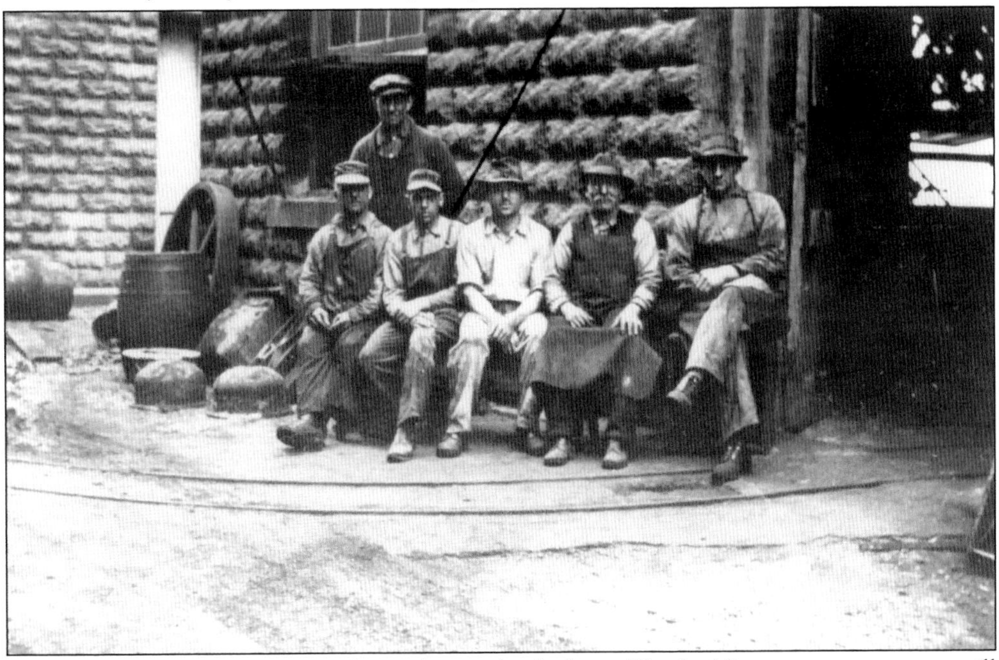

Slaterville Springs Creamery workers relax in the fresh air. The building, now apartments, still stands on the street named in its honor. In recent years, small local creameries are returning as local food gains a foothold, and the Snow Farm Creamery of Caroline is listed on the expanding Finger Lakes Cheese Trail, right beside the wineries.

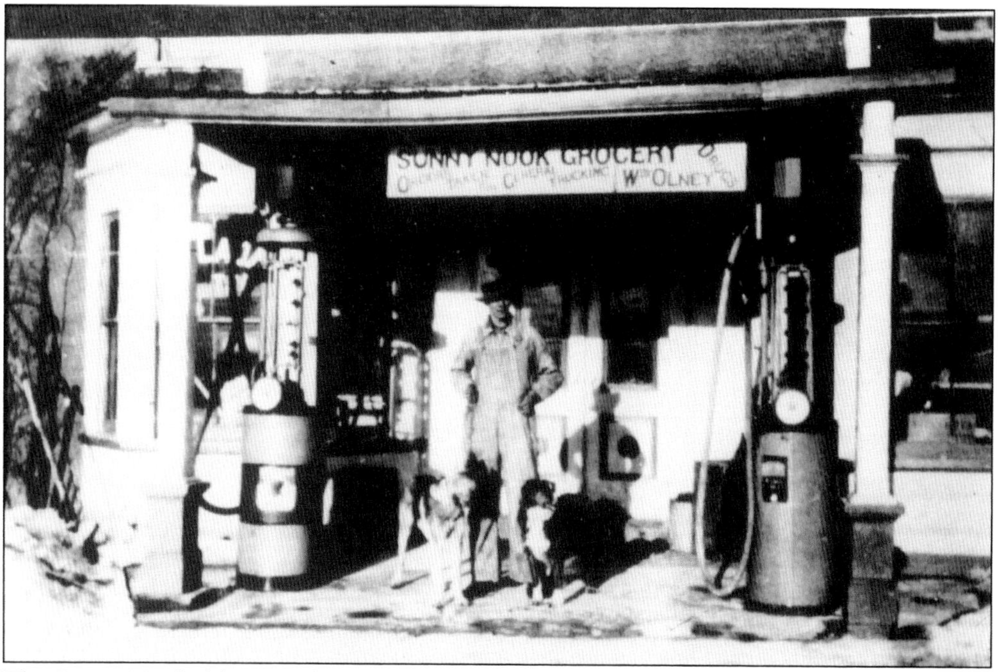

The Sunny Nook, like most hamlet general stores, has a little bit of everything. Such retail establishments might have everything from needle and thread to bear traps, buying some of their stock from traveling salesmen, the city, and local sources, along with growing some of their own.

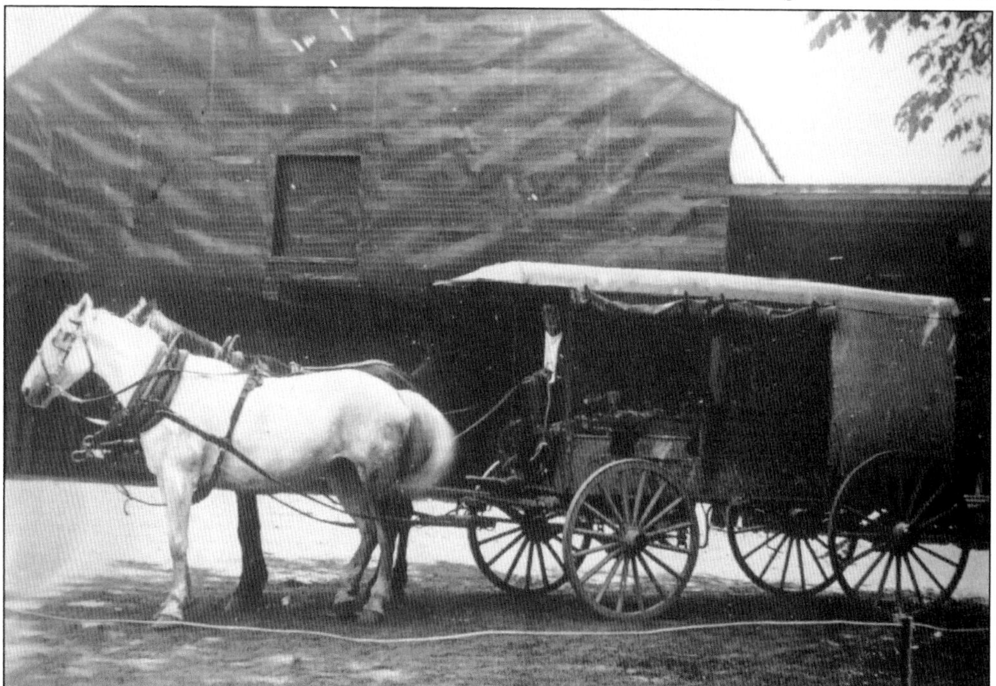
The traveling salesman was an important member of society as he moved from one community to the next, with his wagon stuffed with everything from pots and pans to fabrics. Occasionally, he would sweeten the deal for a housewife by throwing in a hair ribbon or two.

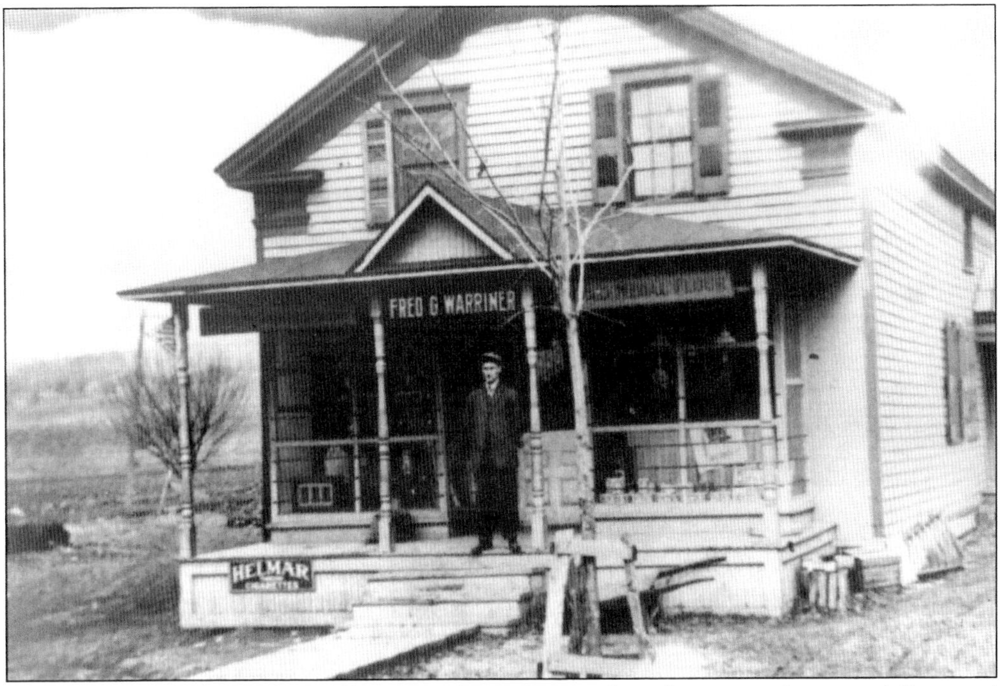

Fred Warriner's store in Slaterville Springs has a fair number of items on the ground floor, and like many rural stores, living quarters are located upstairs. Like his competition in Caroline Center and other parts of town, Warriner took advantage of the signs offered by his suppliers, such as Gold Medal Flour.

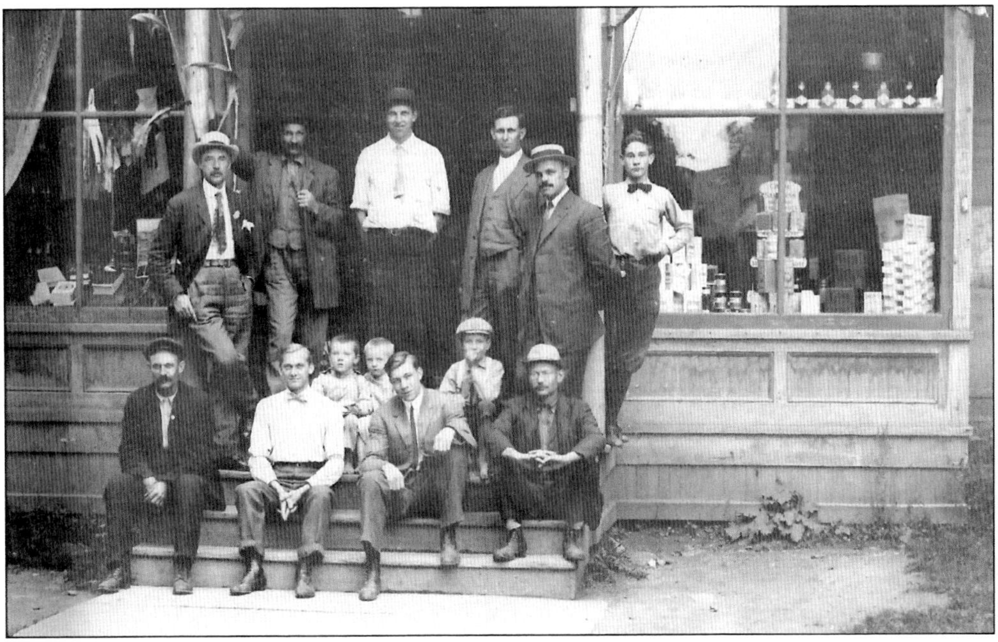

Men and boys hang out at another store in Slaterville Springs. In a less-hurried era, it was not unusual for some people to spend a little extra time catching up on local news and gossip. Perhaps a tourist has stopped by to purchase a souvenir.

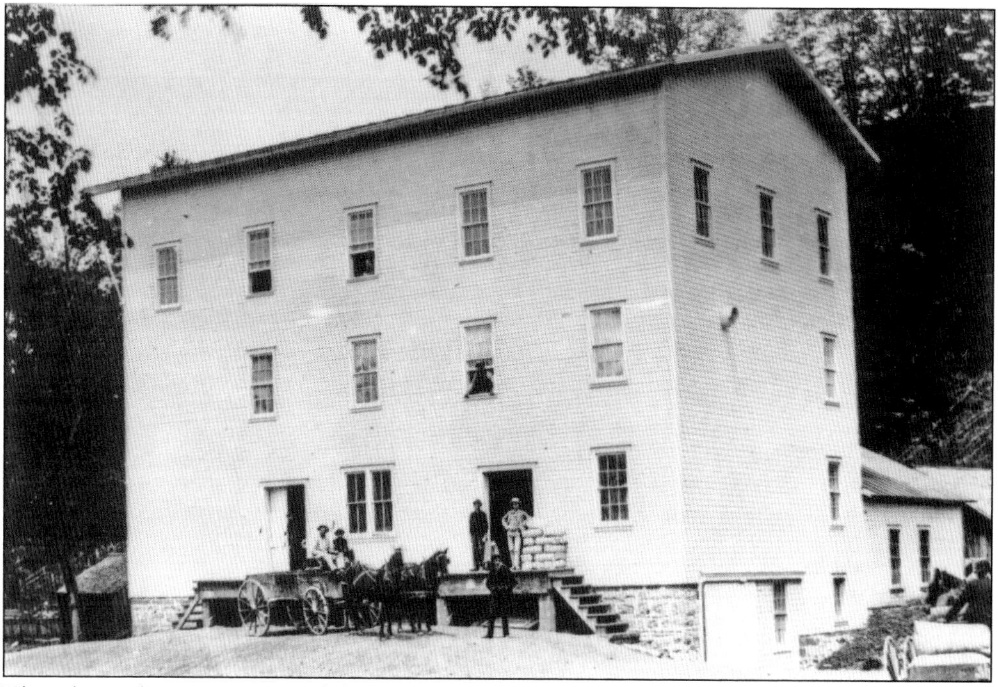

This plaster factory was one of the many businesses in Brooktondale clustered near the lower bridge that crosses Six Mile Creek.

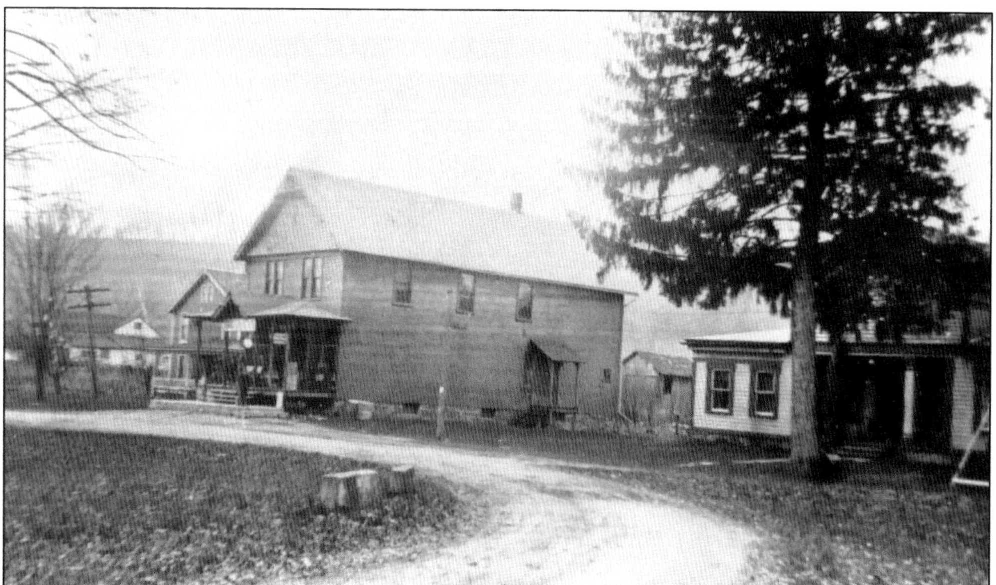

Speedsville is a small hamlet that was once a little bigger. This store, which burned down in 1928, was across the town park from the school and churches. The store had a dance hall and kitchen on the second floor, and it made for a lively town.

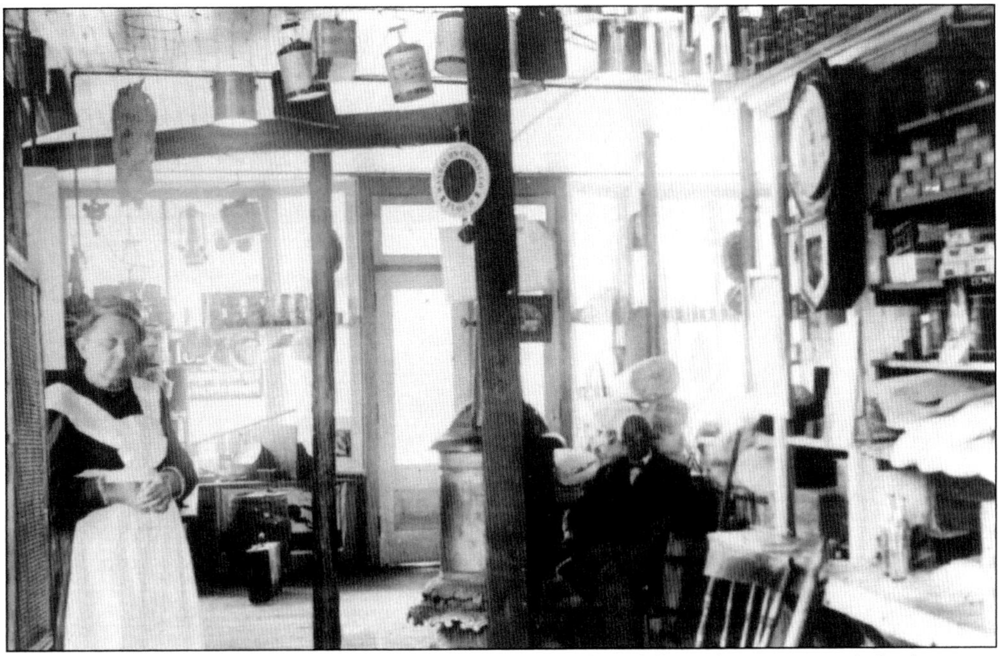

It was not just men who were storekeepers. The task often fell to the women, while the more difficult and physically demanding job of farmwork fell to the men.

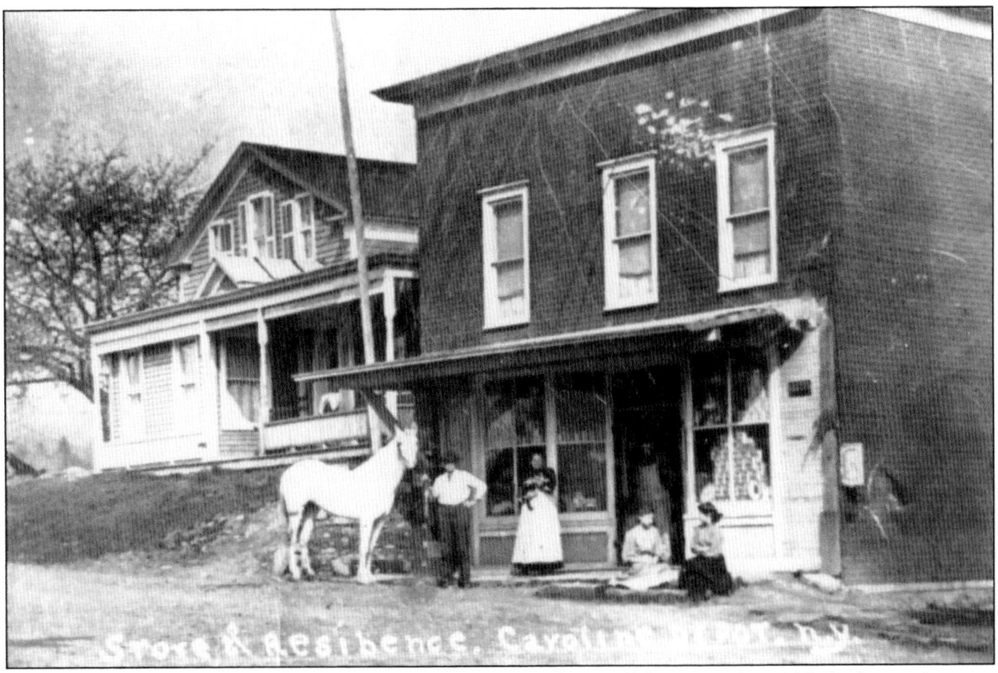

This store and house in the hamlet of Caroline Depot burned down in the 1930s before volunteer fire departments came into being. The store was owned by Henry Personius. Here, Henry and his wife, Frances, and their granddaughter enjoy a little sunshine as a neighbor or customer strolls by. Their house, the former Dutch Reformed Church parsonage, was moved here from West Slaterville Springs.

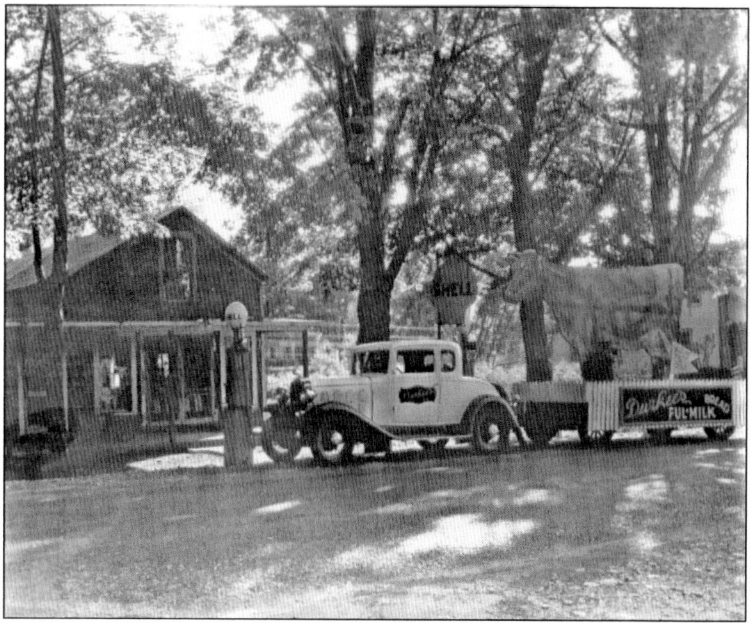

When the age of automobiles arrived, stores might add items to their stock including gasoline, which meant making new arrangements with those who supplied it. Alvin Furguson's store contracted with Shell and had a pump installed. Furguson also apparently dealt in Durkees Bread and Ful Milk, as the eye-catching cow on the trailer advertises.

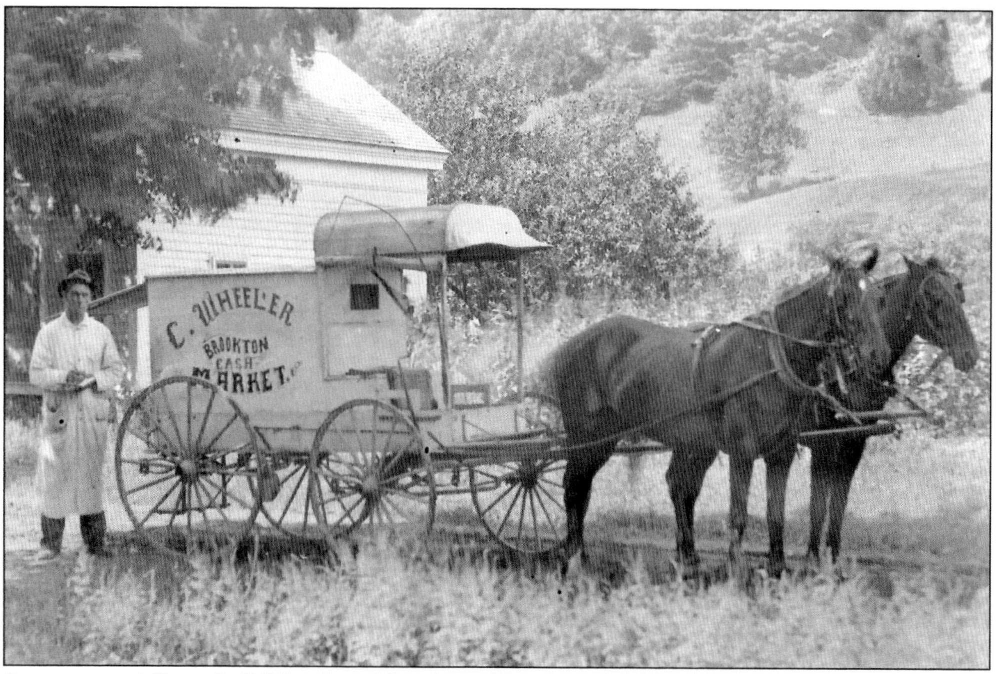

Some stores delivered. C Wheeler of Brookton (Brooktondale) had this very spiffy rig, with two horses to pull it. In the days when many people still worked on the farm or men went to work in factories and mills, leaving the women home all day with small children, the ability to get the essentials brought to a household's door was a great convenience.

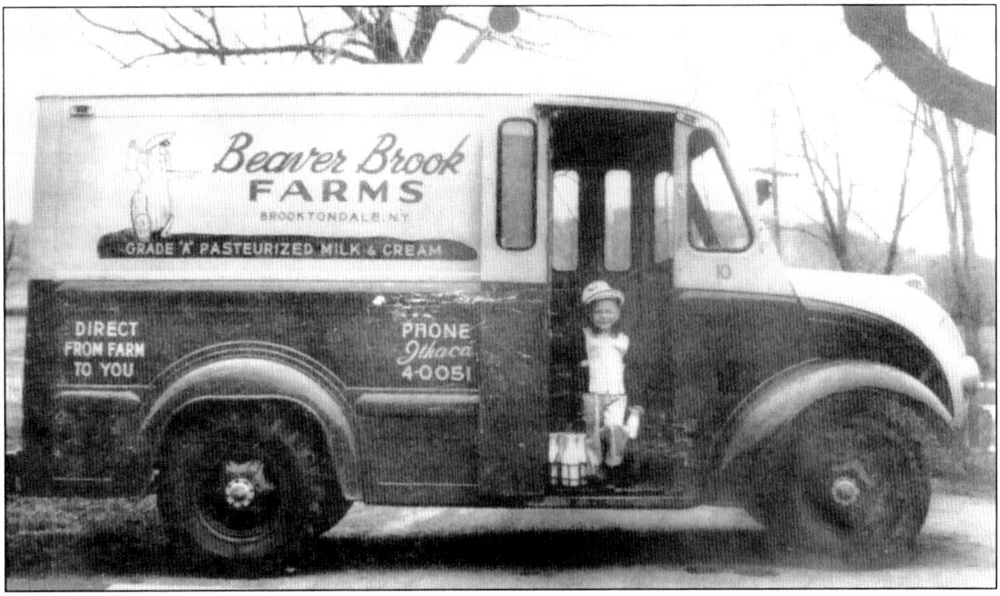

In the early years, the milkman had a horse and wagon, but George Raymond Arsenault's Beaver Brook Farms modernized and advertised its delivery service of pasteurized grade A milk and cream with this nicely appointed truck, with a smiling youngster on the running board. However, it was the slogan and photograph that was most eye-catching: "We Start Early," it declared.

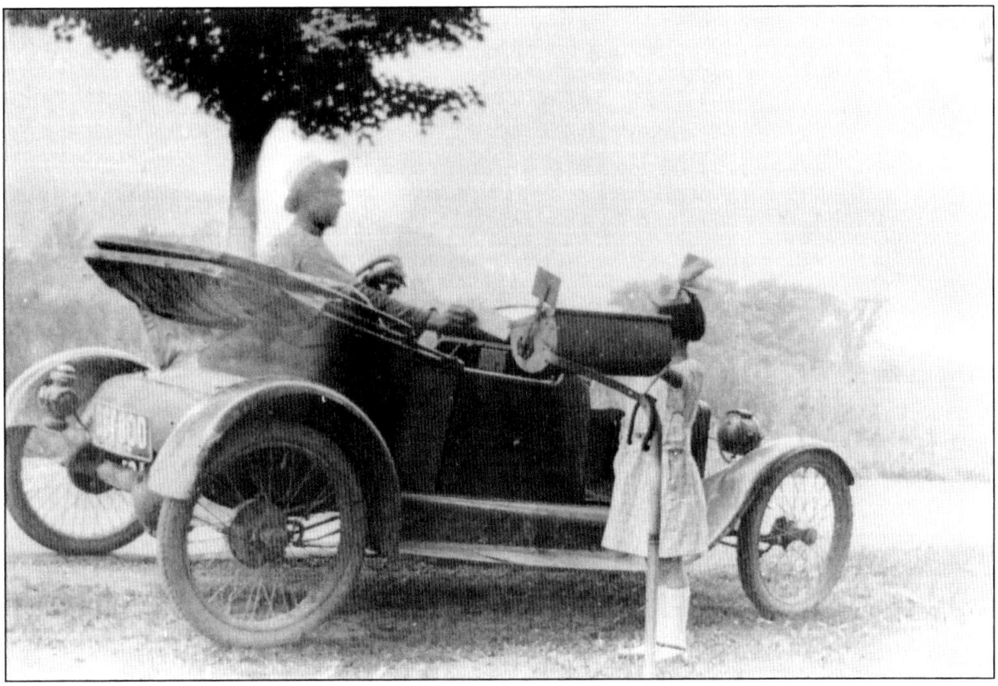

Other deliveries were modernized too. Ben Van De Mark used this roadster, uncovered on warm days, and very unlike the horse-drawn wagons and saddle pouches that were used when Rural Free Delivery mail service first started. This young lady with the big bow in her hair no doubt considers getting the mail one of the most important tasks she is trusted with.

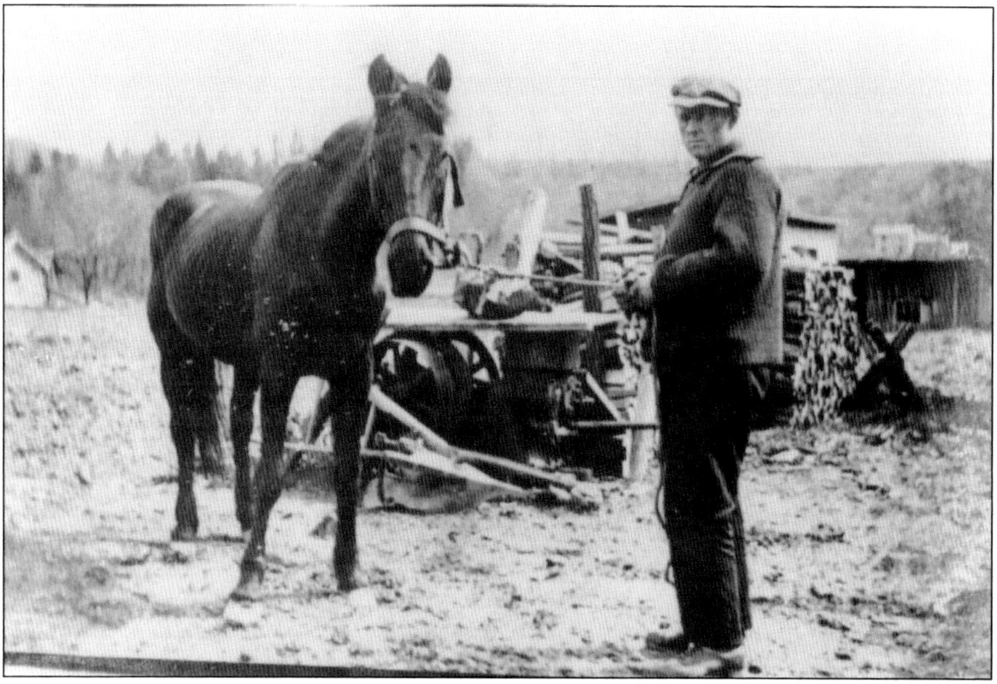

Charlie Weaver, a well driller, was on the cusp of the modern era with a machine to help drive the well point and a horse to pull the machinery to the drilling site. It is unknown if he was a "water witch," one who uses bent rods that dip to indicate underground water, but it was not uncommon then and is still sometimes done today.

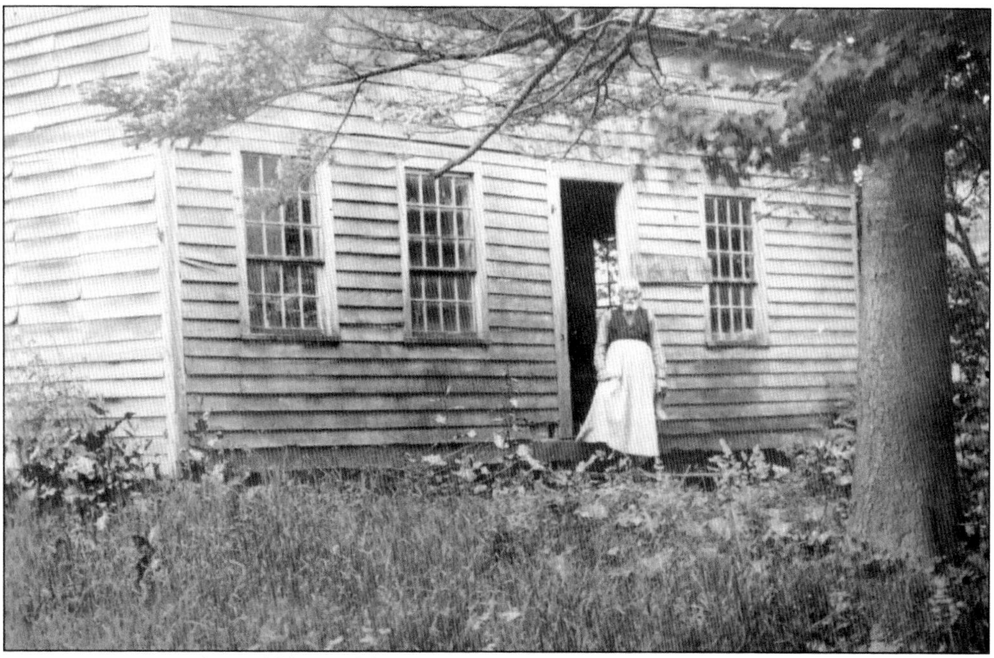

George Nixon ran his cobbler and harness shop from this building for many years. He was an excellent leather worker and an asset to the community. Unfortunately, mass production of shoes and then the automobile came along and put him out of business.

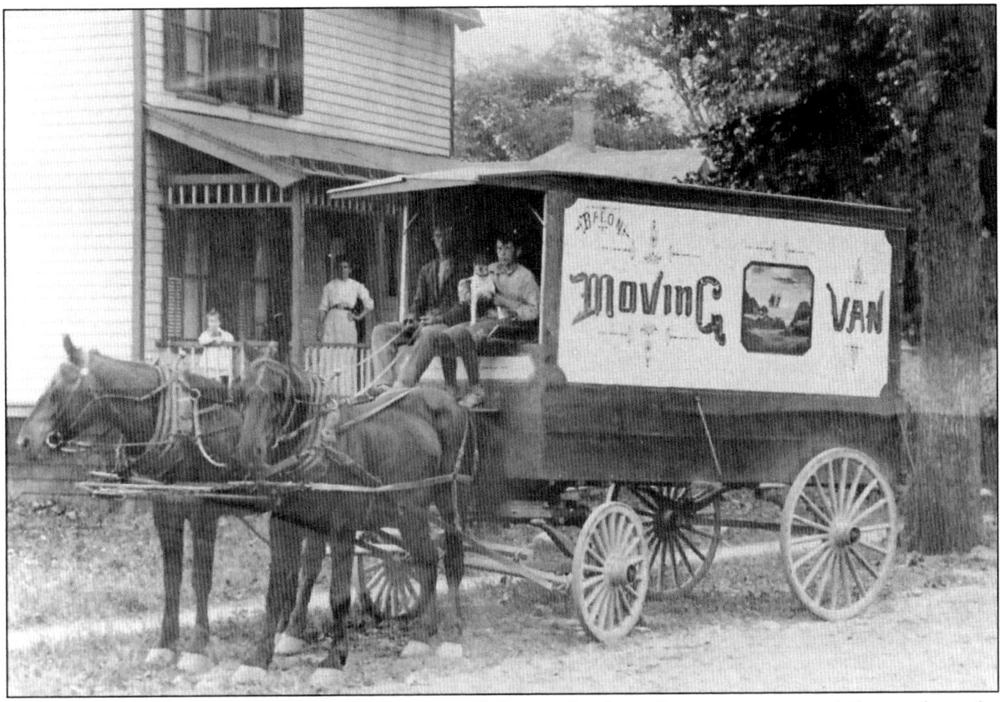

Any number of jobs that used to be done with horses had to change as automobiles and trucks took over the roads. This moving van seems very small by modern standards, but most people did not have the number and variety of items in a modern household, before there were electronics, sectional sofas, and the other things that make modern life so easy and so complicated.

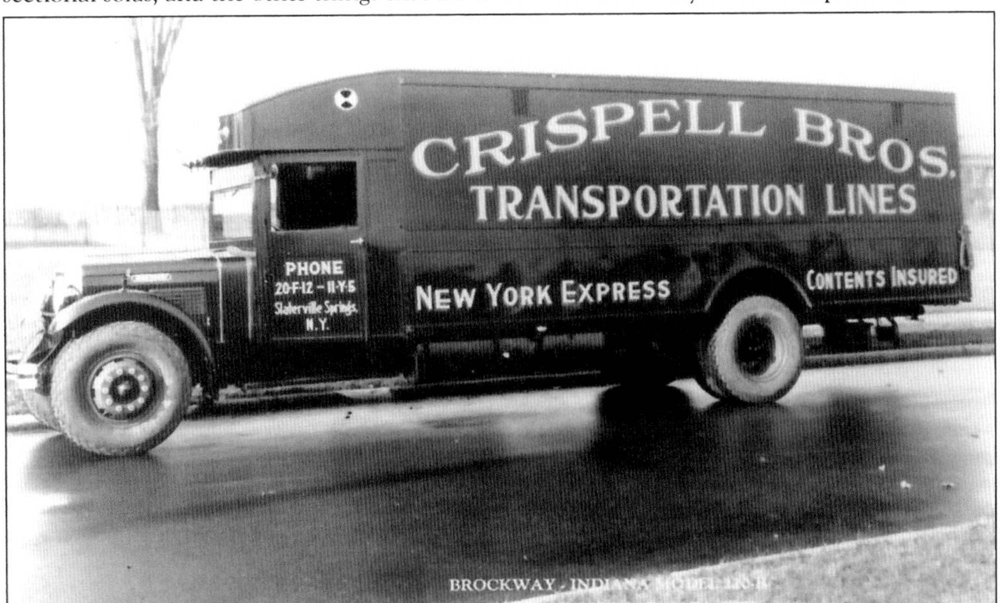

Crispell Brothers Transportation Lines started out with teams of horses and gradually worked up to large delivery vehicles and buses, taking everything from eggs to people as far as New York City, before it sold the fleet and set up shop as truck and auto repairmen. Sadly, that shop closed down just a few years ago, after doing business for over 100 years under the Crispell name.

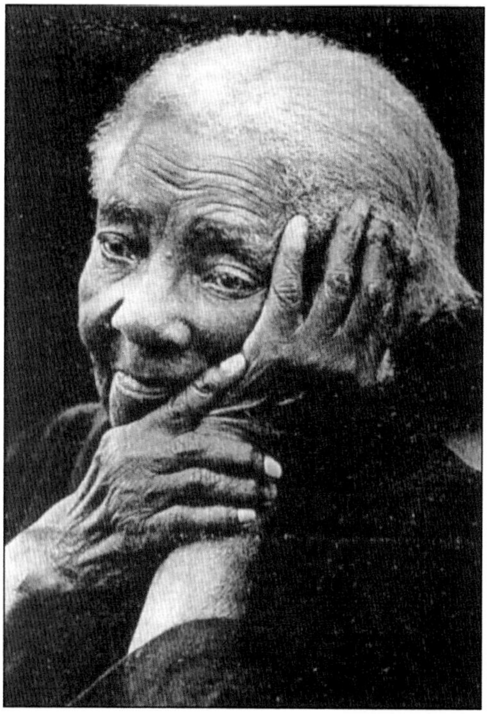

Winifred Bailor, born in 1891, was an unmarried woman, four feet tall, and while she described herself as "a little old runt, nobody wanted me," this spunky young lady was one of the first African American women to attend Cornell University. After graduating in 1921, it was still illegal for her to work as a teacher in the north, so she moved to Mississippi. She later worked at the YMCA in Rochester, passing away in 1982.

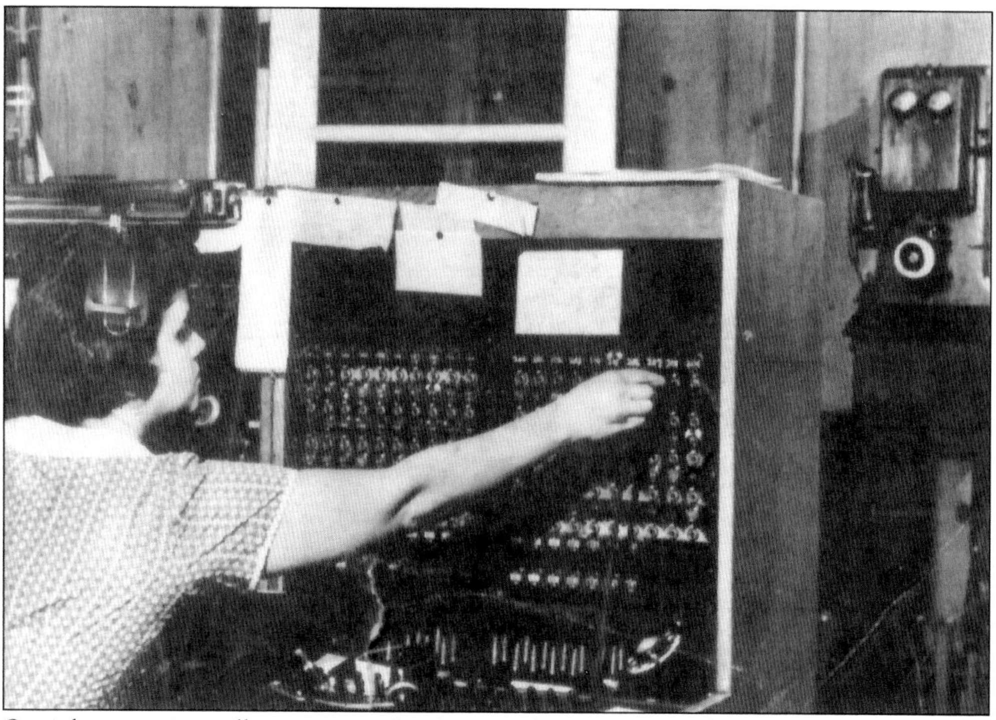

One job women in small towns enjoyed, at least until automatic switching was invented, was that of telephone operator. With the equipment set up in a front room, they could watch the neighbors walk by and often appeared to know everything that was going on in town. Thus, a caller might be told, "Mrs. Smith is not at home. Let me connect you to where she is visiting."

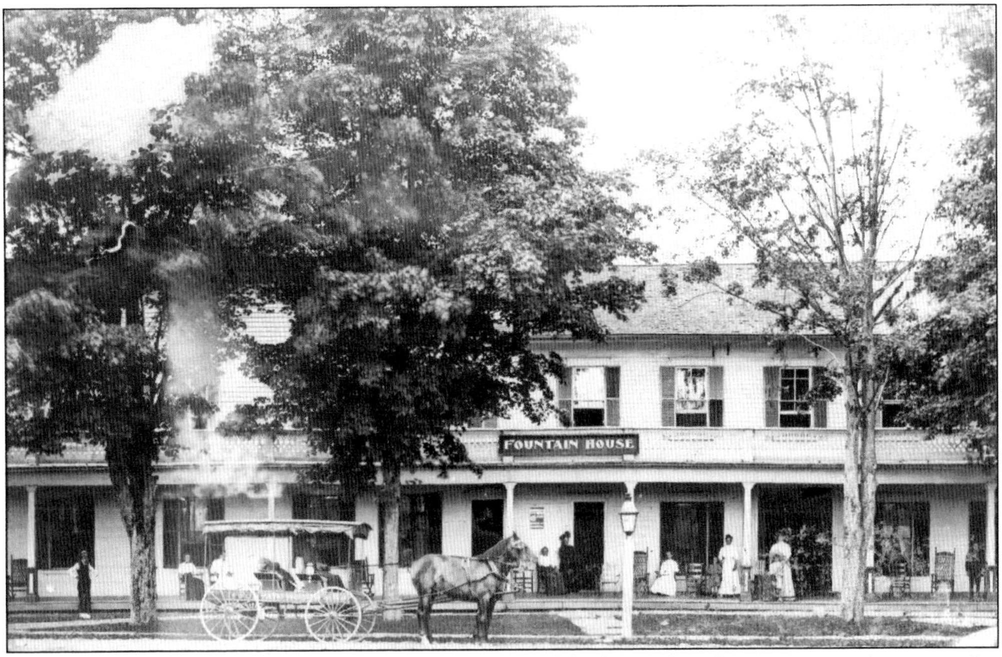

The Fountain House in Slaterville Springs was one of the better hotels to stay in or dine at in the 19th century when the town was filled with tourists from Ithaca or further away still. It was also a place where women without an education could find work away from home or the farm.

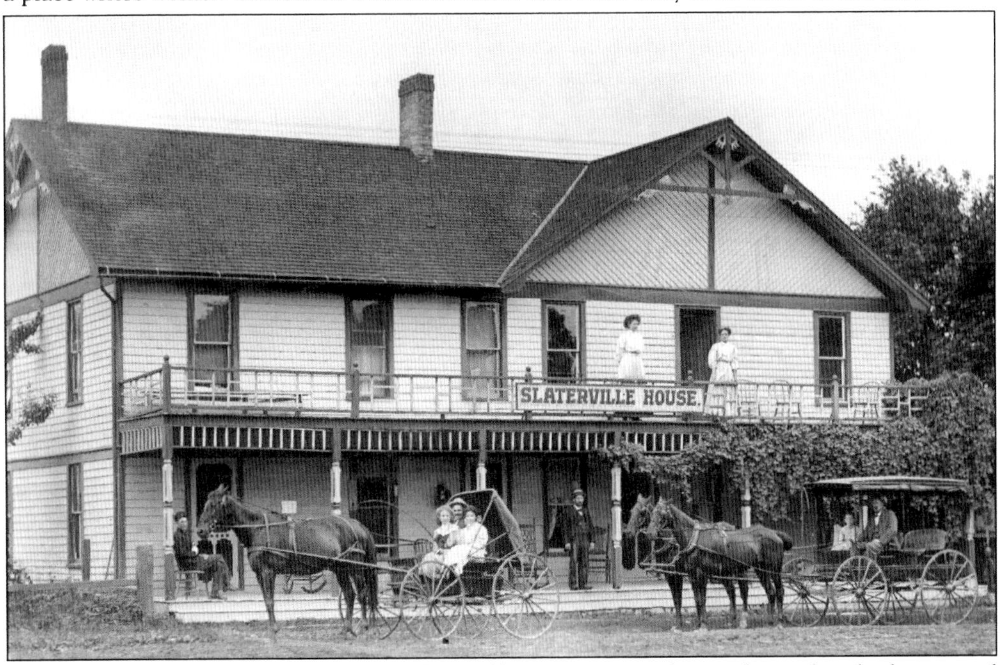

Pleasure-seekers enjoy relaxing at the Slaterville House, one of several area hotels that served guests when the hamlet became a more compact version of Saratoga Springs. People came to drink and bathe in the waters to cure their ills or acquire even greater health. Other businesses sprang up to accommodate visitors from Ithaca, Owego, and beyond, including stables, restaurants, sellers of souvenirs, and eventually, a soda-bottling plant.

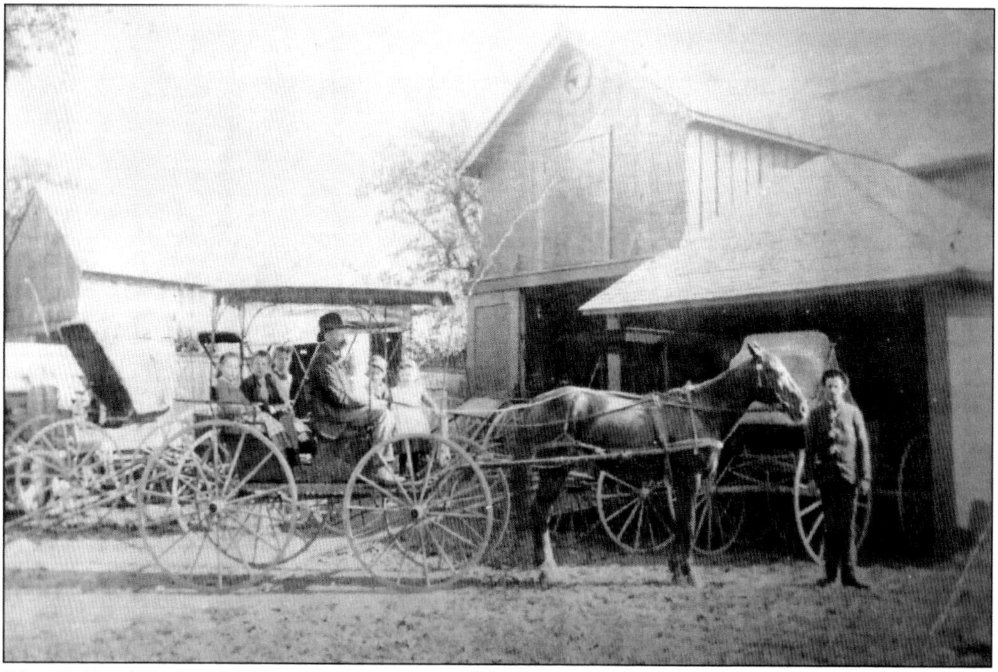

The Holland Livery Stables are one of several businesses that started or grew with the coming of the summer tourists. Visitors had to be picked up at the railroad stations, or if they had come into town with their own horses, the animals had to be fed and housed. Sometimes people would rent a horse or a horse and carriage to explore the countryside. During these years, Slaterville Springs was a very busy town.

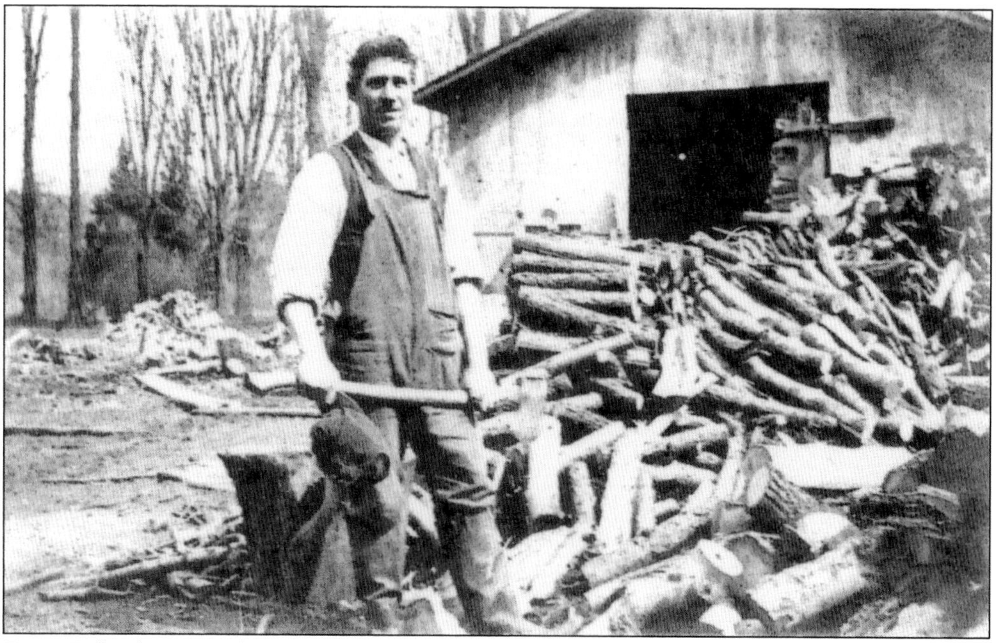

Forest Rills chops wood, one of the many chores that needed to be done to keep a household or hotel warm and supplied with fuel for cooking. With all of the summer visitors also wanting to soak in warm baths, the work probably seemed unending.

Five

Transportation

At first, the only means of traveling to and through Caroline were on foot or horseback. Game trails and those blazed by Indians and explorers were all that was available to those who first looked upon these green valleys. In 1804, a decade after the Earsleys arrived, the Catskill Turnpike was authorized by New York governor DeWitt Clinton, opening up the area for wagon travel and future development. Taverns and towns sprang up near the tollgates, and though at first the road was a dirt track through the wilderness with logs laid in the muddiest sections (called a corduroy road), it was a major improvement to transportation through this developing area.

Later, the Erie Canal allowed people and goods to travel from New York City, up the Hudson River, along the canal, and down Cayuga Lake to Ithaca. After disembarking in Ithaca, the turnpike was then available to shunt goods to Caroline and throughout the upstate area.

When the railroads came in the mid-1800s, that new means of transport further increased the number of people arriving and the options available to them. When paved roads finally came to Caroline, it was both a blessing and a problem, as citizens were not only given options in shopping and work, but also had easier and faster methods of leaving town to work or to migrate to other places, which led to the downfall of several businesses.

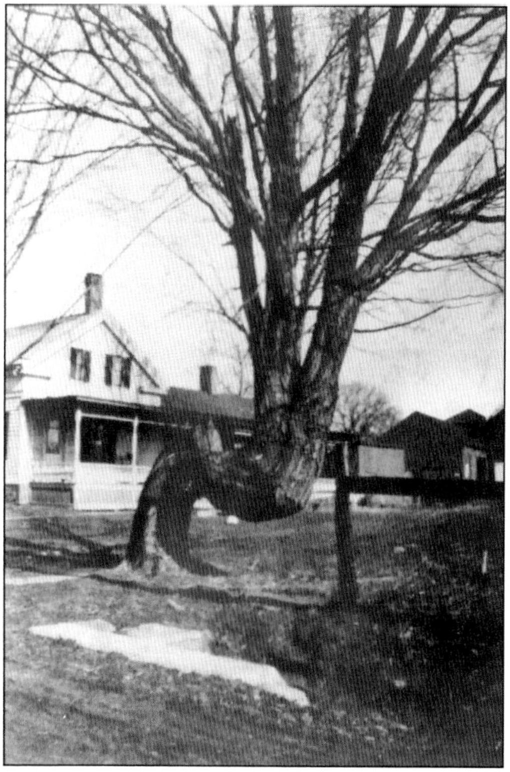

This marker tree was created along what became the Catskill Turnpike in Slaterville Springs. Before roads were blazed by the white man, the Native Americans would deliberately bend and tie trees into these distinctive shapes to mark trails that they regularly used when traveling through the wilderness.

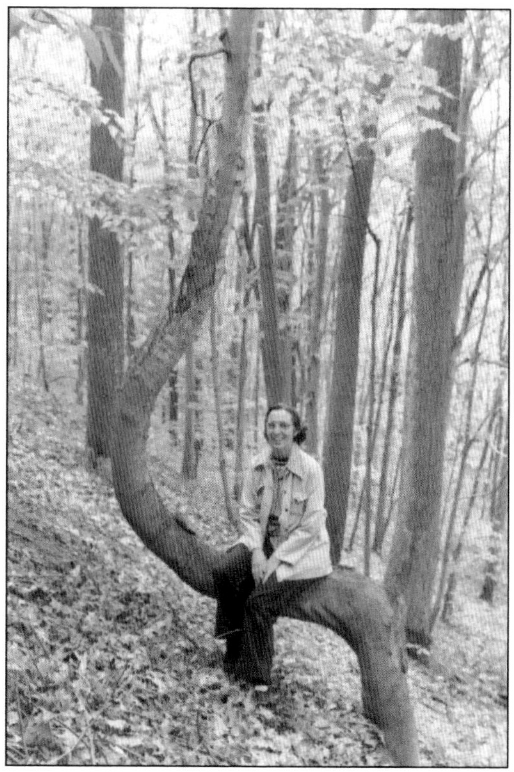

A young Eunice Weber sits on another marker tree, this one halfway up a hillside. A woman interested in history and welfare of the town of Caroline, she passed away some time ago at age 76. These marker trees can still be found sometimes, but most would be over 200 years old now and have likely fallen victim to wind, lightning, and winter storms.

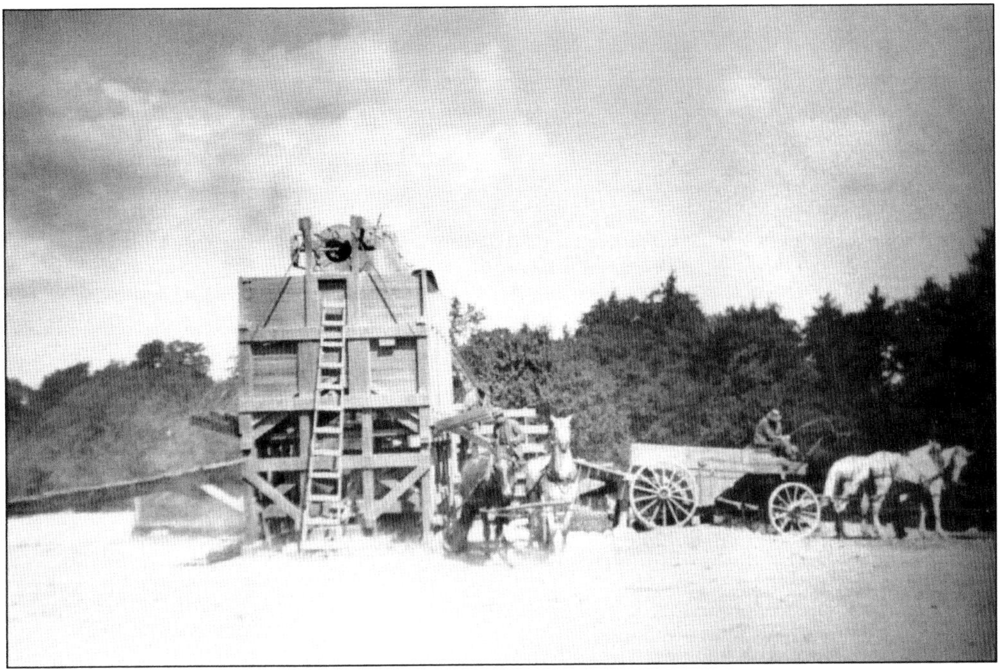

New roads that would accommodate wheeled traffic required a roadbed with various-sized stones. Crushing larger stones into the size required for the job was hard, tedious work, but it made a big difference when one wanted to travel in the springtime without getting hopelessly bogged down in the mud.

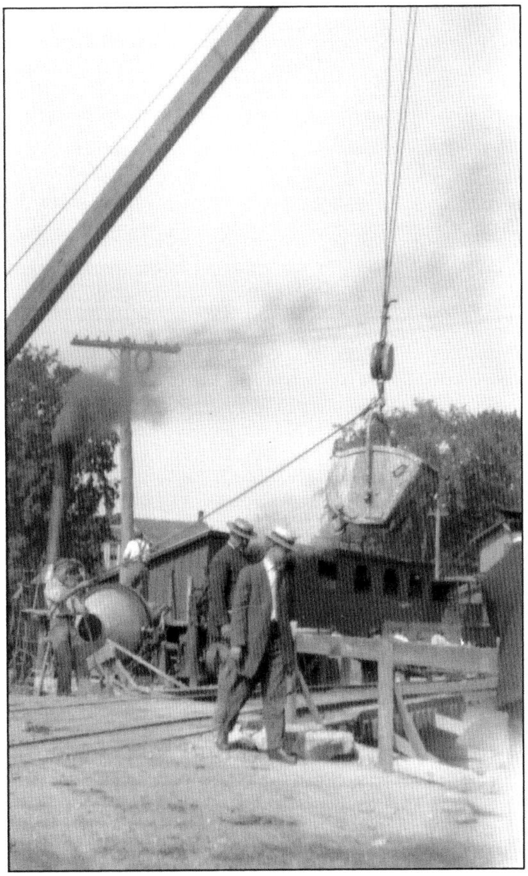

The Besemer Road Bridge was put together in an organized fashion with an engineer as well as a number of skilled workmen. In this photograph, they make sure that the job is being done correctly and concrete was poured properly.

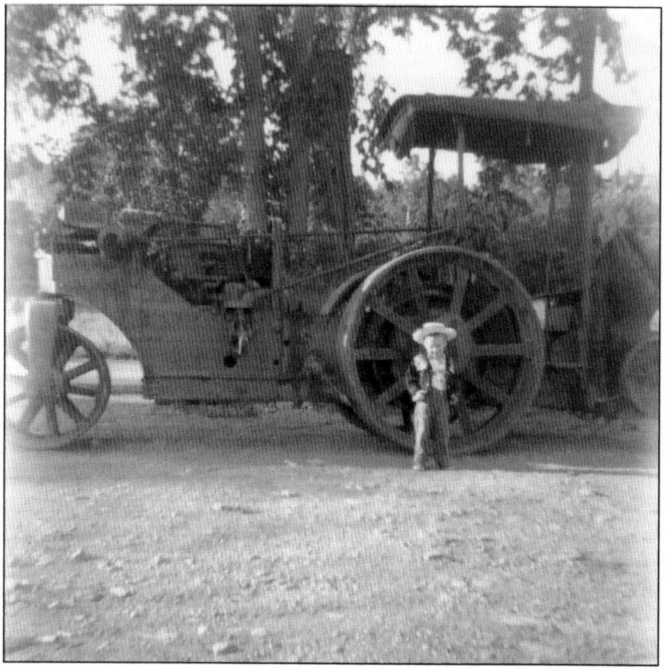

A youngster in a cowboy hat, as fascinated with machinery as any other kid, enjoys being so close to this piece of road repair equipment.

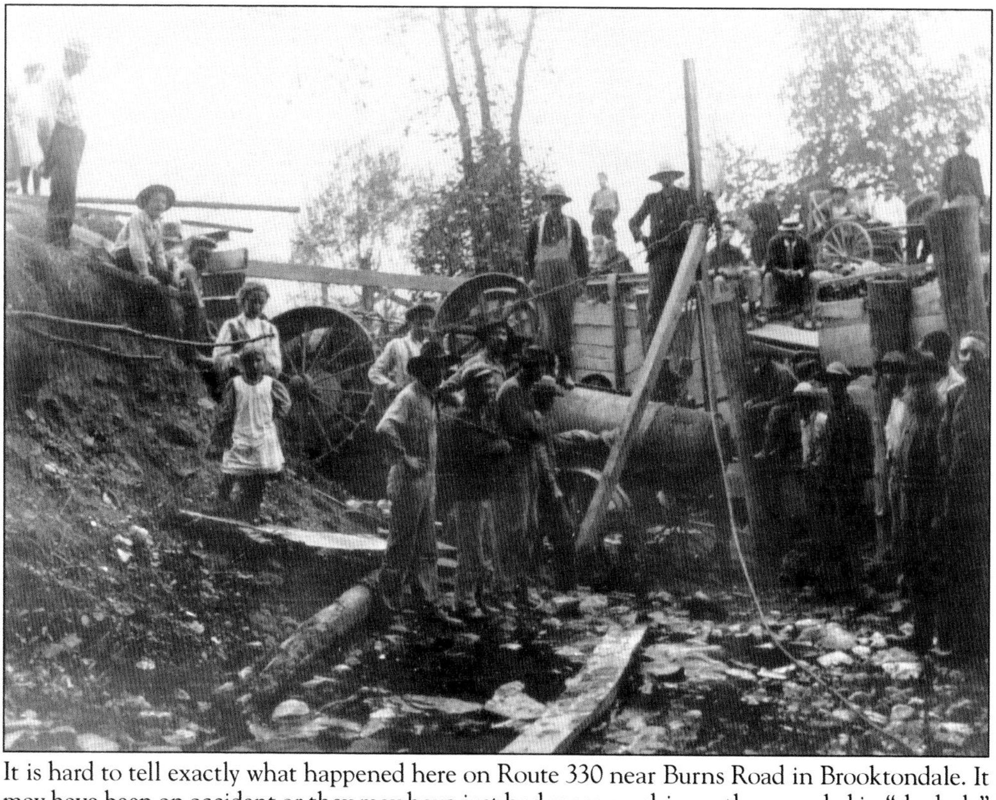

It is hard to tell exactly what happened here on Route 330 near Burns Road in Brooktondale. It may have been an accident or they may have just had more machinery than needed in "the hole" while trying to build a bridge, but whatever the situation, it required a large number of "sidewalk superintendents" to set things right.

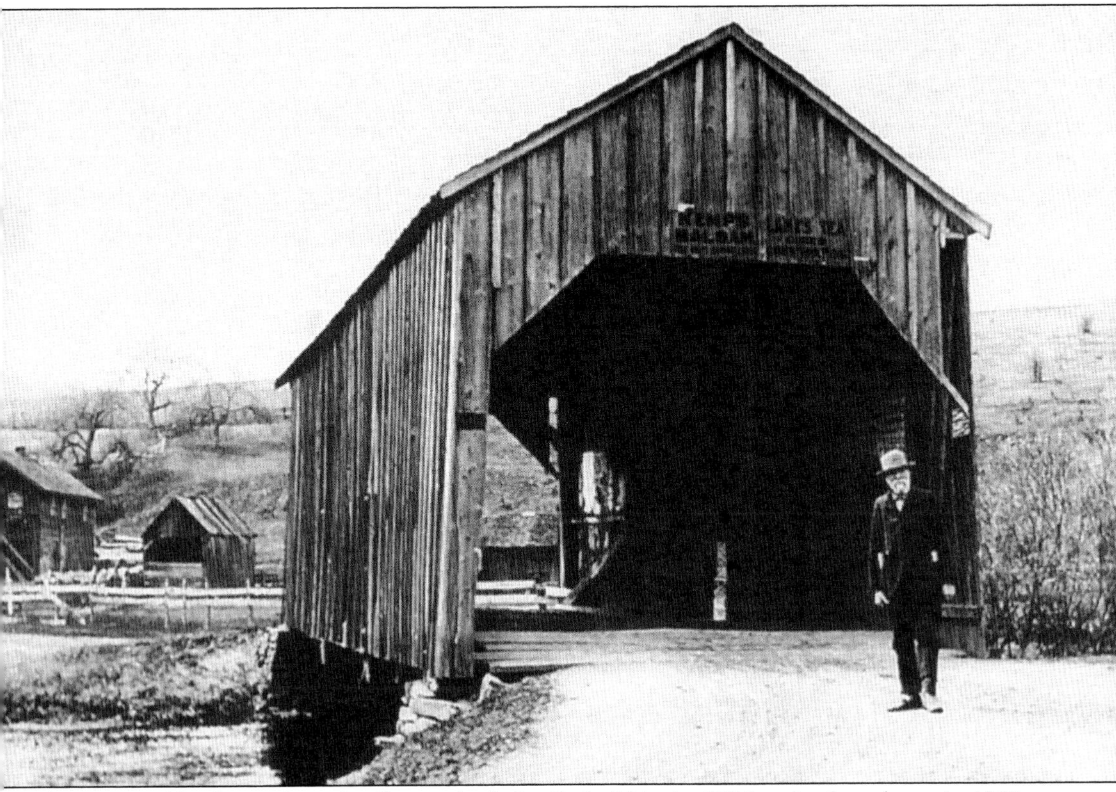

This covered bridge in Speedsville was built by Seth Akin in 1856 and taken down in 1929 when a new metal bridge was installed. There is some debate as to whether covered bridges were useful, keeping the weather off that part of the road, or a nuisance, as during winter, when travelers switched from wheeled wagons to sleds, snow had to be shoveled into the covered part to accommodate the sleds. However impractical, some still find it hard to part with such quaint symbols of America's past.

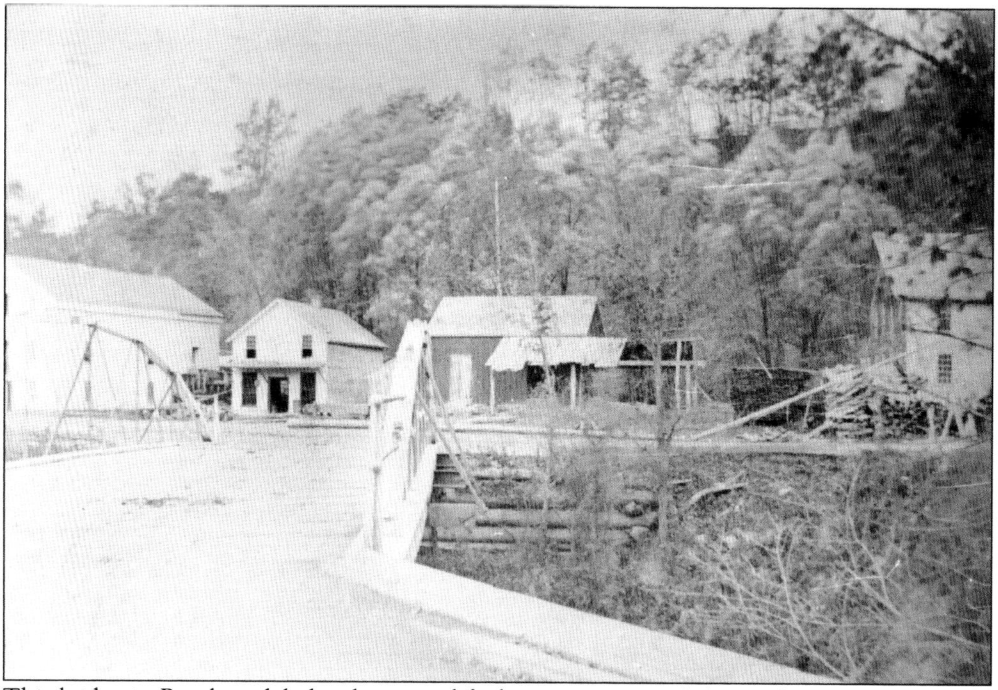

This bridge in Brooktondale has been modified many times, and the road pattern completely changed. The building that looks like a barn is where the Mulks Store, now Brookton's market, stands. To the right is one of the mills, and to the left may be another, perhaps the plaster mill.

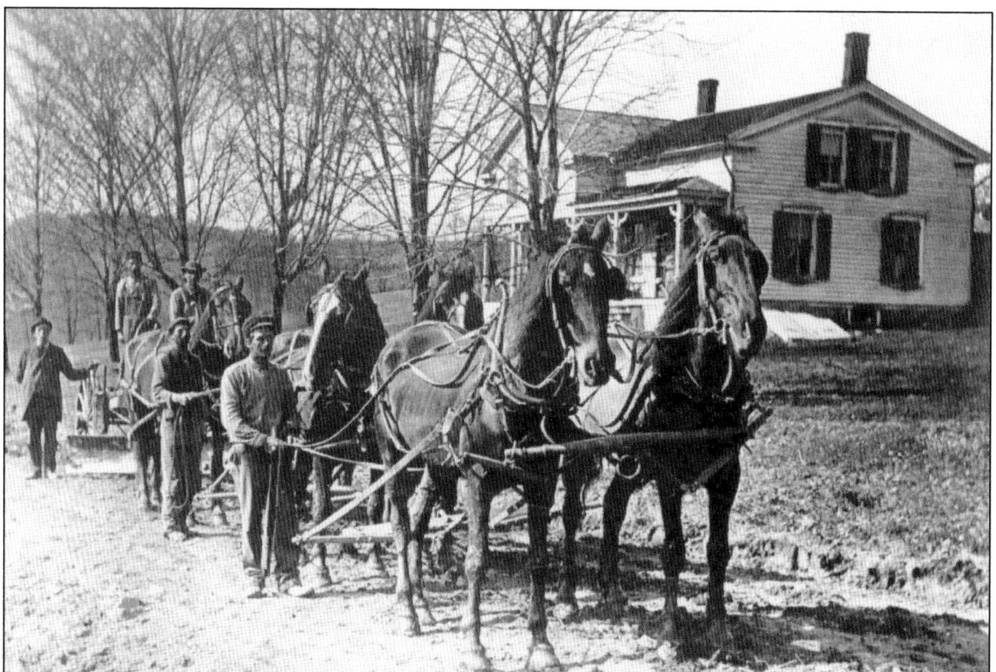

Neighbors gathered with their horses and equipment to repair the roads every spring. Doctors, ministers, the elderly, and the disabled were exempt from this work.

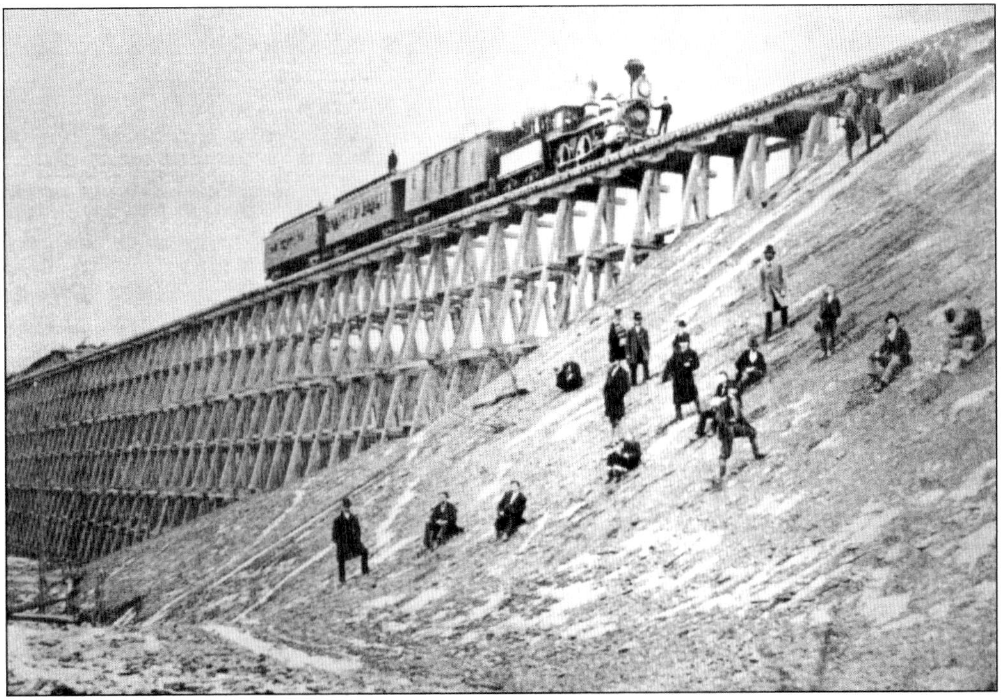

The first train to come through Caroline crosses this wooden trestle, which was built to span the Caroline Valley and completed on December 11, 1875. The Utica, Ithaca and Elmira Railroad used it for many years, until it was replaced by a metal trestle in 1889. When the trestle was dismantled, there were complaints in the hamlet of Brooktondale, just west of this photograph, as it had effectively blocked the cold winter winds while it was there.

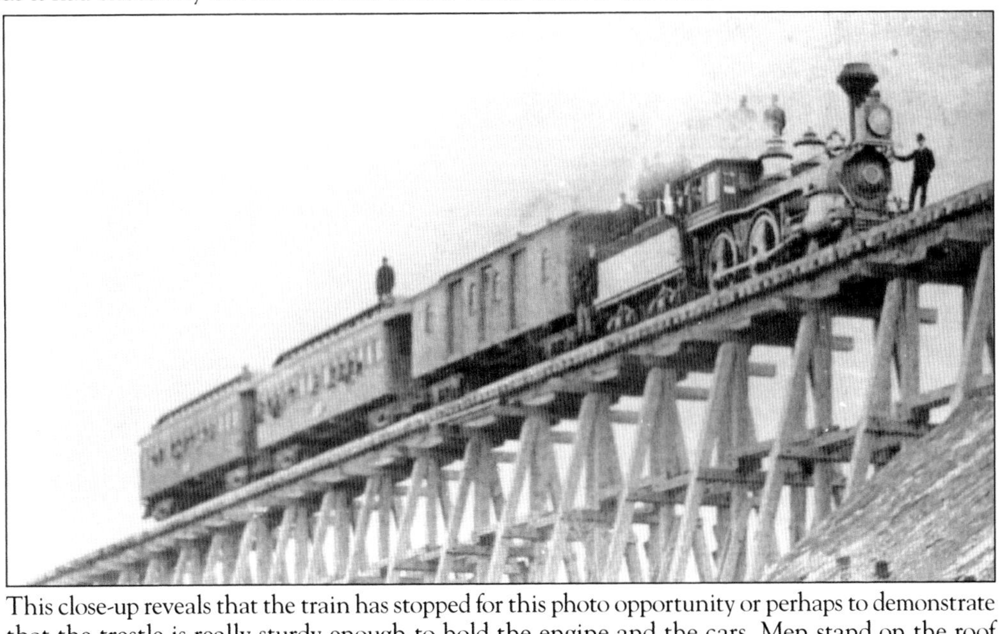

This close-up reveals that the train has stopped for this photo opportunity or perhaps to demonstrate that the trestle is really sturdy enough to hold the engine and the cars. Men stand on the roof of the cab and on top of the cars, hang out of the cab, and stand on the "cow catcher," which occasionally did push a cow off the track, while passengers wave for onlookers.

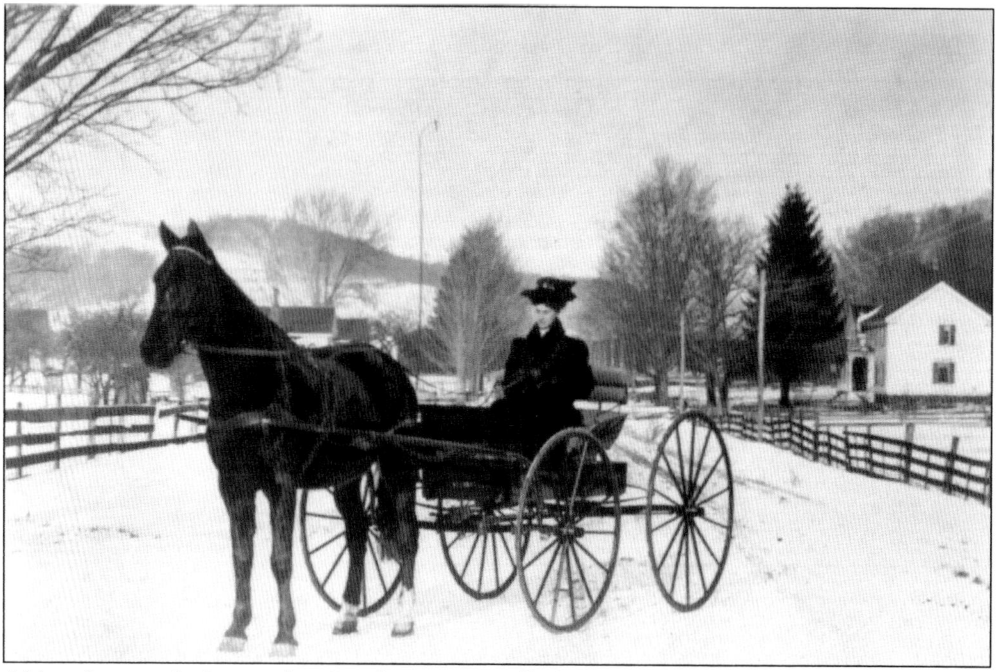

Although trains had arrived in Caroline, it was still a long time before the horse-and-buggy days were finished. Men and women rolled along on the country roads summer and winter, though if the snow became too deep, the carriage was left in the barn and the sled came out.

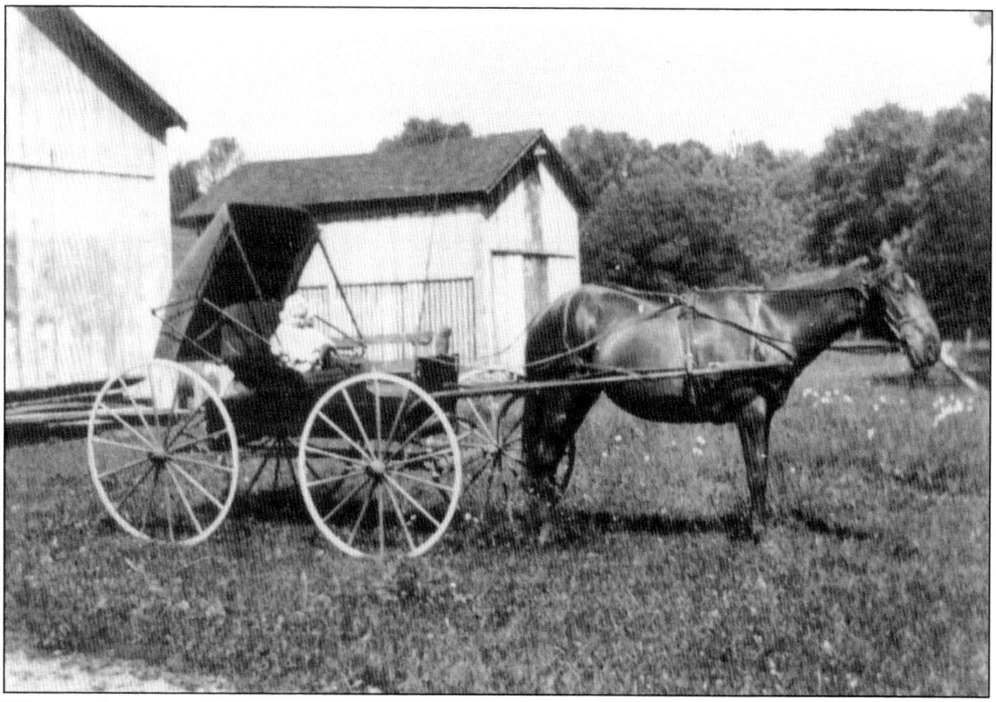

This is either a very well-trained horse or very bold parents, as it is unlikely the baby has mastered the word mama, let along gee and haw. Just as today, people enjoyed taking funny pictures.

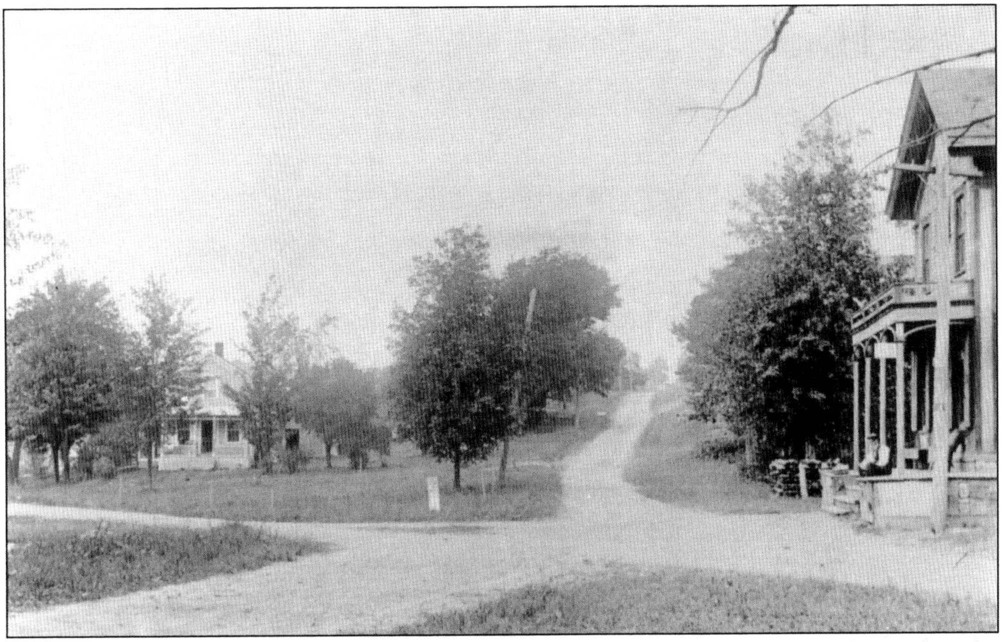

Until the 1950s, most roads in Caroline were dirt roads—dusty in summer and rutted in the spring. Some roads in town still remain unpaved, but with the help of modern machinery, they are kept in better repair.

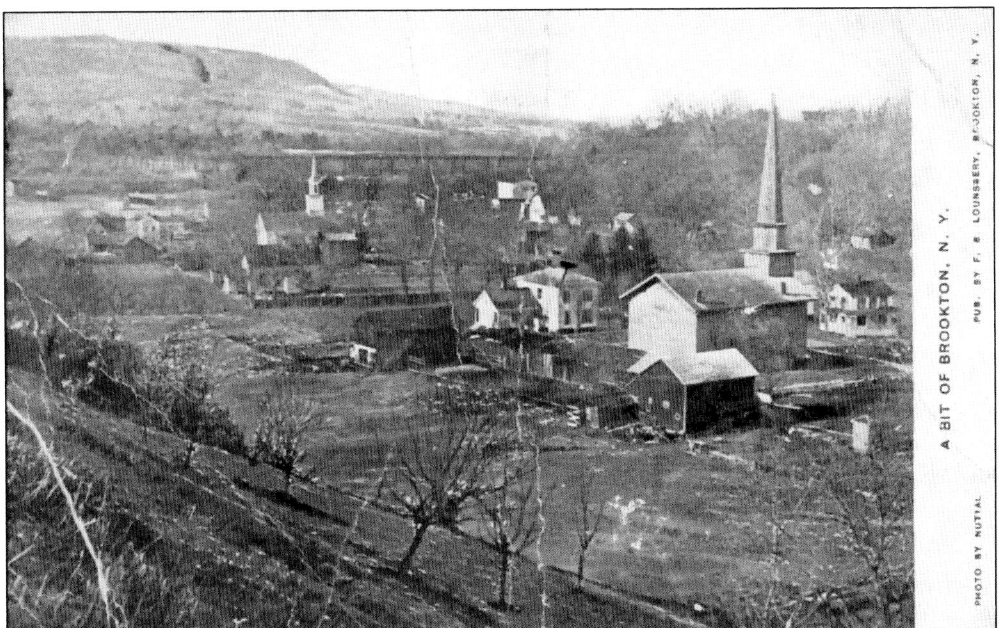

Winter or summer, roads and farm paths must be passable. Horses were often fitted with special ice shoes with cleats on the bottom to keep them from slipping.

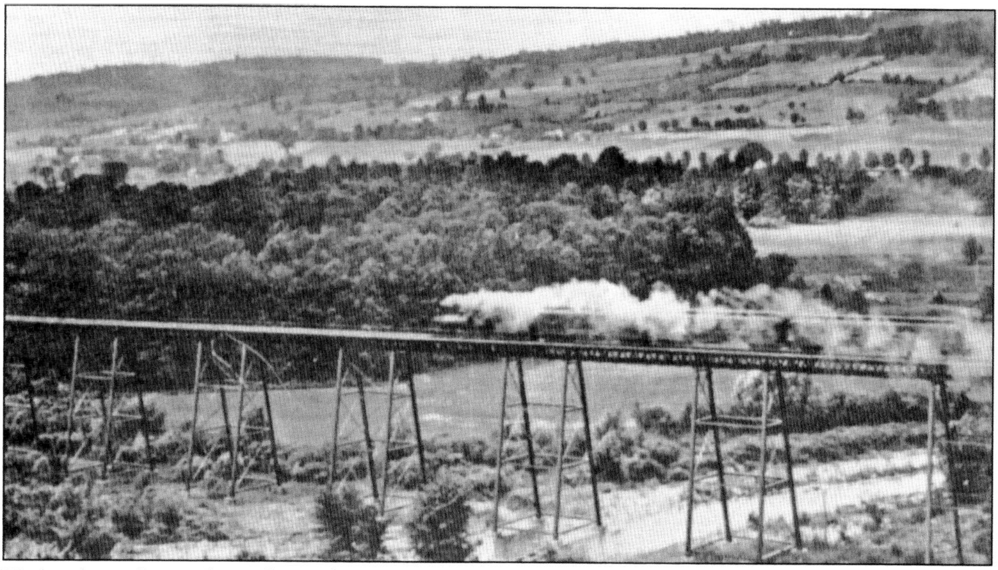

Technology changed rapidly in the 47 years the metal trestle was in use. Here, a steam locomotive heads south, from Brookton Station to Besemer Station. Coddington Road, one of the two roads into Ithaca, is visible in the background along with Six Mile Creek flowing through the valley.

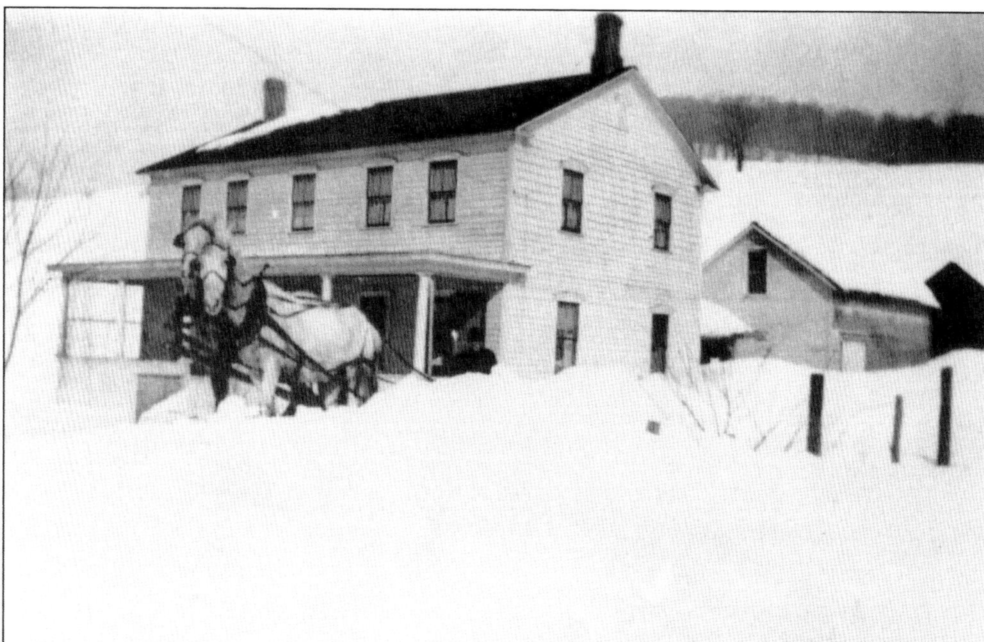

Winter made travel difficult for both people and horses. Few made extended trips, even for important things like school, church, or groceries. Roads were sometimes made more passable for sleds by rolling or dragging a log over the snow.

To get a perspective on the size of this trestle, which was 800 feet long and 85 feet high at its highest point, note the automobile driving beneath it, headed east toward Ithaca on Route 330, which is now called Brooktondale Road.

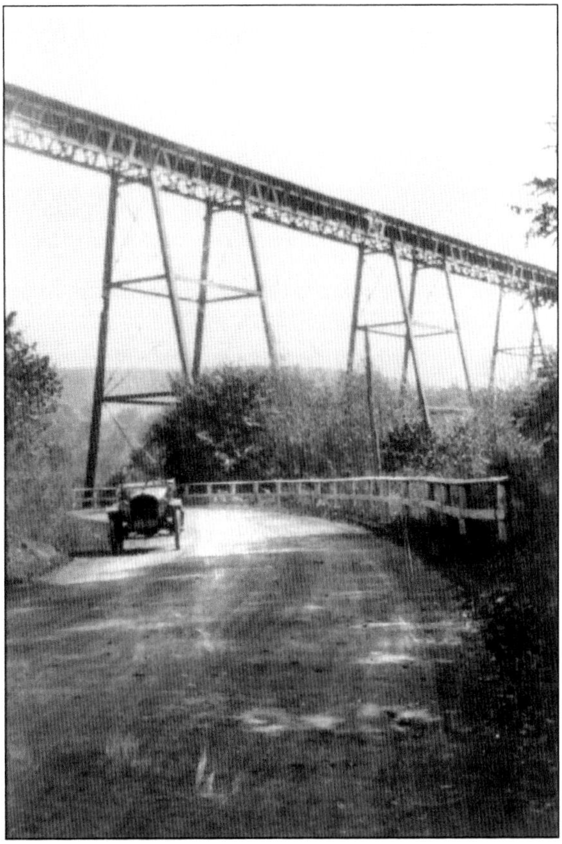

Men at Brookton Depot, located off of White Church Road on Lackawanna Avenue, look for the next train to arrive. A stack of lumber waits to be loaded in the background. The trains, running from one upstate community to the next, took on passengers and cargo that ranged from eggs to wood and were an important part of the supply and transportation system for this area.

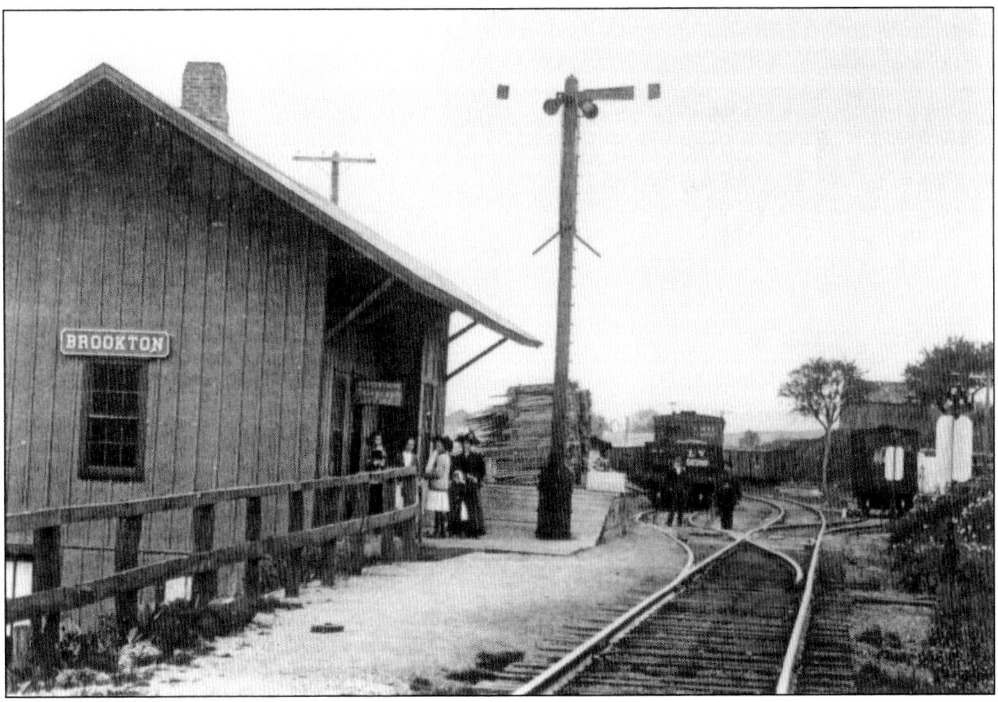

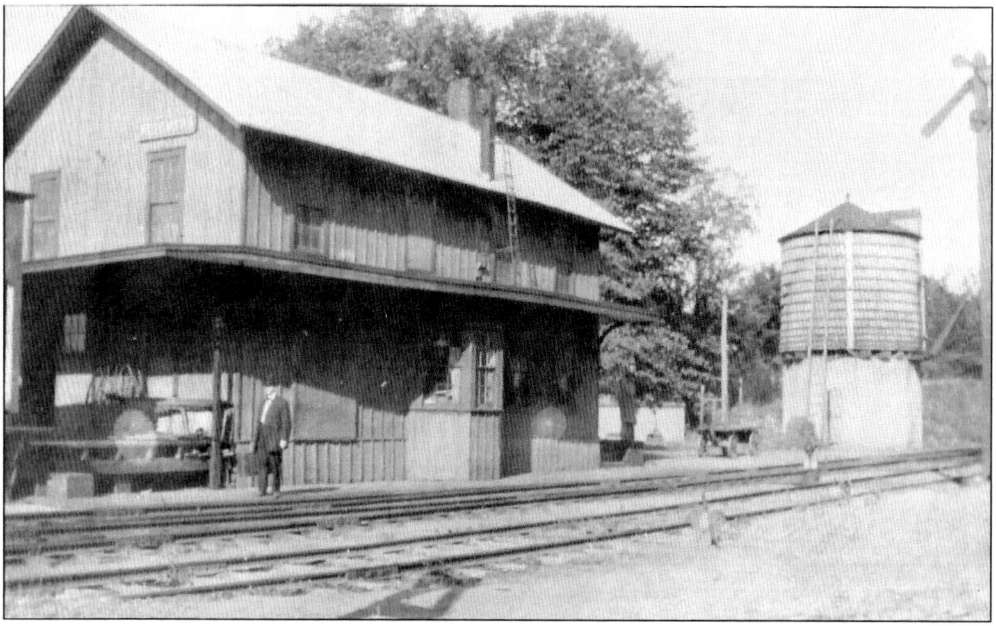

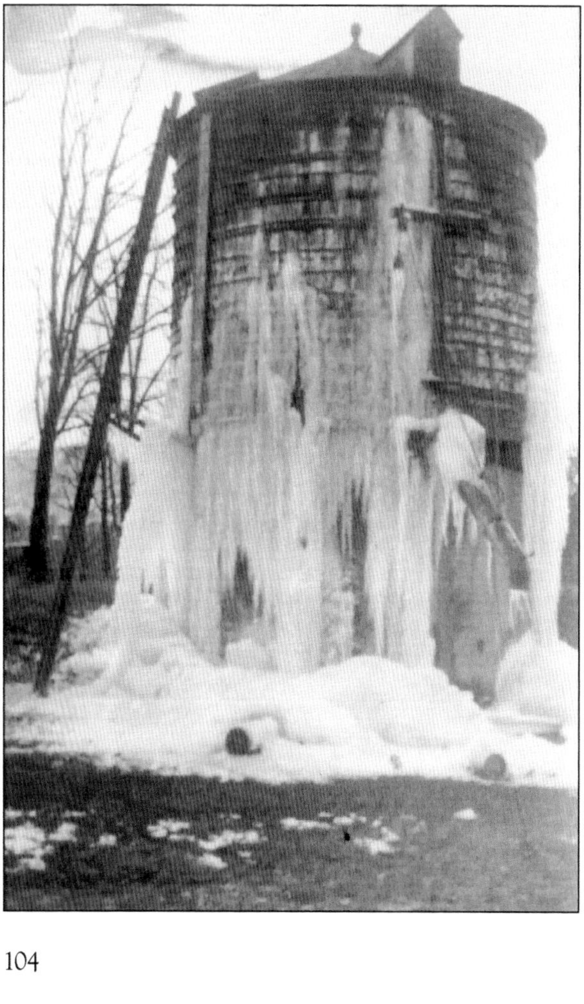

Besemer Station was once located on Route 79, near where it joined with Besemer Road. In the background, the water tank used to supply the steam engines can be seen. The bottom, concrete part of the tank can still be seen just north of Route 79, though it is now almost hidden with vines. The house near the tank was the stationmaster's home.

The Besemer water tank spent a good part of each winter covered with ice. On cold mornings, the ice on the water in the tank and outlets had to be broken in order to make sure that the steam engines could get what they needed to complete their runs.

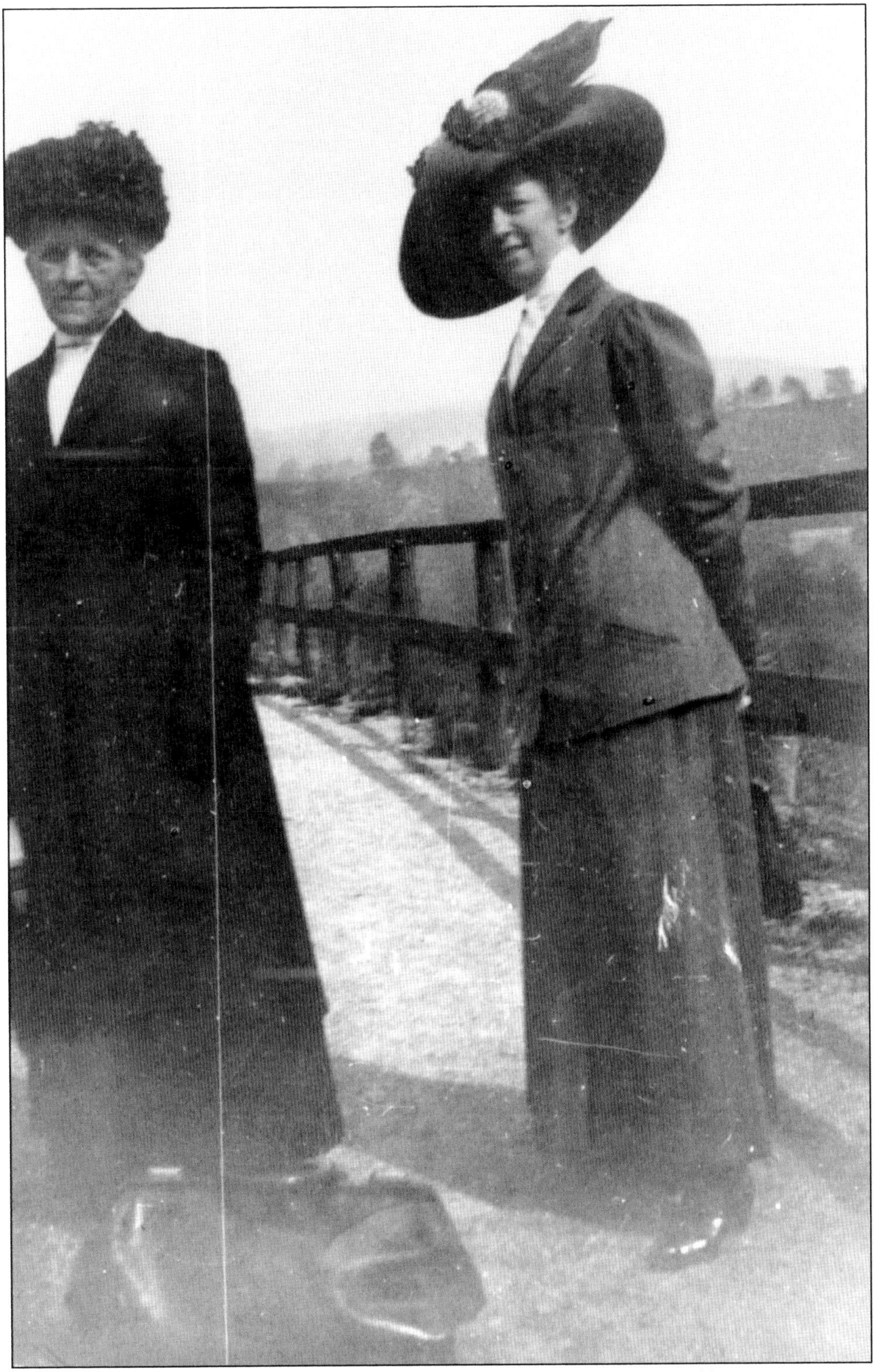

Ladies dressed for the occasion wait for the train near Brookton Depot. Travel by train was exciting and considered a major undertaking, worthy of one's best hat.

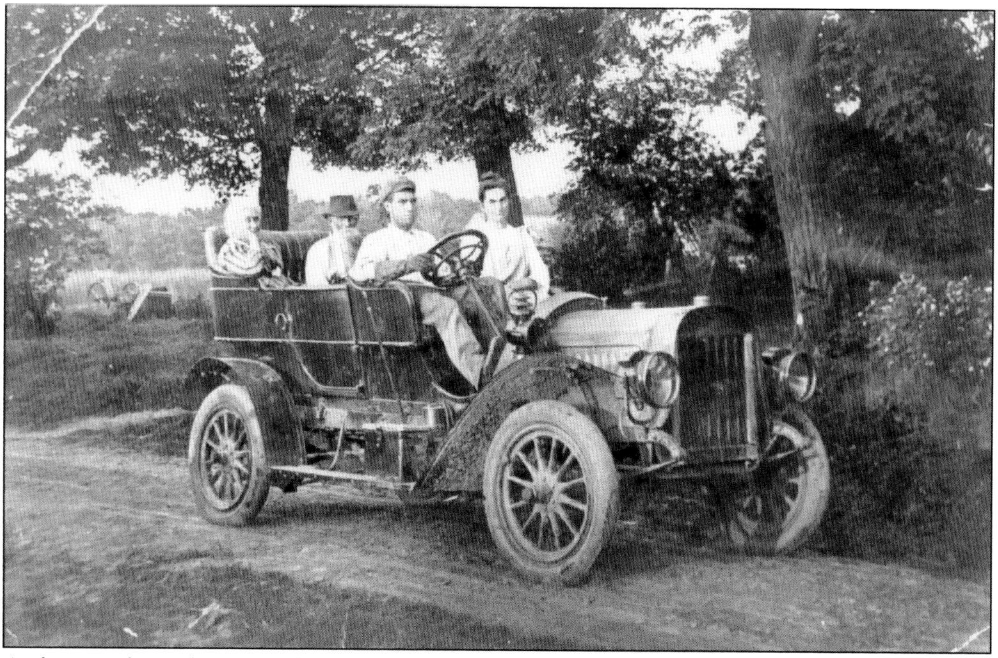

At first, road trips by automobile were mostly summer excursions. There was no heat in the early vehicles, and those with ragtops could be truly miserable in the winter. These young people are making the most of their outing.

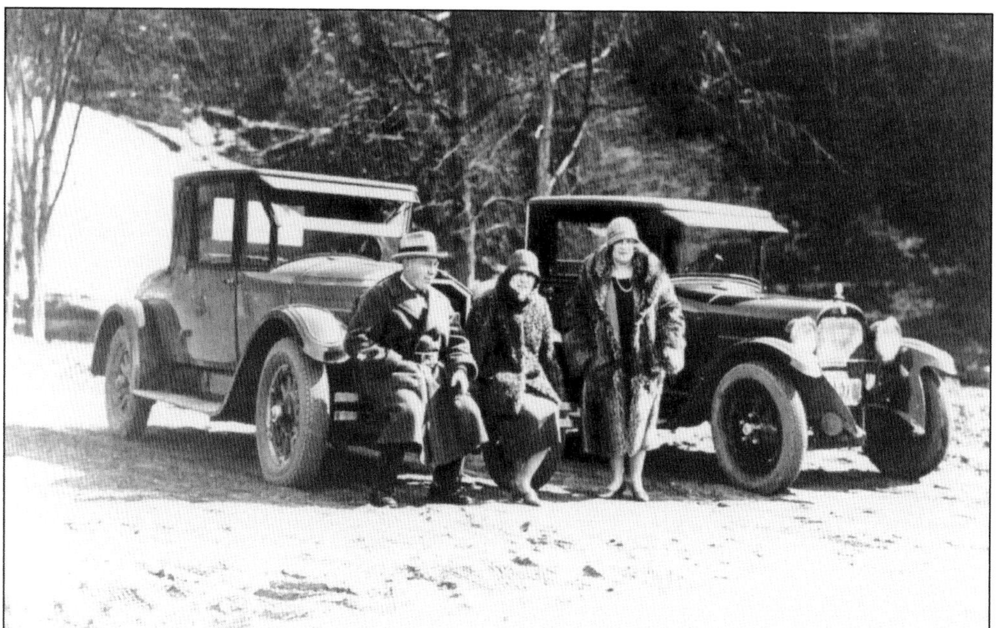

As automobiles became more reliable, the true road trip was born. Women donned pearls and cloche hats, and in the winter, they pulled out their raccoon coats in an effort to be fashionably warm.

Six

Celebrations

From Old Home Days to Fourth of July parades, getting together and celebrating community from the early days on has served to remind Caroline residents of the importance of their friends and neighbors and the need to support each other. The grange used to help farmers and their wives develop skills, but there were also poetry readings, music, and dances. Events were, and are, organized thanks to the efforts of numerous volunteers. Some events are planned only for fun, while others act as fundraisers for the various nonprofits in Caroline. Nowadays, there are school reunions, one for the nearly 20 one-room schoolhouses and one for the Slaterville Springs School. These are organized by the Caroline town historian and still attract former students from as far away as California. The Brooktondale School also has an annual reunion, always located in one of the two buildings now owned by the Brooktondale Community Center, which was erected on the former site of the Brooktondale School. These are generally organized by a former pupil and also attended by people in the community and beyond. What is remarkable is that all of these schools closed in 1959, when the new Caroline Elementary School on Route 79 was built in West Slaterville. Fundraisers, some lasting for over 50 years, include the annual Brooktondale Apple Fest, put on by the Brooktondale Community Center and the Caroline Community Church; a Christmas Country Store craft fair organized by the Caroline Community Church; and occasional events to celebrate fire department anniversaries and other important town events. Monthly dinners are held by the Caroline Center Church, allowing it to keep its historic building open as well as do good works, and other churches in the area also have regular events. Pancake breakfasts and chicken barbeques help keep the volunteer fire companies in business.

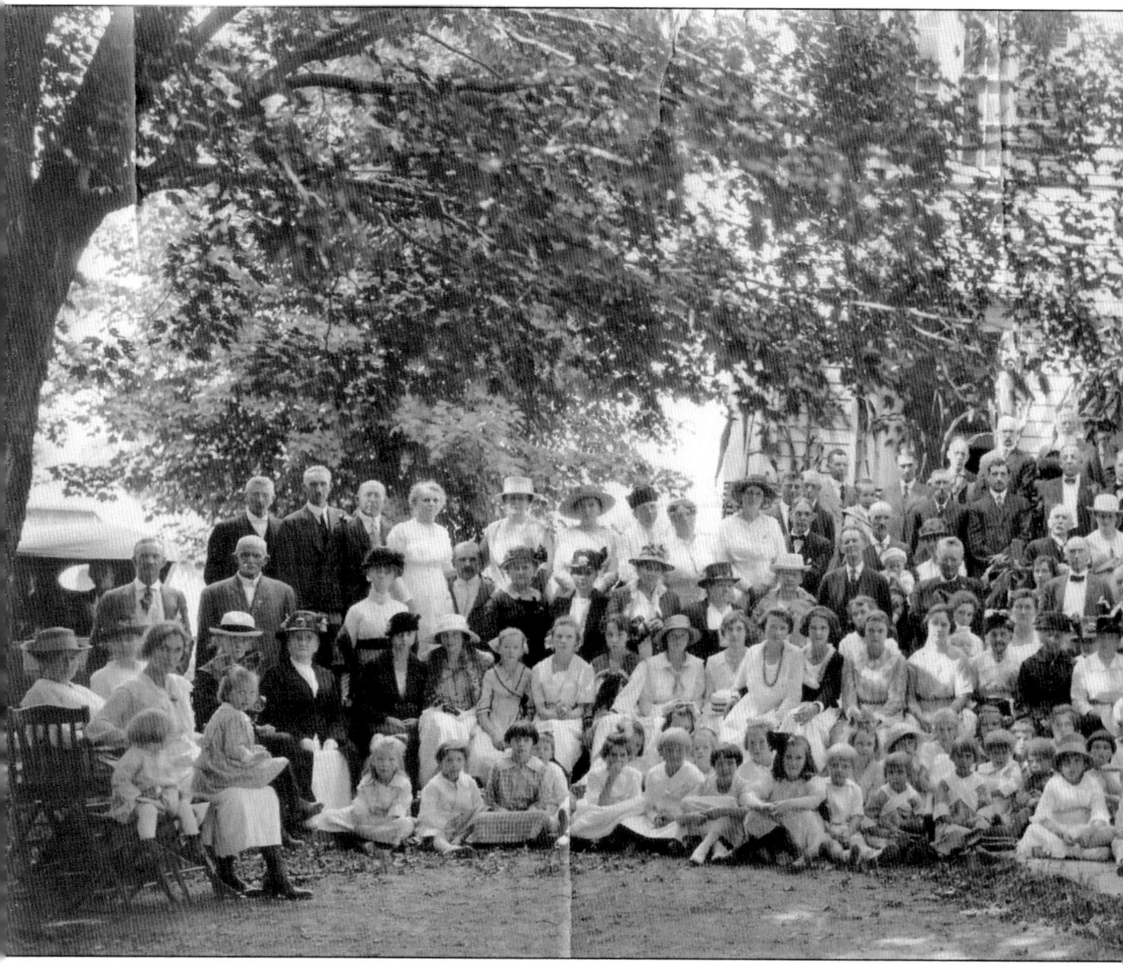

This was one of several Old Home Days celebrations that attracted current and former Caroline residents for a day of picnics, speeches, and patriotic displays.

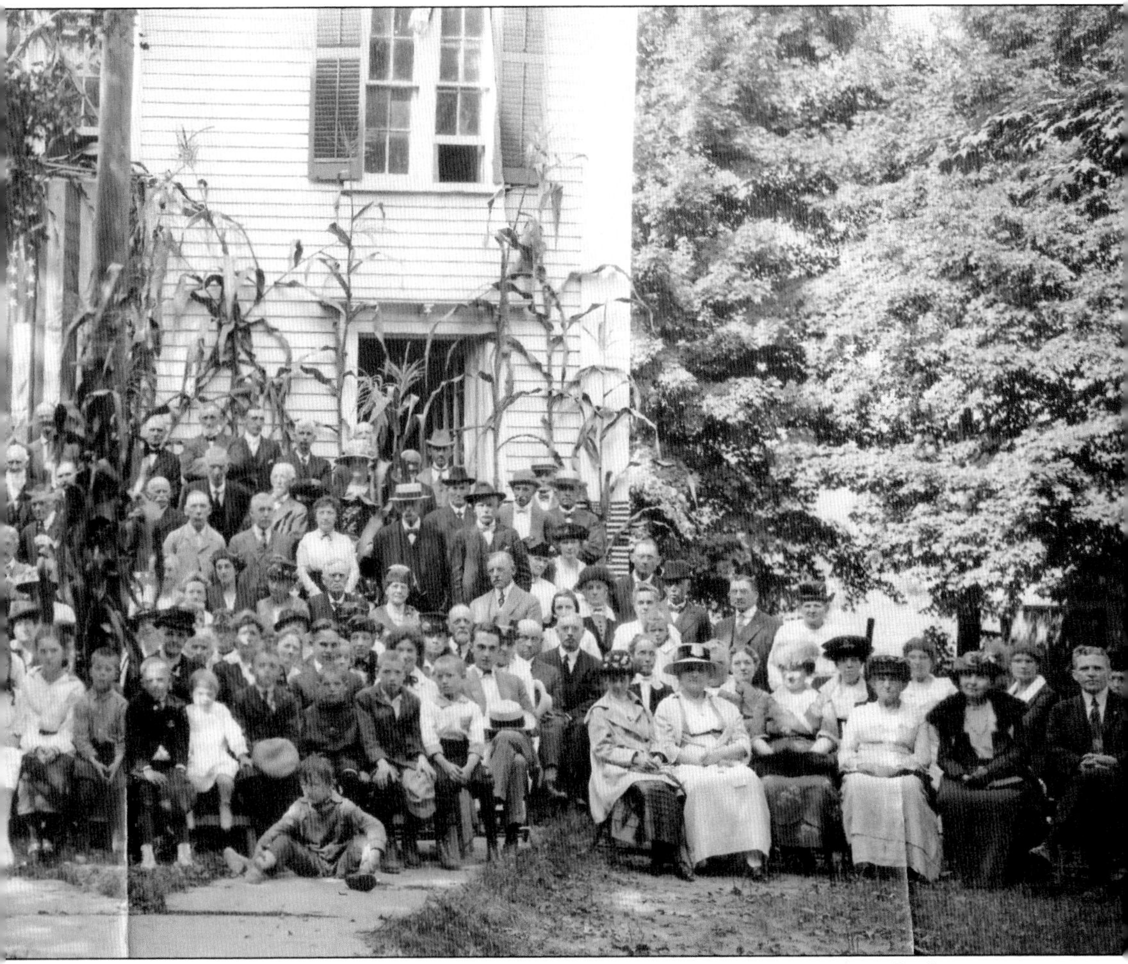

Usually held in the fall, the evidence of a bountiful harvest was encouraging to all who came, from those too young to walk to those nearly too old to do the same.

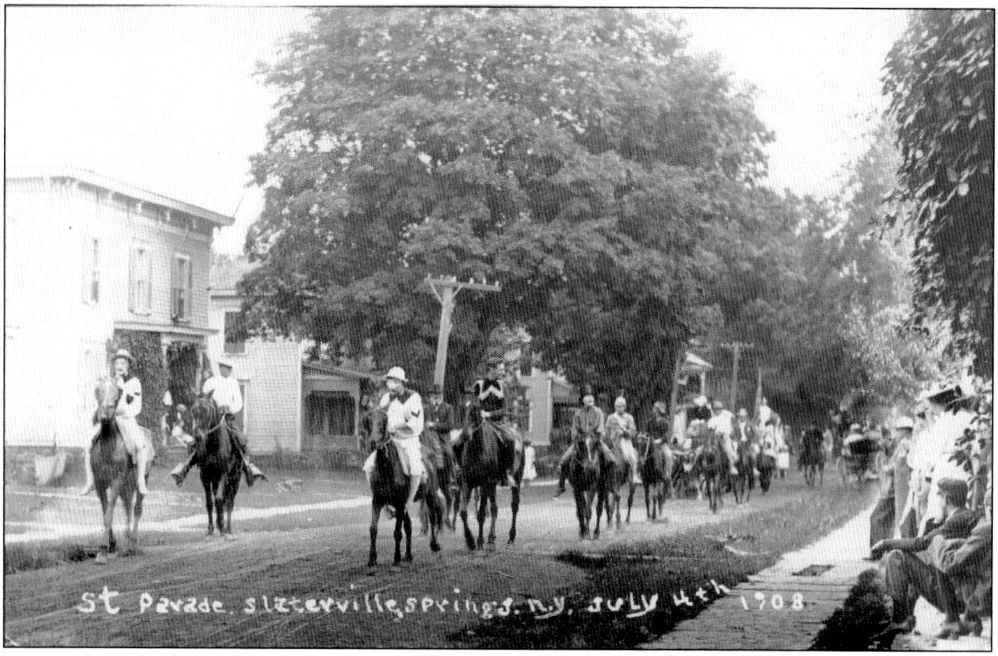

Men on horseback ride into Slaterville Springs for a Fourth of July parade that seemed to encompass the entire community. The photographer, C.B. Childs of Willseyville, took a number of photographs on that 1908 afternoon while everyone enjoyed the merrymaking.

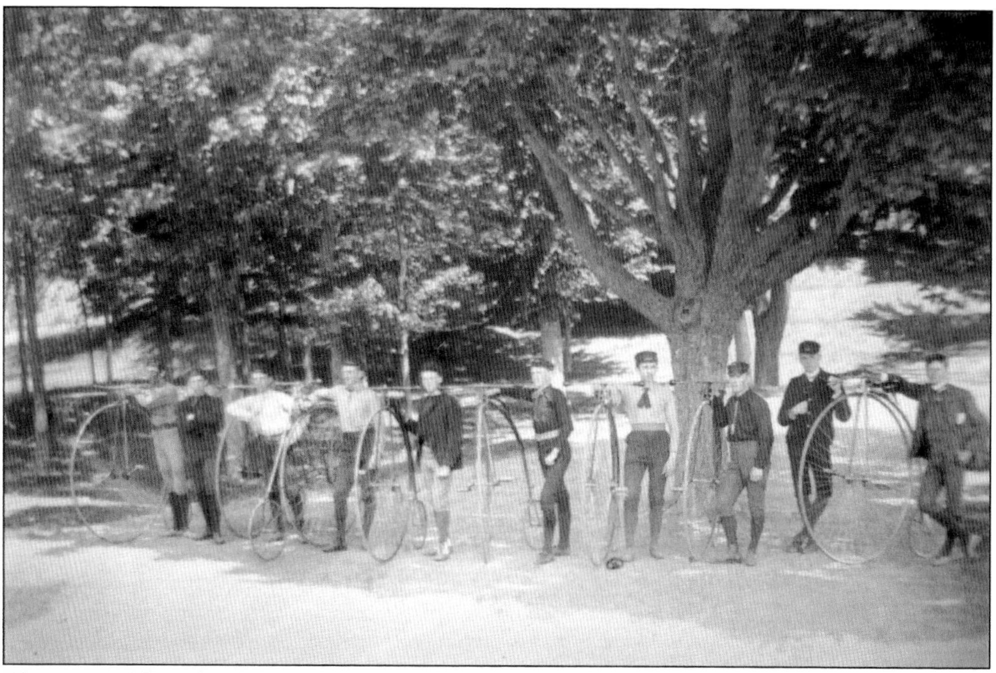

The original big-wheel bicycle racers, young men on penny farthings, prepare to race on the Fourth of July in Slaterville Springs. The first challenge is to get up onto the bicycle.

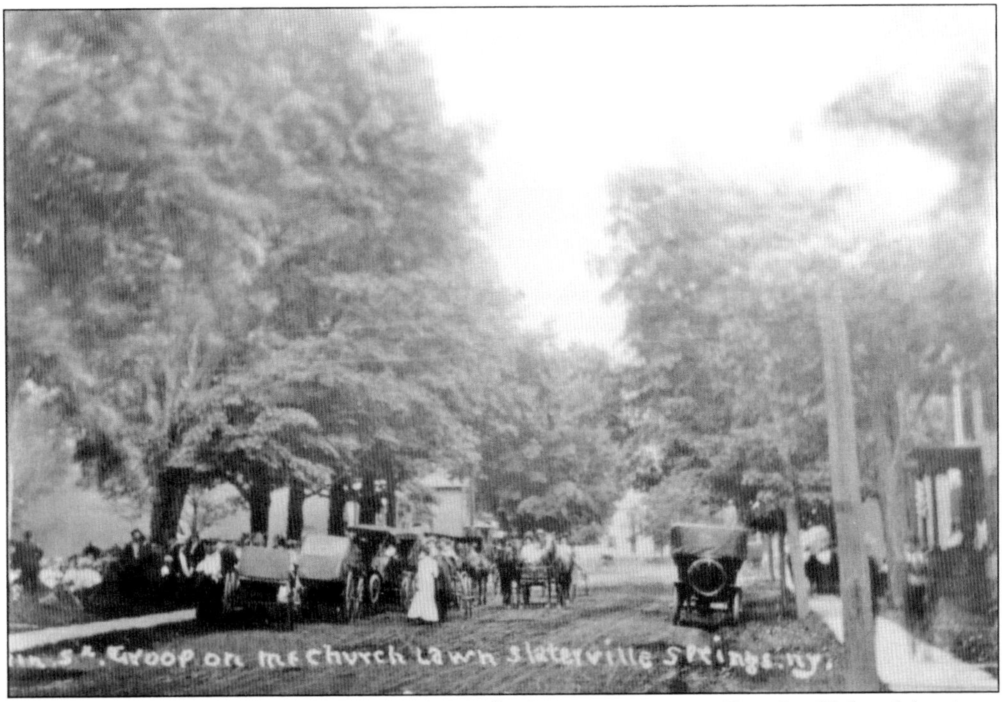

A group of people stroll up the road in Slaterville Springs, enjoying a Fourth of July celebration.

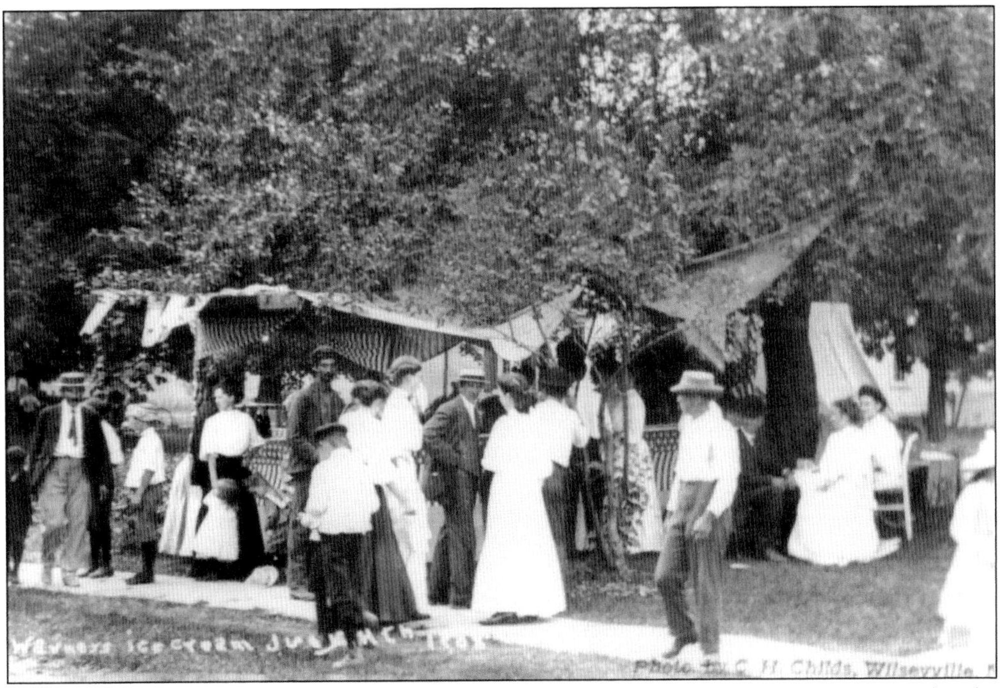

Most people enjoy ice cream on a hot afternoon, and whoever cranked the ice-cream maker for a crowd this size deserved an extra scoop.

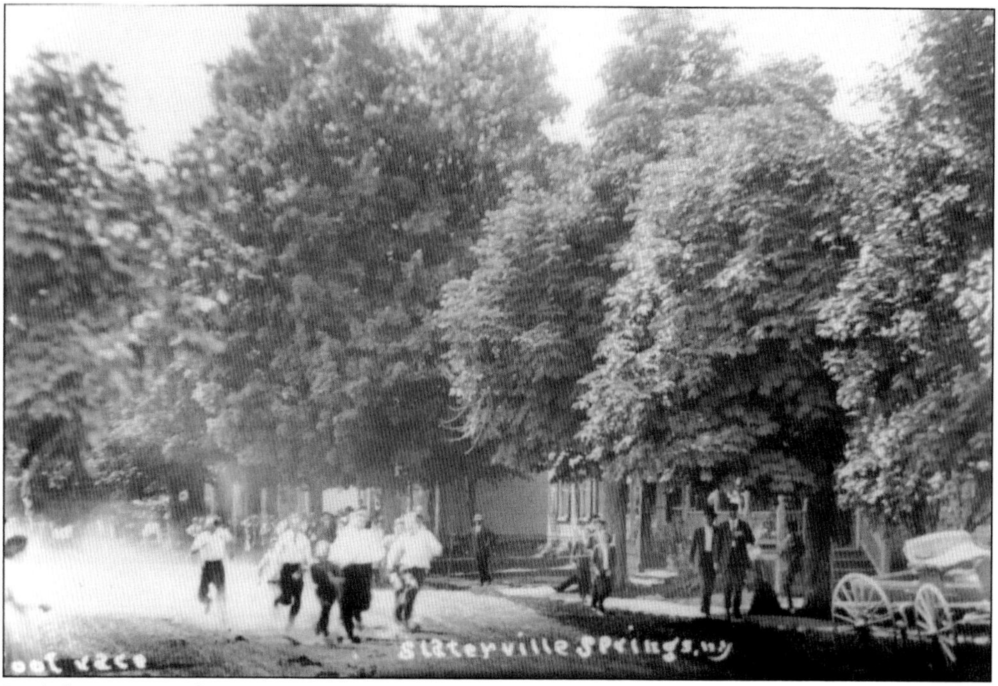

Little boys enjoy a foot race, whatever the excuse, and this happy gang are putting on a fine show on Independence Day.

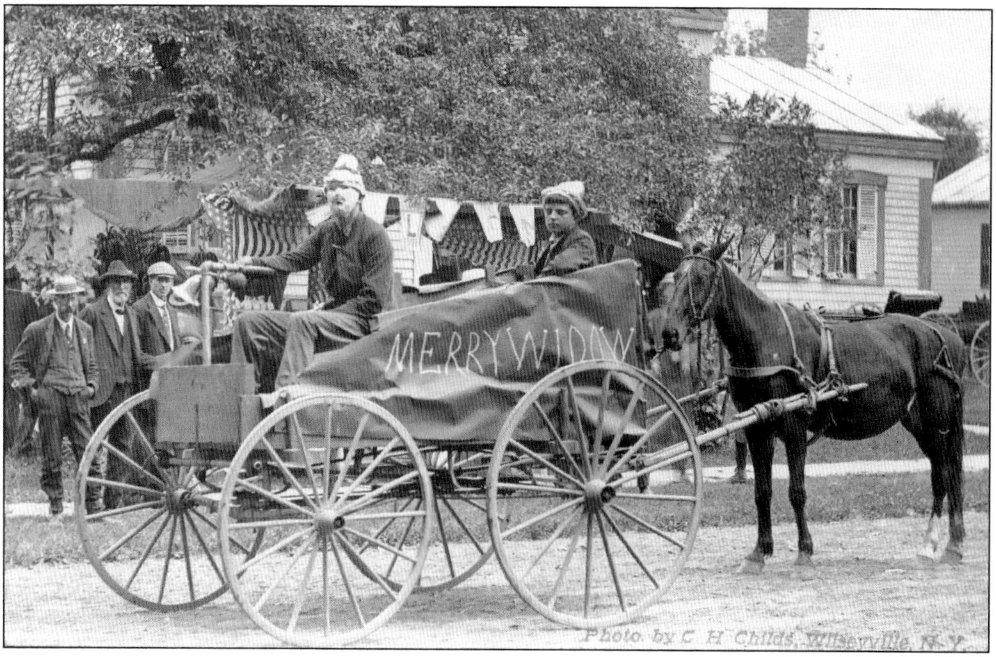

The "Merry Widow" puts the cart before the horse in this very punny float, showcasing a lighthearted display of parade humor.

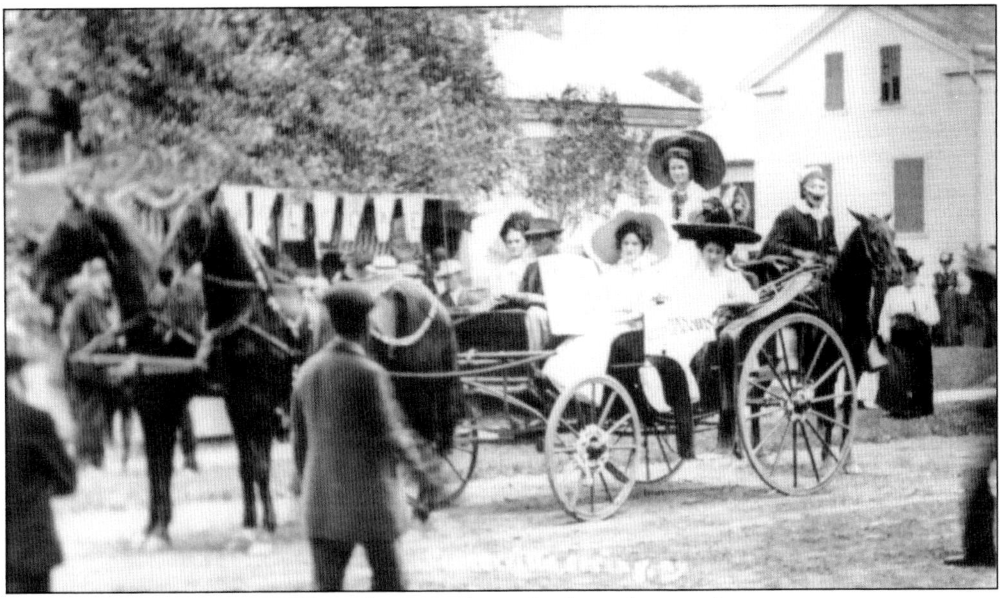

Unidentified ladies show off their finery as they ride along the parade route.

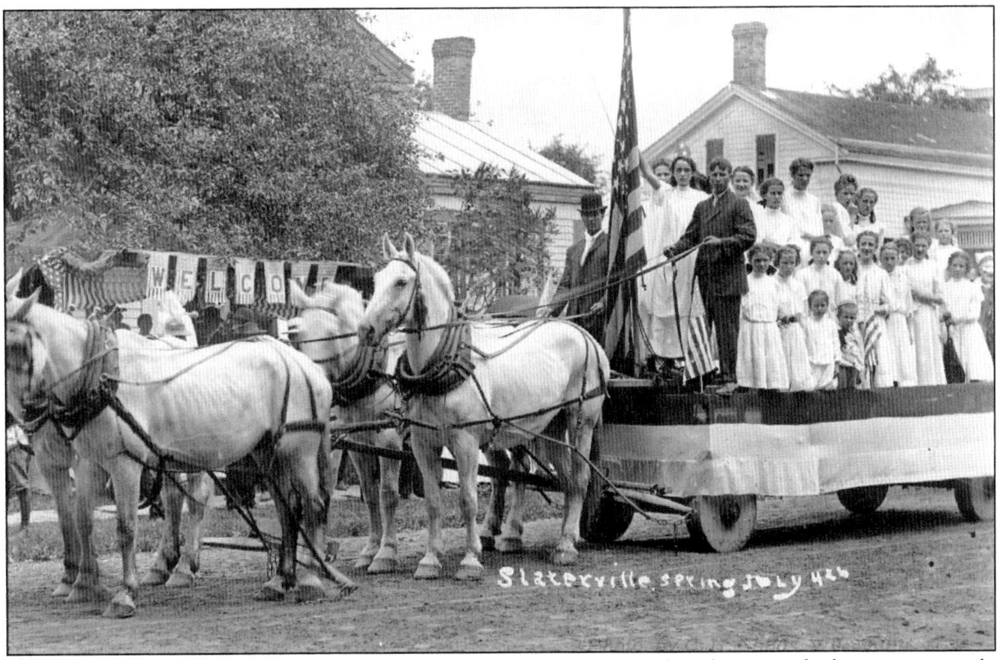

These people, both young and old, ride on the parade route. The photograph does not provide information on this group, but perhaps it is a church group or maybe even a choir.

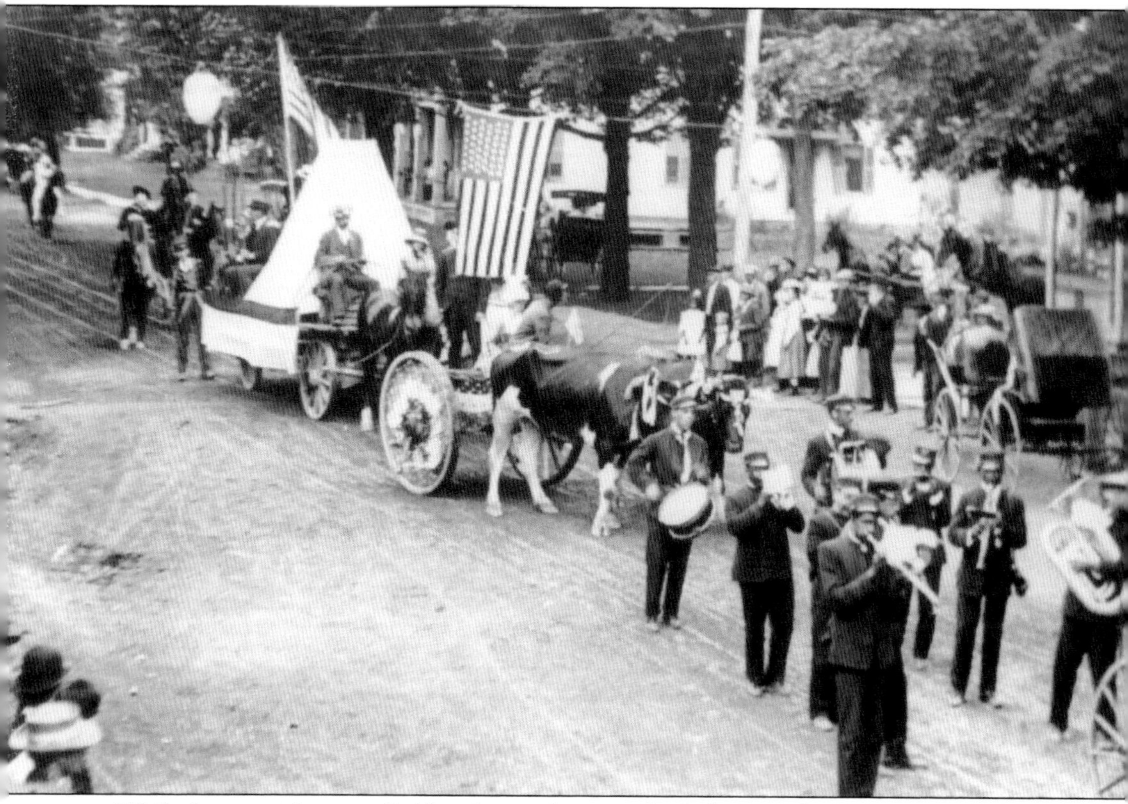

While the tent is being pulled by a horse, the two-wheeled cart in front is being pulled by a cow. Both are being heralded down the street by a brass band.

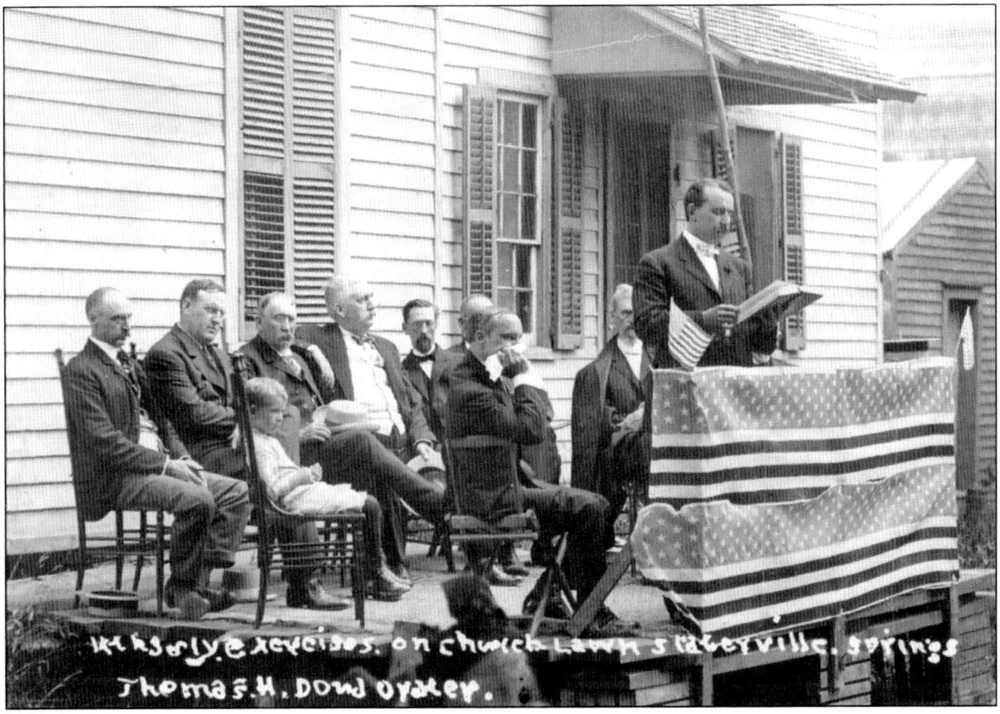

No Fourth of July is complete without a speech, and these gentlemen look like they are capable of both giving a long speech and listening to one intently. Thomas H. Dowd is said to be the orator.

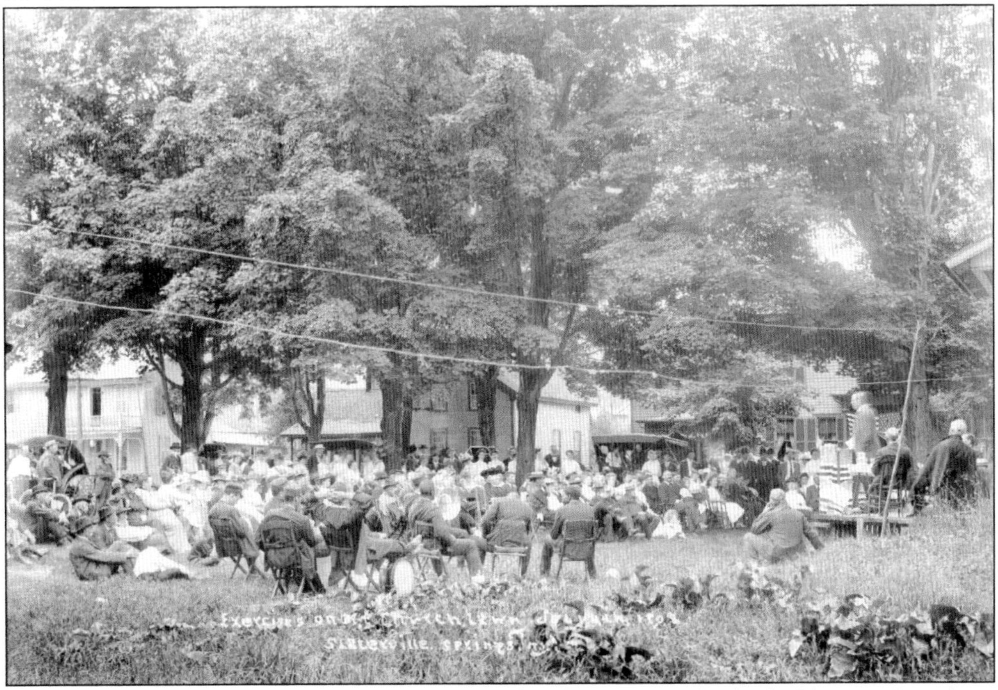

This photograph was labeled "Exercises on the Church Lawn," and it looks like speech making is going on, with a mostly attentive audience.

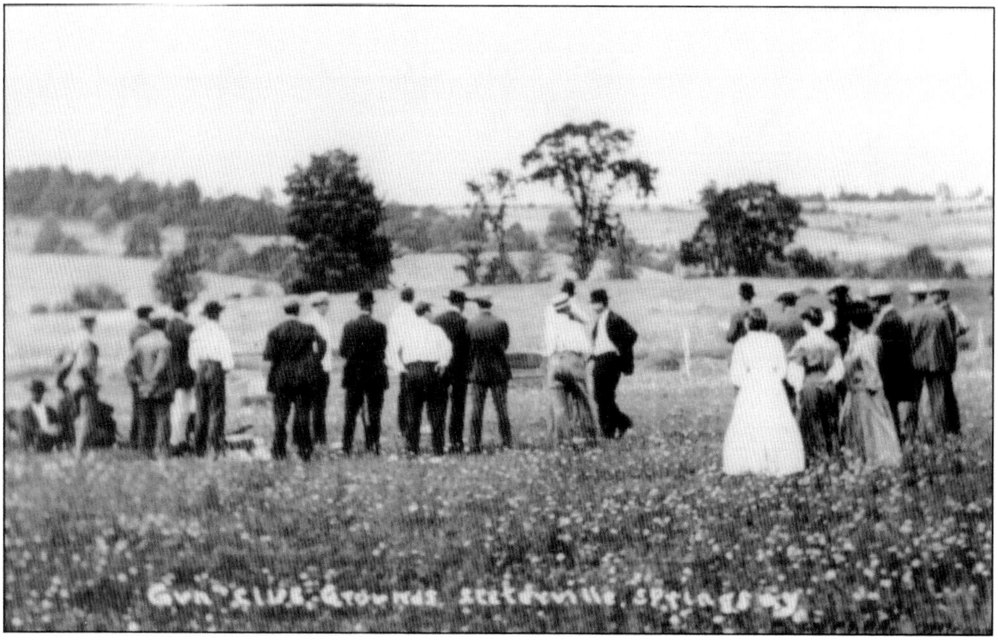

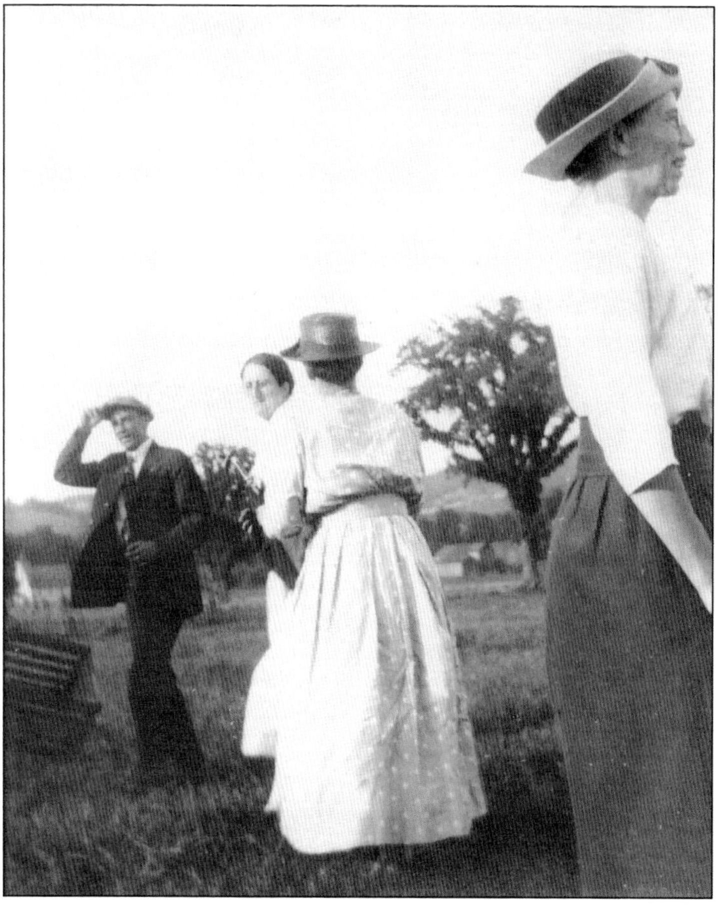

This particular Fourth of July celebration involved going out with the shooting club and trying one's hand at hitting a target or two.

After shooting practice, a picnic was held; it was probably considered the perfect end to a perfect day.

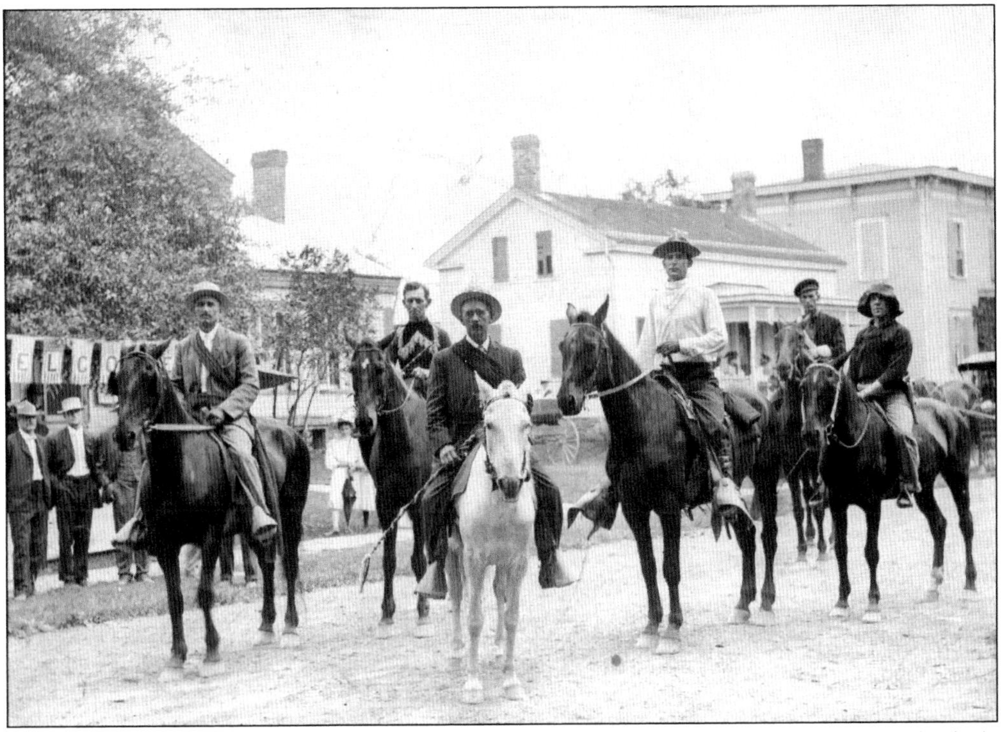

This 1909 photograph is labeled "Mr. Shutt and his crew show up on horseback for the Fourth of July parade." C.B. Childs unfortunately did not provide detailed explanations of his photographs.

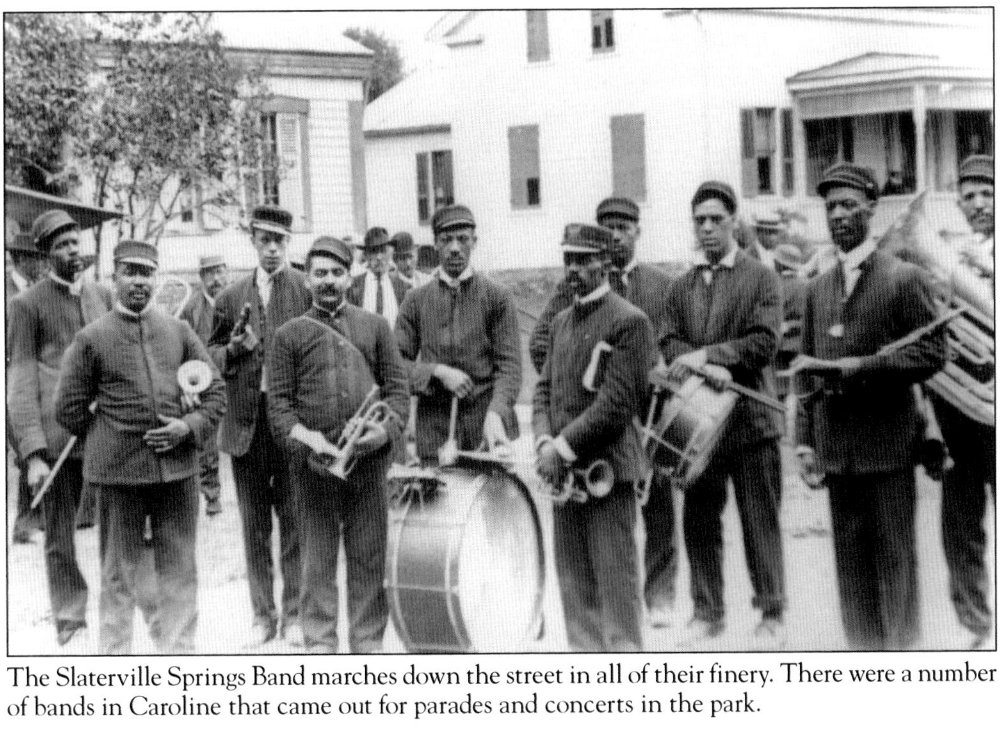

The Slaterville Springs Band marches down the street in all of their finery. There were a number of bands in Caroline that came out for parades and concerts in the park.

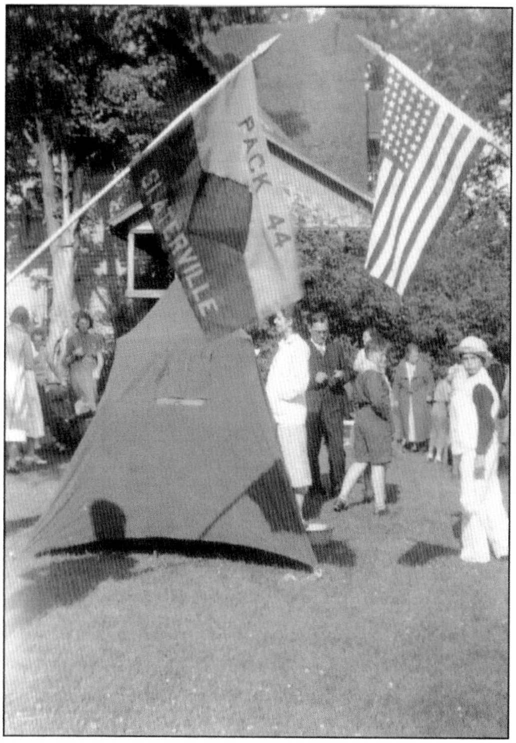

Boy Scouts unfurl their flags at a later-day parade in Slaterville Springs. This photograph was the most understandable of a group of four pictures labeled "Boy Scout parade" with no real explanations and not a lot of connection between the scenes, but it is an intriguing set nonetheless.

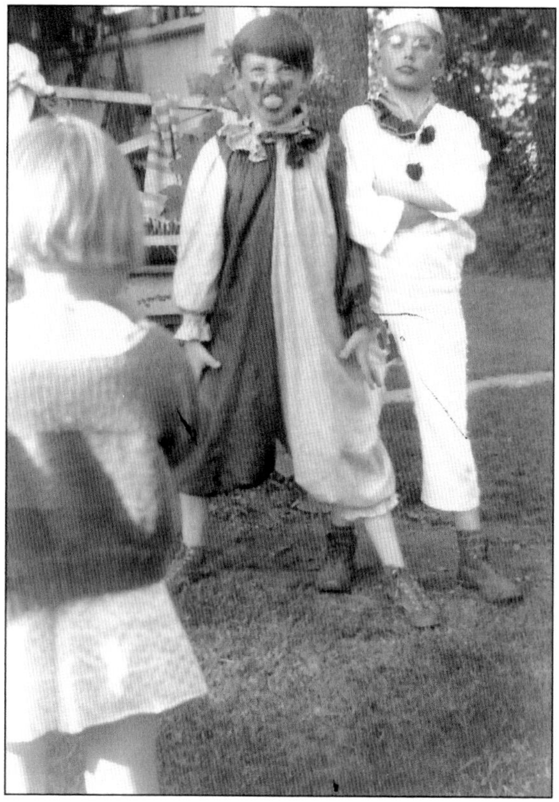

Boy Scouts dress up as clowns on parade day. Just as today, youth groups were welcome at community activities.

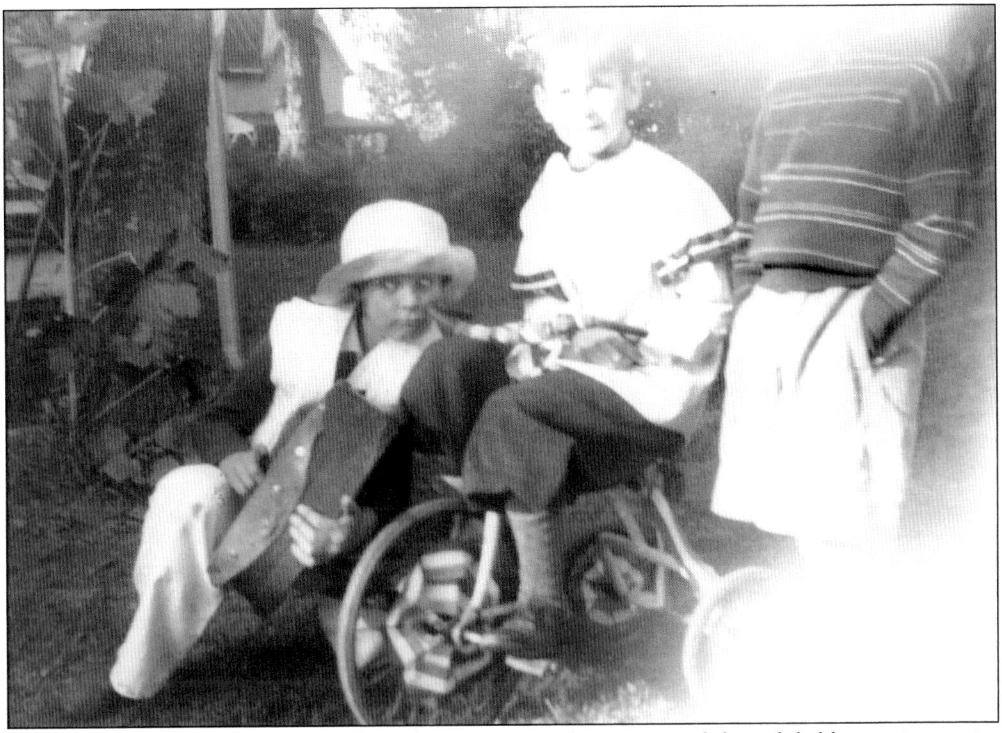

More boys are pictured here dressed up, demonstrating the amazing ability of children to improvise and reinvent themselves.

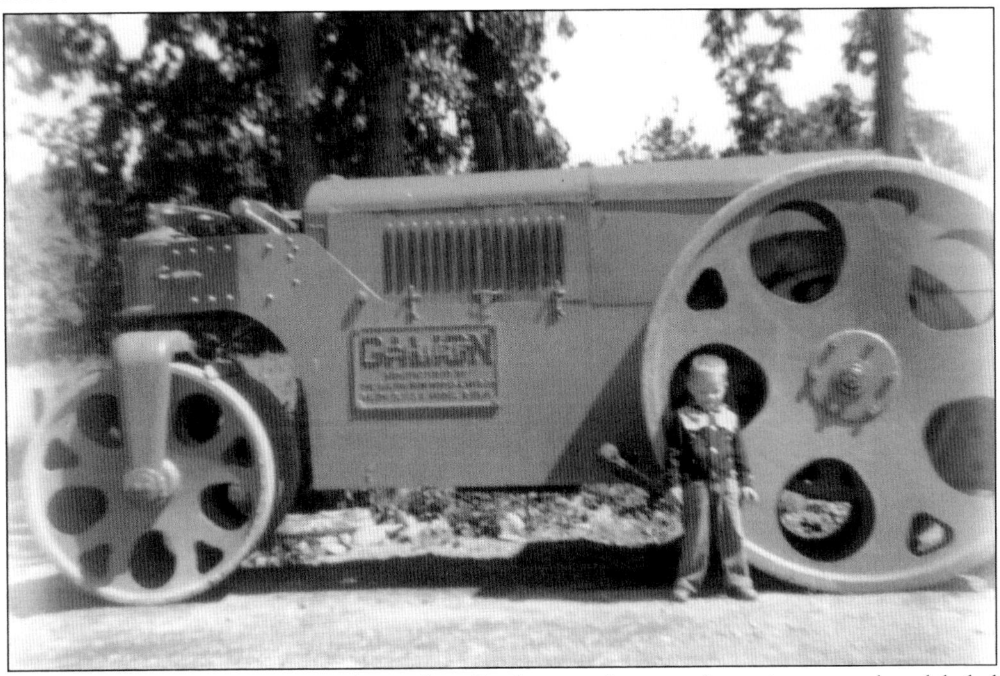

This image of a cute little boy in front of a roller for smoothing roads was in an envelope labeled "Boy Scout parade." Except for his outfit, which does fit in with the rest of the boys pictured in the previous photographs, there is no clue as to why he is displaying heavy machinery.

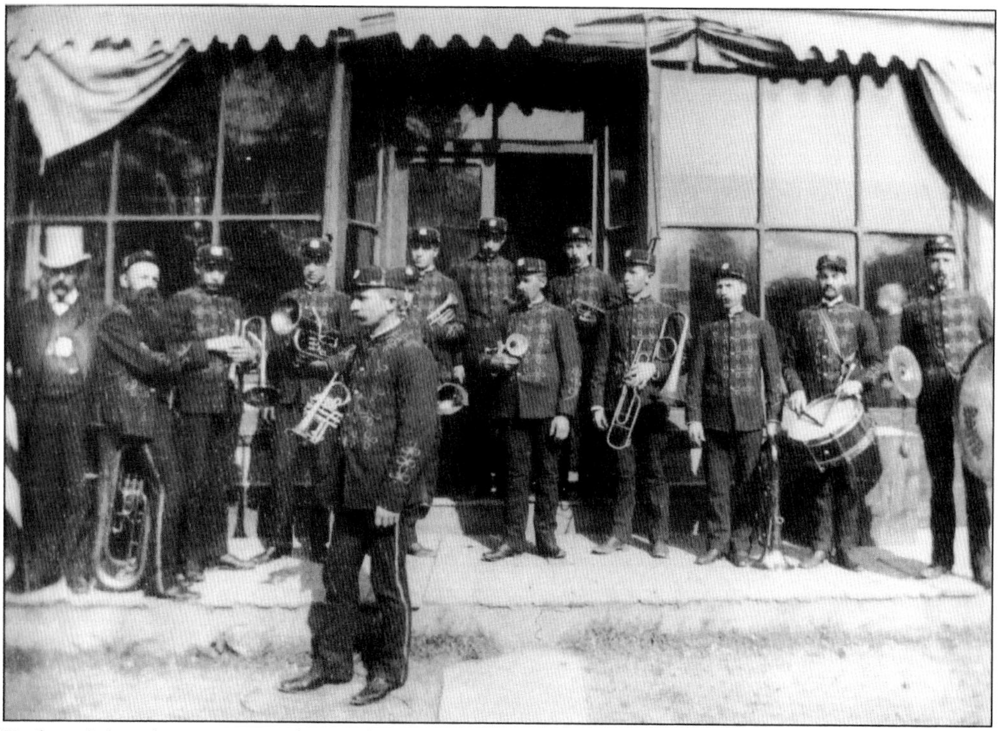

Redman's band warms up in front of a store in Brooktondale. Several bands were organized in the various hamlets of Caroline, and each put a serious amount of work into practice and uniforms.

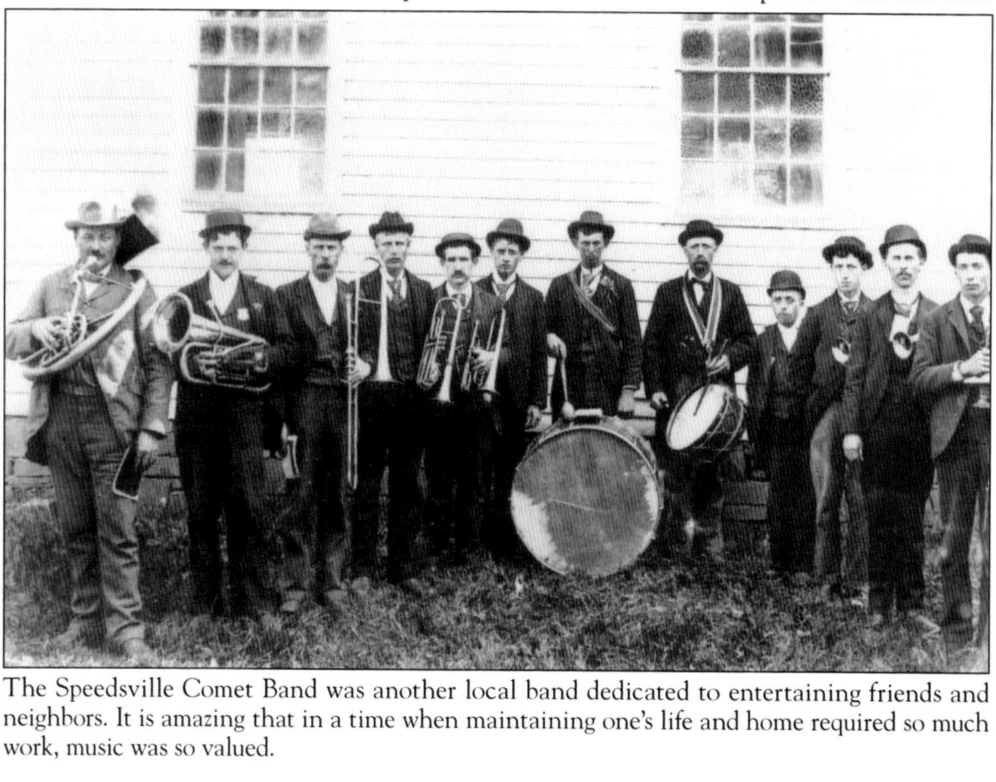

The Speedsville Comet Band was another local band dedicated to entertaining friends and neighbors. It is amazing that in a time when maintaining one's life and home required so much work, music was so valued.

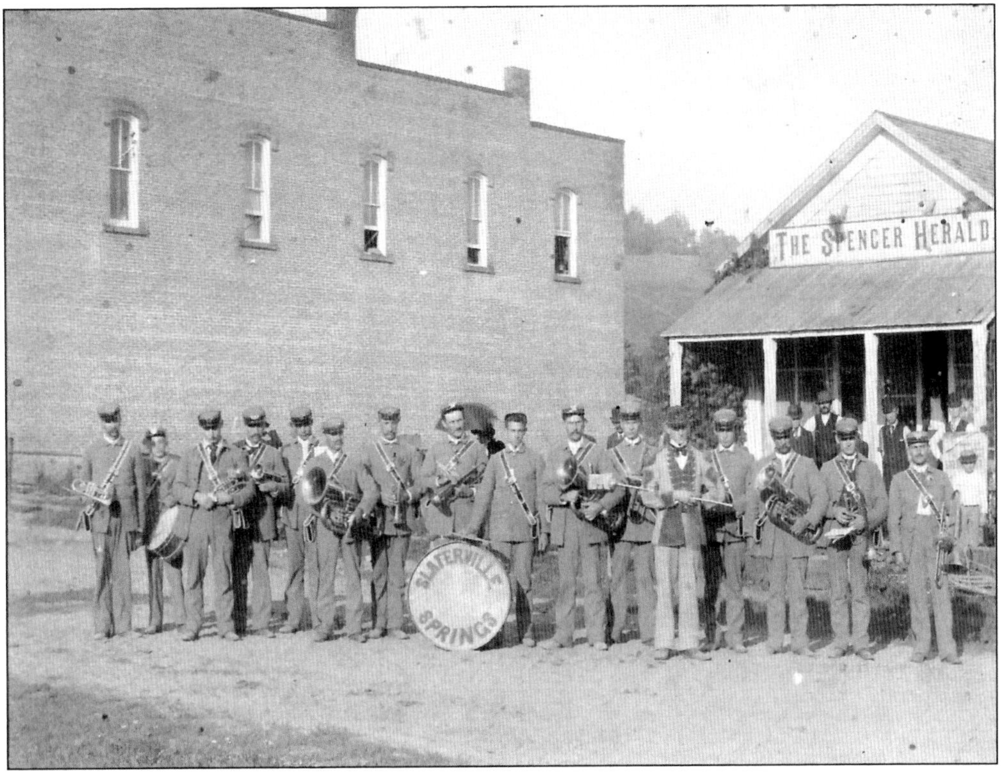

The Slaterville Springs Band takes to the road.

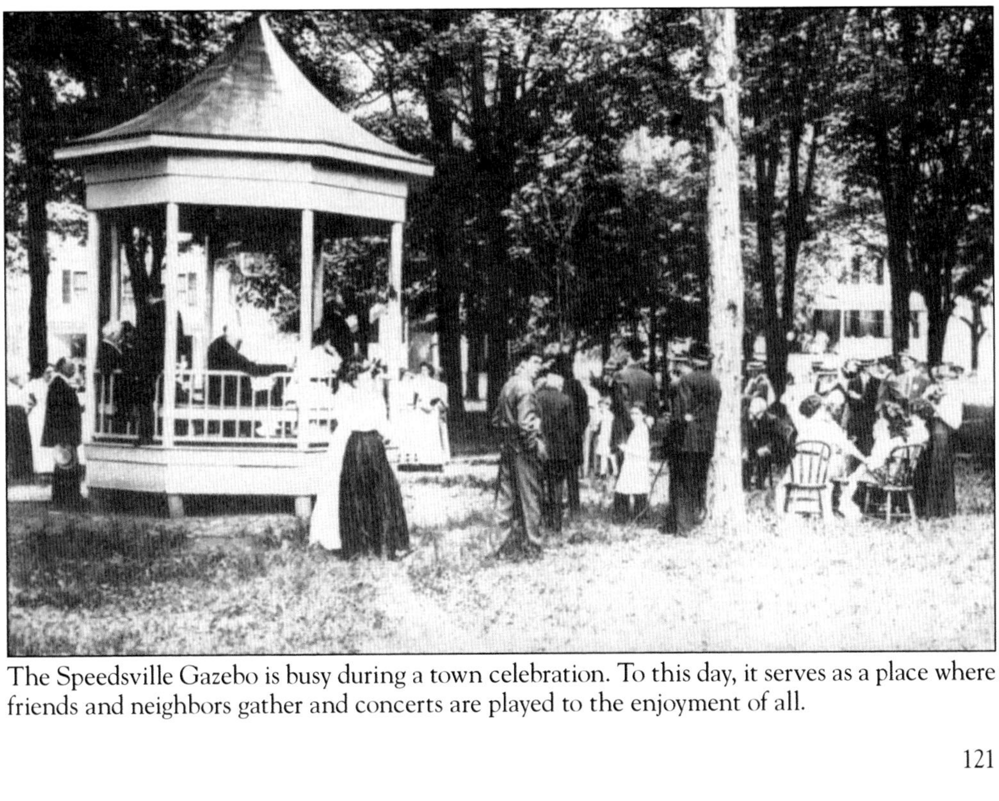
The Speedsville Gazebo is busy during a town celebration. To this day, it serves as a place where friends and neighbors gather and concerts are played to the enjoyment of all.

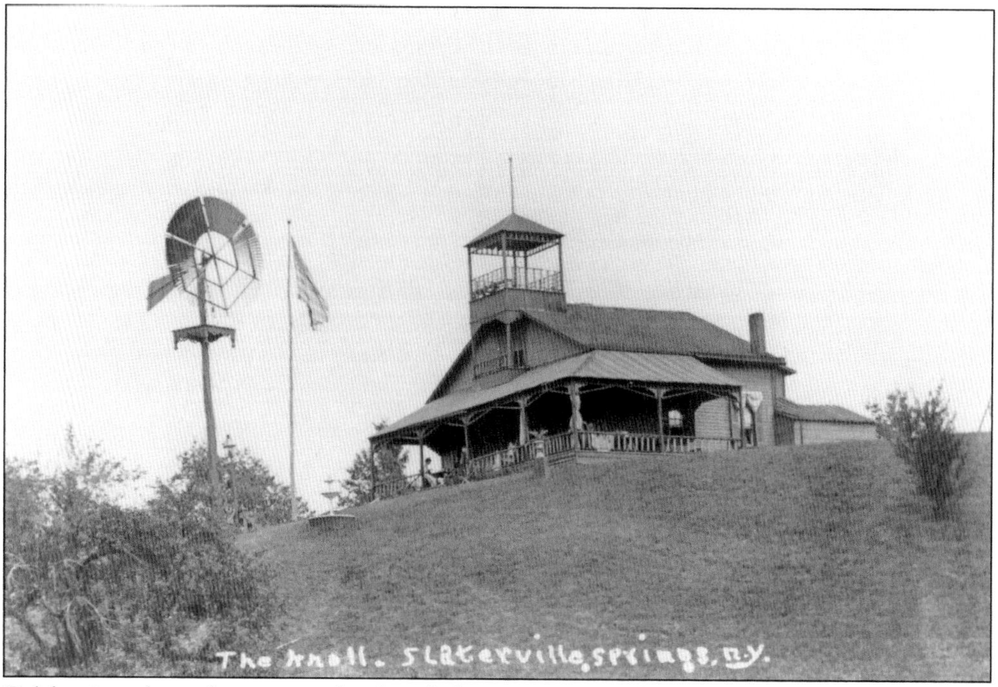

Celebrations do not have to involve the whole community. A family party goes on at the Knoll, a private home in Slaterville Springs. While the house no longer exists, the fountain in the foreground is now installed in front of senior and disabled housing, located right behind the town hall.

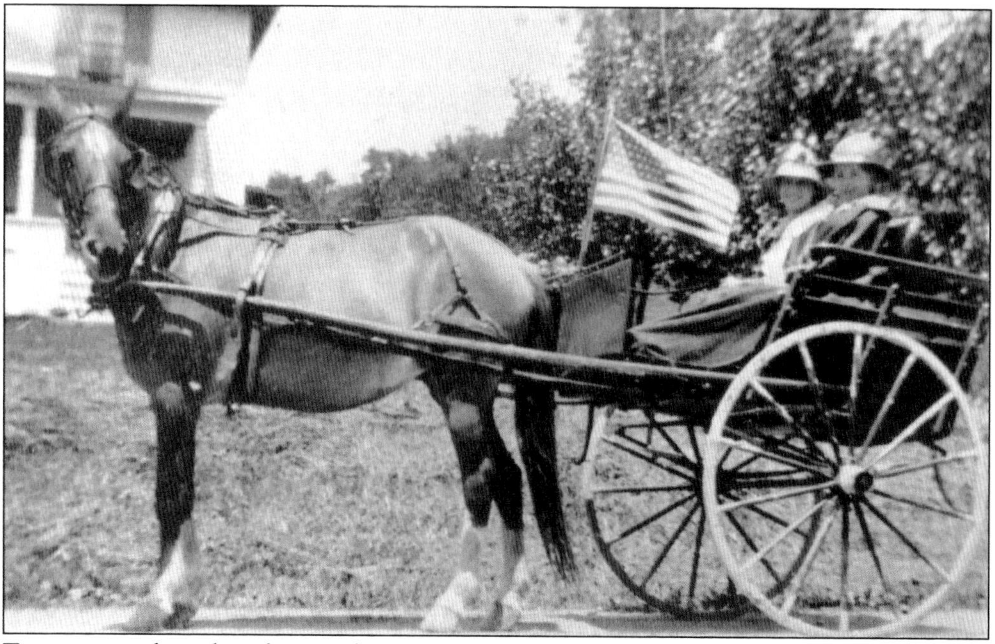

Two women ride in their decorated cart. It is not clear what parade they are in; perhaps they just felt like dressing up for a ride.

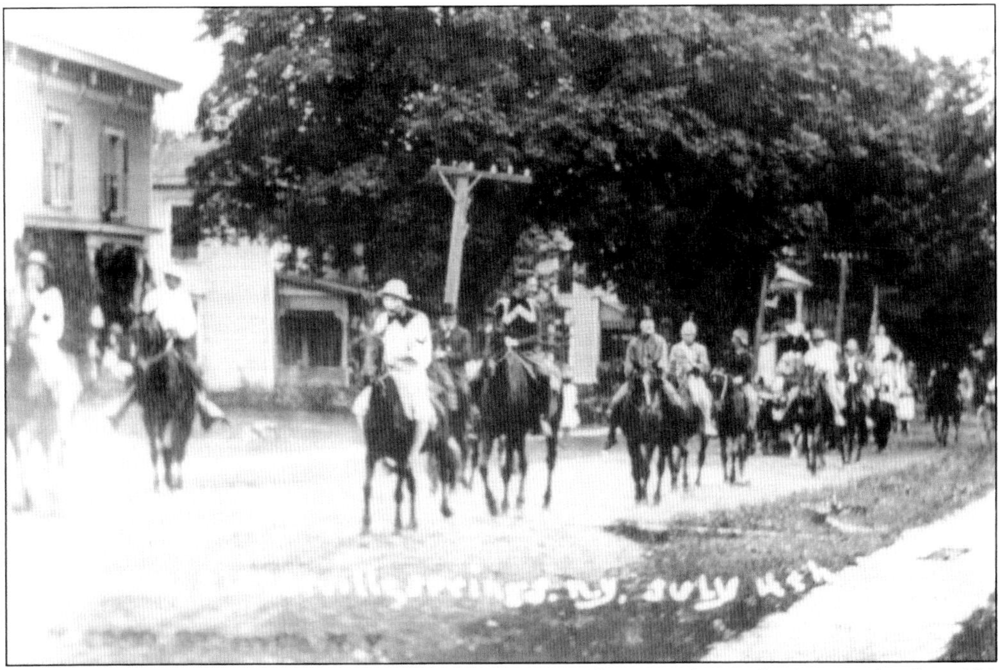

It is not the cavalry, but this group riding tall in the saddle into Slaterville Springs for the 1908 Fourth of July festivities is certainly an interesting bunch. Some don top hats, some are in cowboy shirts, and some wear helmets.

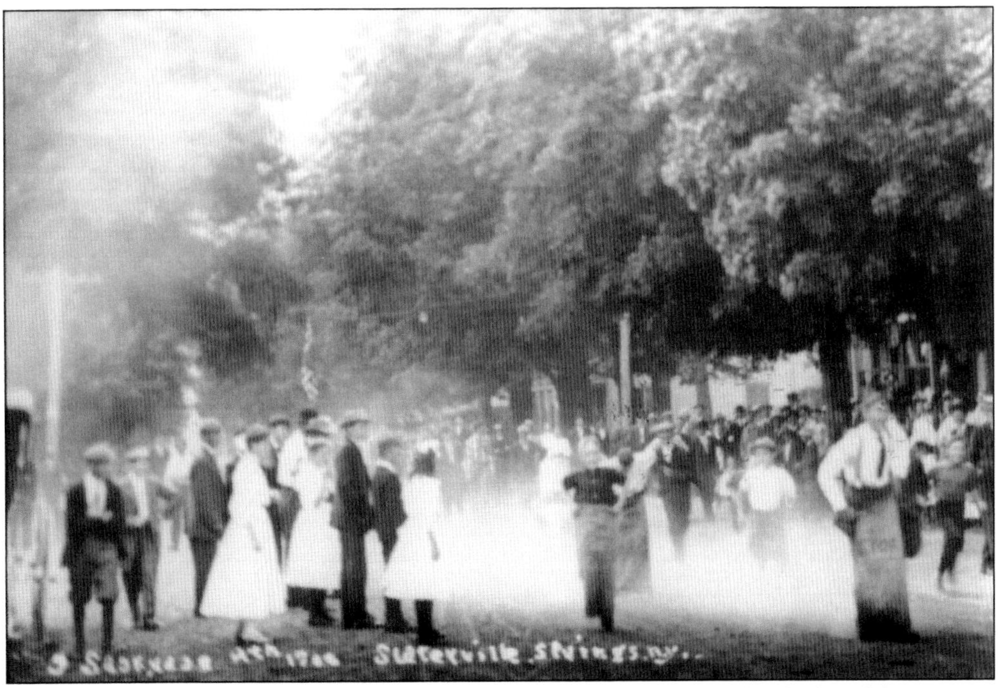

The gunny sack race creates whirlwinds of dust during the 1908 Forth of July celebrations in Slaterville Springs.

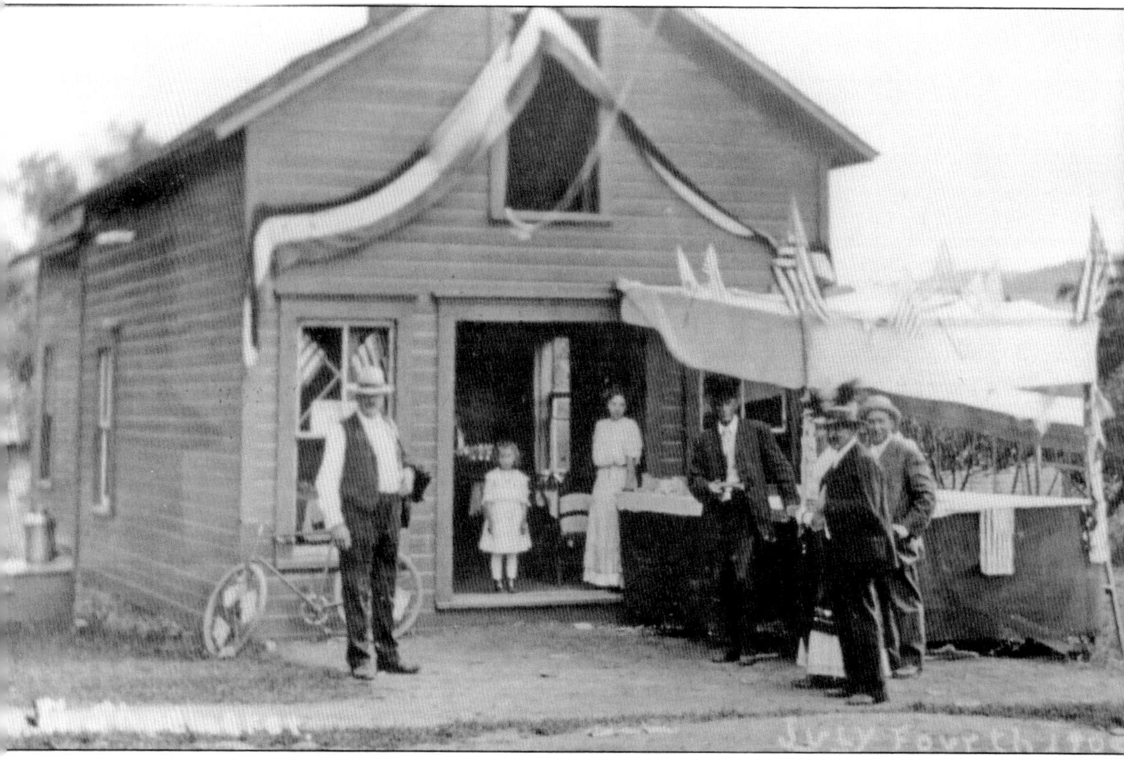

Stores are decorated with plenty of bunting and flags to show their patriotism as well as attract customers.

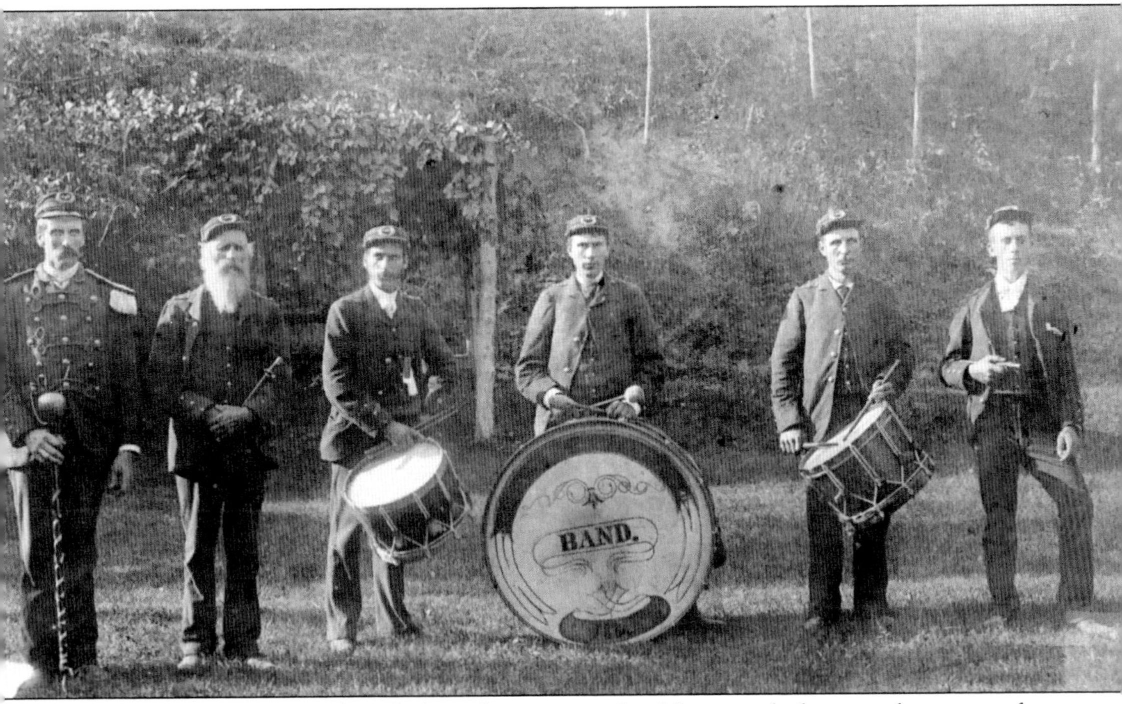

This band is prepared to march with three drums, a couple of flutes, and of course, the master of ceremonies with his extra large baton.

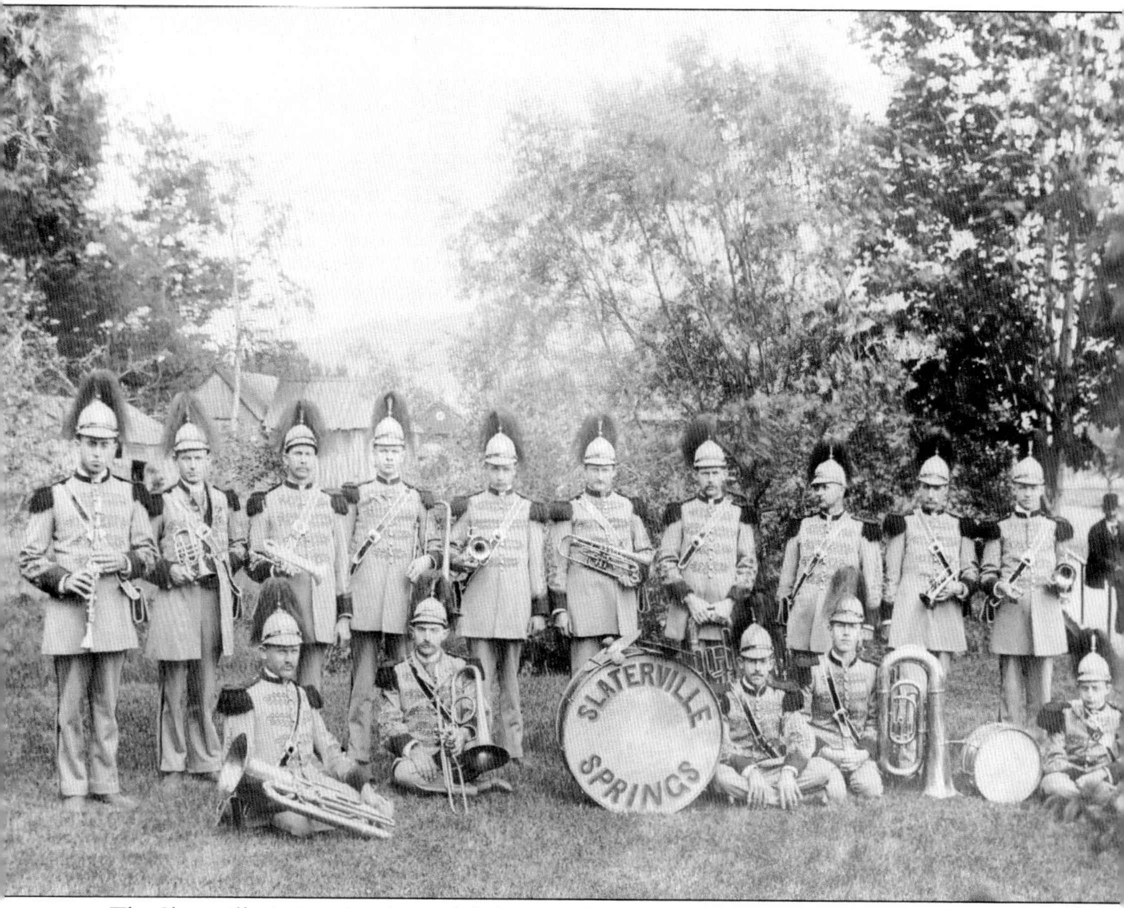

The Slaterville Springs band is in full-dress uniform, complete with helmets and their instruments at ready.

Bibliography

Cook, Kathleen. "Bailor Home Has Seen Slavery and Freedom." *The Ithaca Journal*. October 11, 1965.

Dieckmann, Jane Marsh, ed. *The Towns of Tompkins County: From Podunk to the Magnetic Springs*. Ithaca, NY: DeWitt Historical Society of Tompkins County, 1998.

Drive By Tour of the Town of Caroline, A. Caroline, NY: Town of Caroline Bicentennial Committee, 1994–1995.

Gallway, Sydney. *Peter Webb, Slave-freeman-citizen of Tompkins County, New York*. Ithaca, NY: DeWitt Historical Society of Tompkins County, 1960.

Henninger, Sue. "Notable Locals in History Exhibit." *Tompkins Weekly*. February 2, 2013.

Mix, Barbara. A *History of the Town of Caroline, Tompkins County, New York, United States of America*. Norfolk, NE: Press of Marathon Printing & Publishing Company, 1994.

Olds, Marjory. "From Slavery to Freedom, One Family's Journey Brings Them to Tompkins County." *The Ithaca Journal*. February 23, 2013.